Developing Leaders and Leadership

David V. Day

# Developing Leaders and Leadership

Principles, Practices, and Processes

palgrave
macmillan

David V. Day
Claremont McKenna College
Claremont, CA, USA

ISBN 978-3-031-59067-2 ISBN 978-3-031-59068-9 (eBook)
https://doi.org/10.1007/978-3-031-59068-9



This Palgrave Macmillan imprint is published by the registered company Springer Nature Switzerland AG
The registered company address is: Gewerbestrasse 11, 6330 Cham, Switzerland

Paper in this product is recyclable.

# Preface

Why write a book? It's a great question that I asked myself many times before and during the writing process. The answer to this question came down to the realization that sometimes you just have a lot to say, and that is the case for me with the topic of developing leaders and leadership. My perspective on leader and leadership development is a bit unique—or so I like to think—and a book-length monograph provides a broad canvas to present that perspective.

An important question to consider before committing to writing a book is whether there is sufficient material to motivate such an endeavor. I believe that to be the case now, which was not always so. What has changed over the previous decade is scholarly interest in the core topics has gained momentum. There are plenty of practice-focused offerings on leadership development in the form of so-called airplane books (those books purchased in airport bookstores and read on airplanes) that often have a self-help orientation promising the proven [sic] methods of developing into a world-class leader. That is not the orientation of this volume. The only promise here is that the reader will gain a perspective on developing leaders and leadership that is different from the norm.

It might be easier to identify what this book is not. This book is not about instructing people on how to become a high-potential leader, or how to build a so-called leadership pipeline, or unveiling the five secrets to leadership success, or similar promises. These topics have value (maybe), but here are plenty of offerings to choose from in airport bookstores (or your favorite book retailers) if that is what interests you. The primary audience for this book is someone interested in the scientific study of how people develop as leaders and what we know about how leadership capabilities are developed individually and collectively. This volume is intended as a scholarly contribution to help advance the science of developing leaders and leadership.

That can sound a bit lofty and boring (unless you are kindred scientific geeks), but it doesn't have to be. Another advantage of writing a book is that it gives one license to present complex scientific principles and ideas in an accessible format. I will not go so far to say that this volume is a ripper (i.e., a real page-turner). After all, it is intended as a scientific contribution; however, a scholarly book does not have to read like a terse journal article. One goal in writing this book was to reach a broader audience that is interested in the focal topics, who want to learn more about these topics from a scholarly academic standpoint but are not especially engaged by the writing in a typical peer-reviewed journal article.

Another intended audience is the designers of leadership development interventions, especially faculty and staff in higher education institutions engaged with developing emerging leaders (e.g., college students). The principles, practices, and processes (i.e., developmental pathways) presented in this volume provide innovative ways to design interventions that go beyond one-off leadership development programs. If anything, this volume is somewhat anti-program in its focus because of the inherent limitations associated with trying to develop leaders and leadership using mostly episodic training practices found in most programs rather than deeper long-term developmental initiatives. Indeed, what writing a book and developing as a leader have in common is that both are more of a marathon rather than a sprint. Both endeavors can be grueling, much like running a marathon. The trick is to maintain motivation over a relatively long period of time to successfully complete the project or event.

One big difference between writing a book and developing as a leader is that a book project has a set deliverable date, and once published, the product remains untouched until there is a revised edition. With development, there is no final product or completed deliverable because it is about ongoing, lifelong growth and learning. Not to get too far ahead of ourselves with the content of the book, but this is where the important role of self-views comes into play. Thinking about oneself as a leader motivates the kind of learning and practice that sustains development over years and even decades. Relatedly, thinking of myself as a writer helped to motivate me to sit in front of the computer on those days when I initially wanted to do something (anything) else. A maxim of social psychology is that thinking is for doing. This type of identity-based change is one of those novel development pathways that is explored in this volume.

Here are a few additional key themes that you will find throughout:

- Everyone has leadership potential, some have more of that potential and some with less. But everyone can develop as a leader.
- Self-views—and especially leader identity—are important developmental outcomes along with leadership skills and competencies.
- Programs do little to develop leaders and leadership. What matters more is being embedded in a development system that includes, among other things, feedback mechanisms and the opportunity to grow as a leader through various developmental pathways.
- Development takes time and all things related to leadership develop following different time scales.
- Developing leaders is not the same as developing leadership.
- Collectives (e.g., dyads, teams, organizations) can develop leadership capacity, which is greater than the sum of its individual leaders.
- Social network analysis offers powerful tools and methods for understanding how collectives develop leadership capacity that can be drawn from when facing complex adaptive challenges.
- Adopting evidence-based principles, practices, and processes requires continuous investments in advancing the science of leader and leadership development.

I hope that these themes are intriguing and help motivate you to engage more deeply with them through reading this volume. Even better is to take a few minutes to reflect after reading each chapter using prompts such as (a) what did I learn, (b) how does this material change how I think about leader or leadership development, and (c) how might this change how I study leader and leadership development or engage with developing leaders. It is all about learning because learning is the cornerstone of development. But acting on what is learned is also important because thinking is for doing but it is also the case that doing cause thinking. That thinking–doing–thinking cycle is the core of any developmental system, including those engaged with developing leaders and leadership.

Claremont, CA, USA David V. Day

# Acknowledgments

This book was written while on sabbatical and I gratefully acknowledge the support provided by Claremont McKenna College to complete this project. I also thank Henry and Marie-Josée Kravis for their generous support of the Kravis Leadership Institute at Claremont McKenna, where I serve as the Academic Director and where many of the ideas found in this volume have been honed. There are many other family members and friends who provided valuable forms of support during this project, including my colleagues and the students at the Kravis Leadership Institute. My sincerest thanks to you all.

## Declaration of Competing Interests

There are no competing financial or non-financial interests in relation to the content of this volume.

# Contents

# About the Author

**David V. Day** is Professor of Psychological Science and Academic Director of the Kravis Leadership Institute at Claremont McKenna College (USA). He also holds the titles of Steven L. Eggert '82 P '15 Professor of Leadership and George R. Roberts Research Fellow at the College. He has held previous professorial appointments at the University of Western Australia Business School as Woodside Chair in Leadership and Management, Lee Kong Chian School of Business at Singapore Management University, Penn State University, and Louisiana State University. He is a Fellow of the American Psychological Association, American Psychological Society, International Association of Applied Psychology, and the Society for Industrial and Organizational Psychology. Day has published more than 100 peer-reviewed journal articles, books, and book chapters, many pertaining to the core topics of leadership and leadership development, including the co-authored book, *An Integrative Approach to Leader Development: Connecting Adult Development, Identity, and Expertise* (Routledge/Psychology Press). He has spoken at and worked with organizations around the world on topics related to leadership and leader development. He received the Walter F. Ulmer Research Award from the Center for Creative Leadership for outstanding, career-long contributions to applied leadership research.

# Abbreviations

| | |
|---|---|
| CEO | Chief Executive Officer |
| DDO | Deliberately Development Organization |
| Hi-Po | High-Potential Leader |
| HR | Human Resources |
| IPIP | International Personality Item Pool |
| K (or *k*) | Number of studies in a meta-analysis, number of measurement periods, or higher-level units (e.g., teams) in a multilevel study |
| KLI | Kravis Leadership Institute |
| KSAs | Knowledge, Skills, and Abilities |
| LSE | Leadership Self-Efficacy |
| *N* | Number of participants in a research study |
| P&L | Profit and Loss |
| ROI | Return on Investment |
| SBI | Situation, Behavior, Impact |
| SIENA | Simulation Investigation for Empirical Network Analysis |
| SNA | Social Network Analysis |
| UCINET | Social Network Analysis Software |
| VUCA | Volatile, Uncertain, Complex, Ambiguous |

# List of Figures

# List of Tables

CHAPTER 1

# Overview and First Principles of Developing Leaders and Leadership

## Introduction

> We have barely scratched the surface in our efforts toward leadership development. In the mid-twenty-first century, people will look back on our present practices as primitive.
>
> –John W. Gardner (1912–2002), *On Leadership* (1990, p. xix)

Most people nowadays are unfamiliar with John W. Gardner. For those readers who do not know the name of John Gardner, he was an American statesman, professor, and founder of Common Cause, a nonpartisan, grassroots organization dedicated to upholding the core values of American democracy. He worked with President Lyndon Johnson in designing the so-called Great Society in the 1960s. Gardner cared very deeply about leadership (although no guru) and believed that anyone has the potential to be a better leader. That is a vision embraced in this book as well.

Why does Gardner claim that current practices are primitive? He did not elaborate on this use of the word primitive in his book *On Leadership*, but I have some ideas. He was clear that he believed that there was massive, underutilized leadership potential in the world, which remains the case today. One reason for this unchanged state of the world may have something to do with assumptions about the nature of leadership. One such primitive assumption is that leadership is a rare gift that very few individuals possess or can develop. Gardner believed that every single human being has leadership potential, which is an assumption that this



D. V. Day, *Developing Leaders and Leadership*,
https://doi.org/10.1007/978-3-031-59068-9_1

volume shares. In a more contemporary treatment, it has been suggested that hidden potential is everywhere and resides in us all (Grant, 2023). That includes leadership potential.

Believing that everyone has leadership potential does not mean that any one given individual could be a successful CEO of a multinational company, or elected leader of a country, or even an effective director of a local nonprofit organization. For one thing, *leadership is a process not a position*. Individuals (and collectives) can learn to be more effective in how they participate in leadership processes. But to be effective in these processes, there needs to be preparation and that is what this book is about: Preparing yourself and others for leadership. It is also about how these topics of developing leaders and leadership are studied scientifically.

A question that comes up frequently when this notion of preparing everyone for leadership is if everyone is a leader then who will follow? That notion is mistaken because it partitions people into being either a leader or a follower. Given that leadership is a process it is also a dynamic process whereby who is leading and who is following can change quickly. Some individuals may lead more often than follow (appropriately or not) and others follow more often than lead (again, appropriately or not). We all do both—lead and follow. But as Gardner (1990) also notes, most people go through life using a very small fraction of their potential. One of the greatest untapped human capabilities is that of leadership "gifts" as he calls them (p. xix). It is related to the important question of how might we help people better realize their full potential in life?

Another potentially primitive practice is the reliance on programs as the venue for developing leaders and leadership. Programs are good for vendors because they are easily monetized as a commodity, whether they be open enrollment courses offered offsite or custom ones designed along with organizational stakeholders. The (over) reliance on programs is based on the implicit assumption that you need to take people away from their work to develop. A more advanced and less primitive assumption is that individuals and collectives can develop—and perhaps do so more effectively—while engaged in their work.

There are additional primitive practices that will be discussed in this volume, with an eye toward overcoming their outdated nature to embrace more state-of-the-science development. But the assertion by Gardner (1990) more than 30 years ago is one worth pondering. Are we making progress toward more progressive and less primitive leadership development practices? I think the evidence is mixed and that we can still do much better.

### *Why Leadership?*

An overarching question—or perhaps the proverbial elephant in the room—is why leadership? The research evidence is clear that effective leadership is important for individuals, groups, organizations, and larger collectives. Bad leadership destroys value, ruins interpersonal relationships, and undermines personal wellbeing. There is a rich history, especially in the social and organizational sciences attempting to better conceptualize and understand what makes for effective leadership. Theories abound. Empirical research has provided data galore. Yet there is no one right or best leadership theory. This book is not intended to add to that literature. Rather, it is as much about *development* as it is about *leadership*. Instead of offering another leadership theory or a review of the evidence on various approaches to leadership, this book will take a scientific, evidence-based approach to understanding the study of developing leaders and leadership.

Although there has been progress in developing a science to inform practice, that is not to say that there is any agreed-upon overarching theory of leadership development. Developing leaders and leadership is inherently eclectic. There is a saying among the more cynical academics that the world has problems, universities have departments. There is a siloed approach embedded in colleges and universities for myriad reasons. The leadership development field offers an opportunity to buck that trend. Leadership development should draw from applied psychology such as organizational psychology, more basic branches of psychology such as social and developmental psychology (and especially adult development), as well as learning theories, longitudinal methods, network science, among others. This volume offers an introduction of sorts to the multidisciplinary and wide-ranging field of twenty-first-century leadership development.

Nonetheless, there are restraining forces at work. A major restrainer when it comes to building an evidence-based field of leadership development is the fixation on leadership "gurus" who claim to hold the secrets or magic elixir when it comes to leadership. These guru-centric ideas tend to be presented in the sort of business and popular press books typically authored by a successful leader in business, politics, sport, or entertainment that proposes a personal roadmap of sorts to getting to the top as a leader. These gurus sell lots of books, and make heaps of money as consultants and speakers, but do they actually make anyone a better leader? I have yet to see any evidence of that (hoping this does not sound like sour grapes!). One reason for that is there are no quick fixes or magic bullets when it comes to development. This foreshadows a small set of First Principles presented later in this chapter.

This faddish, popular press albatross is why many academics view the field of leadership with a hefty dose of skepticism in terms of scientific rigor. Leadership development is viewed even more dubiously as a science. The albatross here is the legacy of monetization of developmental programs, practices, and assessments. The underlying values of many providers of leadership development services are financial rather than scientific. This legacy and the skepticism associated with it is starting to dissipate as more theory and research is published in rigorous, peer-reviewed, academic journals. Over the previous two decades, there have also been more junior scholars who have taken up the cause of advancing the evidence-based scholarship of developing leaders and leadership. This book will review a good deal of that work.

An appropriate place to launch this perspective on a different way of thinking about and studying leadership development is with definitions. What is leader development? What is leadership development? How are they different and why is this distinction important?

## Defining Leader Development and Leadership Development

When I first started to think about what is needed to advance the science of leadership development it was evident that there was conceptual confusion about the focus of development. As noted almost 25 years ago (Day, 2000), much of what was presented as leadership development was the development of individual leaders. Developing an individual as a leader does not mean that better, more effective, more complex, or more sophisticated leadership will inherently result. The developmental focus was on the individual and it was assumed that what was learned or acquired would be applied back on the job or other contexts that would help this leader enact better leadership. That is a big assumption. This was the impetus behind a proposed revised terminology of advancing *leader development*, defined as enhancing the capacity of individuals to be effective in leadership roles and processes (Day & Dragoni, 2015; Day et al., 2009; McCauley et al., 2010). The developmental focus is more on intrapersonal or within-person skills and, as will be discussed, self-views that support skill development.

Another term that describes the focus of much of leader development is *human capital*. According to an economic scholar and Nobel Laureate, human capital "is concerned with activities that influence future monetary and psychic income by increasing the resources in people" (Becker, 1993, p. 10). These are usually investments in knowledge, skills, or health/wellbeing that raise the future value of the owner of that capital. In this way, education has been conceptualized and studied as a primary means of enhancing individual human capital. In the leader development field, it is about enhancing the capacity of individuals to be more effective in leadership roles and processes. Enhancing capacity in this way is increasing the human capital value of the developing leader through positive change in intrapersonal attributes.

The processes involved in developing leadership requires a different and more collective focus than developing individual leaders (i.e., there are different levels of analysis involved). Specifically, *leadership development* operates at a more collective level of analysis than leader development. The growth or capacity enhancement is that of a collective (dyad, group/team, business unit, organization) to produce leadership (Day & Dragoni, 2015), which according to some scholars is the collective capacity to produce direction, alignment, and commitment (Drath et al., 2008; McCauley et al., 2010).

Grounding leadership in the fundamental tasks of direction, alignment, and commitment offers a more functional leadership ontology. It also sidesteps the challenges of trying to define leadership succinctly. Many scholars have tried to define leadership—perhaps as many as have studied the construct (Bass, 2008)—but capturing a comprehensive picture of this complex construct has proven elusive. Instead of a definition of leadership, an inclusive, functional ontology addresses new and different questions about leadership. Specifically, leadership theory and research would "seek to explain how people who share work in collectives produce direction, alignment, and commitment" (Drath et al., p. 636).

For this ontological perspective, leadership is anything or anyone—individually or collectively—that brings about direction, alignment, and/or commitment.

Because of the focus on a more collective level of analysis, leadership development is about the creation of *social capital*. This form of capital is not found at the intrapersonal level but interpersonally in the relationships developed among and between people engaged in shared work. According to social capital scholars, it is "the resource available to actors as a function of their location in the structure of their social relations" (Adler & Kwon, 2002, p. 18). The shard work of the collective is what creates and necessitates those social relations. As will be discussed in more detail in Chapter 7, an ideal way to study these relations and the capacities that co-evolve with the growth of social capital is through social network analysis.

The distinctions drawn between leader and leadership development are summarized in Table 1.1. Leader development creates value through enhancing human capital that resides mainly at the individual and intrapersonal levels. It involves the acquisition and growth of individual-level knowledge, skills, and abilities (KSAs) that would help an individual be more effective in leadership roles and processes. It also involves the enhancement of pertinent self-views (discussed in Chapter 4), particularly self-awareness, leadership self-efficacy, and the internalization of a leader identity (Day & Dragoni, 2015). There are more distal outcomes associated with leader development involving aspects of adult development further elaborated on in Chapter 5.

Leadership development creates value through enhancing the social capital that resides mainly at the interpersonal or relational level (i.e., between people). The kinds of capacities that develop more proximally and form the leading indicators of leadership development are conceptualized and measured more collectively such as psychological safety, shared mental models, leadership efficacy, and collective identification; more distal or lagging indicators of leadership development are associated with a collective capacity for leadership (Day & Dragoni, 2015). These are distinct targets for development, but also interrelated in that social capital development can also help develop human capital (Coleman, 1988), and vice versa.

It is not an either/or proposition in terms of either leader development or leadership development. They should both be considered integral

**Table 1.1** Fundamental aspects of leader development and leadership development

| | *Leader development* | *Leadership development* |
|---|---|---|
| Focus | Individual | Collective |
| Capital | Human | Social |
| Level of analysis | Intrapersonal | Interpersonal/ Relational |
| Developmental indicators | | |
| Proximal | KSAs<br>Self-Views | Psychological safety<br>Shared mental models<br>Leadership efficacy<br>Collective identification |
| Distal | Complex meaning-making structures and processes<br>Dynamic skills and abstractions | Collective leadership capacity |

*Note* Adapted from Day (2000) and Day and Dragoni (2015)

parts of a developmental system. The design and implementation of development systems will be addressed in detail in Chapter 2. It is a good design feature to sequence these aspects of development to first focus on individual leader development as a foundation for more collective forms of leadership development. Individuals need to build intrapersonal capabilities before addressing the more complex relational and interpersonal aspects of collective development.

## First Principles of Developing Leaders and Leadership

To integrate leader and leadership development, a good place to begin is to establish work from what is called first principle thinking. It is a well-regarded practice in philosophy and science to derive first principles, especially in designing any coherent logical system. Another way to think about first principles is that they represent the fundamental concepts or assumptions on which a theory, system, or method is based. Each developmental system should be based on its own first principles. What is presented next is a set of first principles that guide the overall thinking in this book. They are also the first principles for a leadership development system adopted by the Kravis Leadership Institute at Claremont McKenna College where I am the Academic Director. Another example of first principle thinking in a university-based developmental system can be found at the Doerr Institute for New Leaders at Rice University (Kolditz et al., 2021).

What follows is a presentation and brief explanation of the first principles guiding the novel approach to developing leaders and leadership in this volume. The focus is mainly on first principles of leader development mainly because of the recommendation to focus on developing individual leaders before attempting to develop collectives. Nonetheless, many of the same principles apply to collective leadership development with some minor tweaks. These will be included as corollaries to individual leader development, just to be clear that there are different levels of analysis at play.

### *Principle 1: You Cannot Make Anyone Develop as a Leader*

Think about it: Is there really any way to make someone become a leader? One answer might be to put someone into a leadership role and ergo that person will become a leader. We know that is magical thinking because we all know at least one person in a formal leadership role who is a terrible leader. They may be perfectly competent in exercising legitimate power as a manager working within the status quo but are not seen as a leader or are considered effective at using other sources of more informal power to enact change. The latter is a hallmark of a leader.

This principle also reflects what we know from the science of adult development (Demick & Andreoletti, 2003; Hoare, 2006). The evidence is clear that individuals can continue to develop over the course of the entire lifespan; however, there is no guarantee that will happen. Development in childhood and adolescence is driven a lot by biological and maturational processes, as well as through environmental forces. For many years it was thought that development ceased once one reached adulthood (around 20 years of age). Theory and research from an emerging science of adult development have proven otherwise, so long as someone is exposed to challenging experiences. In sum, development in the adult years is not a given, but it can occur. A lot depends on owning one's development by exercising personal agency.

Something similar occurs with leader development. Passively sitting through lectures, videos, or reading books is not enough to motivate development as a leader. You need to act, and as will be discussed in subsequent sections of this volume, you especially need to practice mind-sets and behavior that take you out of your comfort zone. Development as an adult is active not passive. One of the reasons why adopting and internalizing a leader identity is so important is because what becomes part of an identity is something that is valued. And if it is valued, we will devote our most precious resource of time to that facet of the self. It is a basic resource allocation issue. Who we are in terms of identity is where we focus our attention and time. This is especially important in motivating development over long time periods, which is discussed in the second First Principle.

**Corollary to Principle 1**: Collectives need to own their development in creating leadership in more shared, collaborative, and networked ways.

### *Principle 2: Development Requires Dedicated Work Over a Long Period of Time*

There are no quick fixes or shortcuts when it comes to development (despite what some might claim). This applies to leader development as well as leadership development. When it comes to any sort of change, there is a need for a longer term commitment. This is one major reason why thinking about development in terms of programs is both limited and limiting. Programs can be helpful in providing tools to practice after the program ends, but it requires someone to own their development (see Principle 1) and continue to practice what was learned. It is unclear how often that occurs, but probably not that often. A meta-analysis (a study of studies) of the transfer of training literature ($k$ = 89, where $k$ is the number of studies) indicated different factors that positively predicted training transfer back to the job, including cognitive ability, conscientiousness, motivation, and a supportive work environment (Blume et al., 2010). This reinforces the point empirically that follow-through on program learning and development is not inevitable.

There is an entire self-help industry that promises to show the way to personal change and growth. Much of this industry is about breaking bad habits or acquiring new ones, which has relevance for developing leaders and leadership even if it is not addressing those concerns directly. There is a lot of unhelpful, ad-hoc advice (i.e., not empirically based) in many of these books, but there are some that are worth their price. One of the best in my mind is *Atomic Habits* (Clear, 2018). The volume is grounded in scientific evidence to complement the author's personal experience, with a focus on making small changes that can lead to big results. Too often there is a tendency to believe that one needs to make a really big life change to bring about long-term growth, development, or change. It tends to be just the opposite.

Take the example of individual personality. Can someone change their personality traits? The old-school thinking on this was somewhere along the lines of personality is destiny. Given that personality is largely genetically determined, psychologists reckoned that it probably did not change much after someone reached adulthood. More recent scientific research suggests otherwise. One example (Hudson et al., 2019) reported on a 15-week study that used an intensive longitudinal design with multiple waves of data collection ($M = 11.25$, $SD = 4.16$ of data waves). Participants ($N = 377$) provided self-report ratings of the Big 5 personality factors (or traits) of Openness to Experience, Conscientiousness, Extraversion, Agreeableness, and Emotional Stability (or Neuroticism) and nominated one that they would like to change. They were invited to try out relevant challenges tailored to each specific personality trait. Personality was shown to change over time; however, just accepting behavioral challenges did not predict trait changes. Participants needed to complete small challenges by performing trait-typical behaviors to accomplish personality change over time. It also wasn't the difficulty of the challenges that predicted trait change, but the consistency with which participants engaged in these trait-consistent behavioral challenges. Small changes can lead to big results, even in changing personality traits.

**Corollary to Principle 2:** Collectives need to work together intensively over time to develop their leadership capacity.

### *Principle 3: To the Extent that Leadership is Learned, It Is Learned Through Experience*

This principle owes a debt of gratitude to Morgan McCall, who included it as one of his "seven sure bets" regarding what we know about using experience for developing leaders and leadership (McCall, 2010, p. 3). A long-standing debate concerns whether leaders are born or made. Is leadership something based on inherited qualities (i.e., nature) or a product of environmental forces (i.e., nurture)? The answer turns out to be: Yes!

Leaders are both born and made, nature and nurture. Some individuals are born with greater leadership potential than others. This does not mean there is a specific leadership gene (although see De Neve et al., 2013 for a provocative alternative perspective); rather, inherited attributes such as intelligence and personality play a large role in who emerges as a leader. Who others see as a leader is important because being perceived as a leader provides more latitude to influence others than not being seen as a leader. A classic example of this is Extraversion being positively associated with leader emergence, which researchers are still examining in new and innovative ways (e.g., Landis et al., 2022). More sociable and outgoing individuals are more likely to be seen as leaders relative to those who are more introverted.

What this means is that some individuals have an advantage when it comes to being perceived as a leader (emergence) and performing effectively as a leader (effectiveness) (Judge et al., 2002). Others lacking these attributes can still be seen and engaged effectively as leaders, but they will likely need to work harder to achieve the same ends as the more fortunate individuals with the purported "right stuff." We all know individuals who are blessed with certain gifts whether in sport, math, leadership, or other domains but who never work to develop those gifts. They rest on their laurels in terms of what the raw talent provides them. These individuals typically lose out in the long run to those with less talent but who have the work ethic and personal discipline to keep working at learning and getting better in a specific domain (see Grant, 2023). Consider it a version of the parable of the tortoise and the hare. It's the long game that matters.

This brings us to the role of fun in leadership development. There are any number of games and other kinds of purportedly fun activities that are used in the name of development. Most of these are bad. By bad, I mean that they have little if any effect on development. They are a waste of time and money. As observed by colleagues at the Doerr Institute for New Leaders at Rice University:

> We use the term "leader-tainment" to characterize activities that are sold as leader development but amount to little more than a few laughs and feel-good moments. That's the type of program that our research found predominates the current leader development landscape in U.S. colleges and universities. (Kolditz et al., 2021, p. 18)

I dare say that these kinds of leader-tainment activities can be found in the corporate leader development world as well. Fun is all well and good, but it should not be the criterion used to choose which developmental activities to implement. Just because an activity is fun or enjoyable does not mean it is developmental. It perpetuates the predominant mindset that leadership development is a like a pass to an amusement park. You go on a bunch of rides, maybe play some games, have a laugh or two, and write it off as your developmental investment in leadership for the year.

Leader development is more like buying a gym membership. What do we know about gyms and those who buy memberships? A lot of those people who buy memberships don't bother going to the gym or if they do it's more to socialize than to sweat. To change your muscle mass or aerobic capacity you need to work out, push yourself beyond current capabilities, and do it regularly. That is why evidence-based leadership development is more like buying a gym membership than spending the day at an amusement park. And by the way, your leader development gym is all around you. It comprises your ongoing, everyday experiences.

**Corollary to Principle 3:** Developing a collective capacity for leadership is more about regular hard work with others who share work than offsite teambuilding activities in which having fun or providing a "memorable experience" is the chosen criterion.

### *Principle 4: The Foundation of Any Meaningful Developmental Experience Includes Assessment, Challenge, and Support*

Not every experience has an equivalent "developmental punch" (Tesluk & Jacobs, 1998, p. 323). Some experiences have greater developmental potential than others. It is also the case that different experiences develop different types of skills, competencies, and mindsets. A great example of a received doctrine in leadership development (i.e., something that everyone tends to believe about leadership development but has no basis in fact or evidence) is the so-called 70–20-10 rule about how to best develop leadership talent. The rule is more of a heuristic or rule of thumb, but it prescribes the best mix of developmental experiences are 70% challenging assignments, 20% other people (e.g., developmental relationships), and 10% programs (McCall, 2010). Note the relatively small emphasis on formal leadership programs. And yet, the practice space is still dominated by leadership programs with little emphasis on the other 90% of experiences.

Researchers from the Center for Creative Leadership have offered a complementary perspective. In their handbook of leadership development (Van Velsor et al., 2010) it is proposed that any experience can be made more developmental to the extent that it includes the core aspects of assessment, challenge, and support (McCauley et al., 2010). This recommendation is grounded mainly in their 50+ years of working in the leadership development space rather than any particular research study or studies. From this perspective, formal classroom programs can be made more developmental by including assessment, challenge, and support activities. Conversely, challenging assignments or challenge experiences may not be very developmental if they lack aspects of assessment and support to complement the challenge. This happens all too frequently when individuals are put into very demanding work assignments that lack either assessment mechanisms or support. Leader development is not—or should not be—a sink or swim proposition. That is just bad developmental practice.

Assessment, challenge, and support are the cornerstones of a sound developmental system. A system transcends any one program or any given assignment or other experience. It offers the potential for an integrated system that enhances learning from experience. That important point should not be overlooked: It is not so much about providing experiences to promote the development of leaders and leadership as it is about doing things that enhance learning from experience. That might sound like a trivial distinction, but it is the case that learning from experience is not easy or inevitable.

In a commentary piece to the McCall (2010) article, I noted several obstacles that prevent people from learning from experience (Day, 2010). These learning obstacles when it comes to experience include that there may not be an awareness that there is something to learn (e.g., the focus is on performance rather than learning); it is not clear what is to be learned from the experience (e.g., there is no guidance or support to reinforce what is to be learned); and it is unclear if or when learning has occurred. As noted in the commentary, "All of these issues are magnified when the experience in question is a challenging stretch assignment in which there are major career implications at stake and the primary focus is on performing well rather than learning well" (Day, p. 42). Enhancing the learning that comes from a well-designed development system is the key factor (also called a mediator variable in the psychology literature) in enhancing the development of leaders and leadership. Further details about what kinds of things are considered aspects of assessment, challenge, and support will be taken up in Chapter 2 with the topic of developmental systems.

**Corollary to Principle 4:** Assessment, challenge, and support are just as relevant to the design and delivery of collective leadership development experiences as they are to an individual leader development system.

### *Principle 5: There Are Evidence-Based Practices That Support the Development of Leaders and Leadership*

It should go without saying (but I'll say it anyway) that just because something costs a lot of money does not mean it is any good. This is especially the case in the world of leadership development. A prime example is the phenomenon of the leadership speaker. These are usually "world renown" leadership experts mainly by virtue of having held an important, visible leadership role that was associated with some successful outcomes. The thinking on this is something like "Let's hear what this individual has to say because it might help us become just like him/her/them."

There are any number of assumptions embedded in the hope that such leadership gurus will contribute to the development of others as leaders. A quick reality check is to ask someone a few days after attending one of these talks what was learned or even what is something that can be remembered. Often there is just a stunned silence. Huh? But if something can be articulated about what was learned that was related to leadership, then what specific action was taken to implement this learning in ways that would enhance development? Usually, no actions were taken. But even if there were articulated leadership lessons, and some change in behavior, what kinds of evidence is there that such longer term change is common? As noted by Kolditz et al. (2021), there is no empirical, quantifiable data that the considerable monetary sums paid to leadership gurus to give talks has any developmental impact on those who attended such talks (this often goes for guest speakers in college classes on leadership as well).

Organizations should invest more wisely in their developmental initiatives, otherwise there is a real risk of simply wasting valuable resources in time and money. To avoid this potential waste, decision-makers should choose to invest in evidence-based practices and processes. There is a trend beginning with medicine and now moving into other fields such as management to value being evidence-based. According to Denise

Rousseau (2006), "Evidence-based management means translating principles based on the best evidence into organizational practices" (p. 256). These principles are based in research evidence and translated into practices that help solve organizational problems. Applied to the more specific organizational problem of developing leaders and leadership, evidence-based leadership development looks to use research evidence to design the developmental pathways for building more effective leadership in organizations. It is maximizing investments in those practices and processes that have evidence to support that they work. Evidence-based leadership development is the *sine qua non* of a more scientific approach to developing leaders and leadership. Science is based on empirical evidence.

## Implications of the First Principles

The five First Principles presented in this chapter form the backbone of a developmental system that is coherent and cohesive. These principles also represent fundamental assumptions about how to go about developing leaders and leadership in ways that can help create a competitive advantage in organizations. But they also represent assumptions about the individuals and collectives engaged in meaningful developmental activities. What follows is a brief discussion of the implications of those principles and their underlying assumptions.

First Principle #1 that you cannot make anyone develop as a leader goes beyond a decision whether to make leadership training and development mandatory. It goes to the issue of who owns leader and leadership development. Is it an organization's Human Resources (HR) department or the individual aspiring to be a better leader? If you assume that HR or some talent development function owns development an implication (often implicit) is that an individual waits around for HR to give them some sort of developmental assignment such as attending a leadership development workshop or program. Waiting around for HR to tell you what to do is probably never a good practice, especially when it comes to leadership. Individuals need to own their development and be more proactive and less reactive in finding suitable and impactful practices and processes.

First Principle #2 proposes that developing as a leader takes consistent effort over a relatively long time span. Don't expect miracles! This principle is based on evidence stemming from the considerable body of scientific research in the field of expert performance (Ericsson et al.,

1993). You might have heard the adage that it takes a minimum of 10 years or 10,000 hours of dedicated practice to become an expert in any field (e.g., music, chess, gaming, and other skill-based endeavors). The research evidence generally supports this assertion although there are important individual differences based on the underlying talent that someone brings to a field. The same can be said about becoming an expert leader (Day et al., 2009). An implication of this principle is that attending a few workshops or programs spread out over time is not going to do much in terms of developing expert-level leadership. There needs to be an ongoing commitment to practicing one's leadership to get the time and amount of deliberate practice to become that expert leader.

An implication of First Principle #3 is that to develop as a leader the right kinds of experiences need to be found—or designed. Avoid the siren song of meaningless leader-tainment activities. There is a great deal of evidence about the kinds of experiences that have evidence-based impacts in developing leaders and leadership. Knowing the kinds of activities that help promote development and those that are a general waste of resources is an important part of owning your own development.

Using assessment, challenge, and support to design your own developmental curriculum will enhance the power of leveraging experience for development. An assumption behind First Principle #4 is related to the notion of proactivity. Experiences do not just happen to us (at least not all the time); rather, they are often things we self-select into and out of as well as design in intentional ways. Although "fun" might be the criterion used to design experience, it is the wrong standard to use. Identify those experiences that will challenge you the most (within reason), which first means building some level of self-awareness, and one way to do that is through assessment. Complementing assessments to find out what you are like with experiences designed to challenge you to get out of your comfort zone with the support needed to maintain practice over a long period of time are paramount to effective development. Experiences can be designed and chosen with some deliberation. Use the most appropriate criteria in doing so.

An assumption supporting First Principle #5 is that there is a science of leadership and its development. It does not mean that there is any "Grand Unified Theory" or that we know everything there is to know about leadership. It is also the case that there is an art to leadership as well. Leadership involves performance and some will be better performers than others; however, any leader can become more effective by adopting

**Table 1.2** Summary of the first principles of leadership development and implications

| |
|---|
| **First Principle #1: You cannot make anyone develop as a leader** |
| *Implications*: Individuals need to own their development and be proactive in choosing and designing developmental experiences |
| **First Principle #2: Development requires dedicated work over a long period of time** |
| *Implications*: No one should expect miracles when it comes to development. It is like developing expert performance in any domain: Consistent practice over many months or years is needed |
| **First Principle #3: To the extent that leadership is learned, it is learned through experience** |
| *Implications*: Leadership involves both nature and nurture. Leaders are both born and made. Experience molds leadership talent into more effective leaders so choose developmental experiences carefully |
| **First Principle #4: The foundation of any meaningful developmental experience includes assessment, challenge, and support** |
| *Implications*: Some experiences are more developmental than others. Know how to design into experiences those aspects of assessment, challenge, and support that make an experience more developmentally meaningful |
| **First Principle #5: There are evidence-based practices that support the development of leaders and leadership** |
| *Implications*: Science may not know everything about leadership and its development, but there is research evidence that can help design and implement better practices and processes for enhancing the development of leaders and leadership. Know that evidence and use it |

*Note* First Principles are the fundamental concepts or assumptions on which a theory, system, or method is based.

an evidence-based perspective on their lifelong journey as a leader. These First Principles and their implications are presented in Table 1.2.

## Overview of the Volume

This opening chapter provided an overarching framework and motivation for the volume. A central thesis is that there is a need for more scholarly treatment of the science behind developing leaders and leadership. Instead of presenting what individuals need in the way of prescribed knowledge, skills, abilities, competencies, traits, and on and on, the approach presented in this volume will be focused on the scientific study of leader and leadership development. How has the research been conducted methodologically? What are the kinds of variables used in related research? A major component of this introductory chapter presented and discussed a set of innovative first principles that underpin how the development of leaders and leadership can be considered scientifically, along with a discussion of their implications.

### *Chapter 2: Developmental Systems*

This chapter focuses on the important role of systems thinking in developing leaders and leadership. Implicit in the First Principles is that effective change and growth (i.e., development) are more likely to occur if supported by a coherent developmental system. A standard definition of a system is a group of interacting, interrelated, or interdependent elements forming a complex whole. This is contrasted with the more typical program-centric approach to developing leaders and leadership. Programs tend to be bounded and episodic events with little in the way of system feature such as interacting, interrelated, and interdependent elements. Programs also tend to be designed more around closed systems than open systems. The essential features for developing leaders and leadership are assessment, challenge, and support. These essential features are discussed along with concrete examples, including how to design an initiative with true systems features.

### *Chapter 3: Individual Leader Development*

The focus of this chapter is on individual leader development. Most claims of leadership development are instead focused on the development of individual leaders. There is nothing wrong, per se, about this focus; however, it creates the erroneous expectation that developing leaders inherently develops leadership. Essentially, it is a level of analysis issue. This chapter elaborates on the fallacy that developing leaders will develop leadership and its importance in terms of using an appropriate developmental focus. Another relevant distinction discussed in this chapter is the difference between leadership training and leader development.

### *Chapter 4: Self-views and Leader Development*

Time plays an important role in development. Knowing what develops more proximally and what develops more distally allows researchers to propose and test better research hypotheses. At a more proximal level, developing leaders not only acquire knowledge, skills, and abilities (KSAs) related to leadership but these are complemented and reinforced by self-views. One such self-view involves a leader identity. Internalizing an identity as a leader along with other important self-identities helps to motivate the kinds of practice needed to develop over the long term. People allocate their most valuable resource (i.e., time) to what they value the most. What is highly valued becomes an integral part of one's self-construal (i.e., identity). Other relevant self-views in leader development include self-awareness and self-efficacy, especially regarding leadership KSAs. This chapter reviews the role of self-views in leader development focusing on leader identity, self-awareness, and self-efficacy. It also elaborates on how self-views and skill development are mutually reinforcing processes in leader development.

### *Chapter 5: Considering Adult Development in Leader Development*

Continuing with the theme of time and development, this chapter examines the more distal outcomes of leader development that are associated with adult development. These distal outcomes—or lagging indicators of leader development—are related to mental complexity in which the leader's "operating system" is enhanced in ways that allow for deeper connections to be understood among various external forces. The role of subject–object transitions is discussed in facilitating the development of mental complexity. Another focus is on the development of epistemic cognition involving the origin, limits, and justification of human knowledge. This type of reflective judgment process is ultimately about gaining a deeper understanding of the causal forces in the world and those that shape who we become and why. In this manner, there is an inherent connection between the self-views presented in Chapter 4 and the adult development lens for understanding longer term developmental outcomes. Enhancing the interior lives of leaders is proposed to help developing leaders better adapt to complex changes in the external environment, also known as requisite complexity.

### *Chapter 6: Developing a Collective Capacity for Leadership*

This chapter represents a shift in focus to a more collective level of analysis (e.g., group, team, organization). As such, the focus is on leadership development rather than individual leader development. Although different in terms of focus and scope, the development of leaders and the development of collective capacity for leadership are not mutually exclusive endeavors. Whereas leader development is mainly about human capital development, leadership development focuses on social capital as the relevant outcome. Instead of focusing on the intrapersonal development of an individual leader in enhancing the potential for leadership, a collective focus recognizes that leadership is found in the interpersonal connections among individuals engaged in shared work. Leadership is conceptualized as an output shaped by systems structure and processes rather than considering it solely as an input into the system. Much less is known about collective forms of leadership development than those related to individual leader development; however, there have been some notable work in recent years summarized in this chapter. As with leader development, time is an important consideration. Proximal and distal outcomes of leadership development—leading and lagging indicators—will be presented and explained.

### *Chapter 7: Networks and Development*

Social network analysis is the application of network science to groups of people linked together through some common purpose (e.g., shared work). Social networks comprise links or ties among nodes (i.e., individuals or agents) in a bounded but permeable space. A social network is a way to understand the informal organizing structure among any group of people. It is argued that through interactions and appropriate interventions a collective capacity for leadership emerges in a network of actors involved in shared work. Network theory and social network analyses offer a useful lens and sound methodological/analytical approaches to understanding leadership capacity at a collective level of analysis. A related concept is that of social capital, or the value inherent in the relationships developed among people in a network. In this way, leadership resides between people in their links or ties rather than the leader-centric assumption that a leader is the sole cause of leadership in a system.

### *Chapter 8: Advancing the Science of Developing Leaders and Leadership*

This volume presents a scholarly perspective on the emerging science of developing leaders and leadership. Where available, scientific evidence is presented to support the choice of appropriate developmental pathways (i.e., processes and practices) that enhance the likelihood of effective leader and leadership development occurring. This chapter concludes with a focused summary of key points to consider for future research and practice. It also presents a set of research questions to help guide further advances in the nascent science of developing leaders and leadership. The mandate going forward is to advance the scientific study of developing leaders and leadership, elevating the field to something on par but different from what is found in the leadership literature and the voluminous self-help types of books that promise to make someone a great leader.

## Chapter Summary

- There is an emerging science of developing leaders and leadership that is grounded in empirical evidence.
- Developing leaders (i.e., leader development) is not equivalent to developing leadership (i.e., leadership development) because they involve different levels of analysis.
- The focus of leader development efforts is on enhancing the human capital capacity of individuals to be effective in leadership roles and processes.
- The focus of leadership development is on enhancing the social capital capacity of collectives (groups, teams, organizations) to draw forth and enact leadership.
- A set of First Principles (see Table 1.2) summarizes the fundamental concepts or assumptions on which the developmental system is based.
- The implications of these First Principles reflect that anyone can become a more effective leader to the extent that they own their development and leverage experiences in appropriate ways to enhance that development.

## References

Adler, P. S., & Kwon, S.-W. (2002). Social capital: Prospects for a new concept. *Academy of Management Review, 27*(1), 17–40. https://doi.org/10.5465/amr.2002.5922314

Bass, B. M. (2008). *The Bass handbook of leadership: Theory, research, and managerial implications* (4th ed.). Free Press.
Becker, G. S. (1993). *Human capital: A theoretical and empirical analysis with special reference to education* (3rd ed.). The University of Chicago Press/ National Bureau of Educational Research.
Blume, B. D., Ford, J. K., Baldwin, T. T., & Huang, J. L. (2010). Transfer of training: A meta-analytic review. *Journal of Management, 36*(4), 1065–1105. https://doi.org/10.1177/0149206309352880
Clear, J. (2018). *Atomic habits: An easy and proven way to build good habits and break bad ones*. Avery.
Coleman, J. S. (1988). Social capital in the creation of human capital. *American Journal of Sociology, 94*(Supplement: Organizations and Institutions: Sociological and Economic Approaches to the Analysis of Social Structure), S95–S120. https://doi.org/10.1086/228943
Day, D. V. (2000). Leadership development: A review in context. *The Leadership Quarterly, 11*(4), 581–613. https://doi.org/10.1016/S1048-9843(00)00061-8
Day, D. V. (2010). The difficulties of learning from experience and the need for deliberate practice. *Industrial and Organizational Psychology: Perspectives on Science and Practice, 3*(1), 41–44. https://doi.org/10.1111/j.1754-9434.2009.01195.x
Day, D. V., & Dragoni, L. (2015). Leadership development: An outcome-oriented review based on time and levels of analyses. *Annual Review of Organizational Psychology and Organizational Behavior, 2*, 133–156. https://doi.org/10.1146/annurev-orgpsych-032414-111328
Day, D. V., Harrison, M. M., & Halpin, S. M. (2009). *An integrative approach to leader development: Connecting adult development, identity, and expertise*. Psychology Press.
De Neve, J., Mikhaylov, S., Dawes, C. T., Christakis, N. A., & Fowler, J. H. (2013). Born to lead? A twin design and genetic association study of leadership role occupancy. *The Leadership Quarterly, 24*, 45–60. https://doi.org/10.1016/j.leaqua.2012.08.001
Demick, J., & Andreoletti, C. (Eds.). (2003). *Handbook of adult development*. Kluwer Academic/Plenum Publishers.
Drath, W. H., McCauley, C. D., Palus, C. J., Van Velsor, E., O'Connor, P. M. G., & McGuire, J. B. (2008). Direction, alignment, commitment: Toward a more integrative ontology of leadership. *Leadership Quarterly, 19*(6), 635–653. https://doi.org/10.1016/j.leaqua.2008.09.003
Ericsson, K. A., Krampe, R. T., & Tesch-Römer, C. (1993). The role of deliberate practice in the acquisition of expert performance. *Psychological Bulletin, 100*(3), 363–406. https://psycnet.apa.org/doi/10.1037/0033-295X.100.3.363

Gardner, J. W. (1990). *On leadership*. The Free Press.

Grant, A. (2023). *Hidden potential: The science of achieving greater things*. Viking.

Hoare, C. (Ed.). (2006). *Handbook of adult development and learning*. Oxford University Press.

Hudson, N. W., Briley, D. A., Chopik, W. J., & Derringer, J. (2019). You have to follow through: Attaining behavioral change goals predicts volitional personality change. *Journal of Personality and Social Psychology, 117*(4), 839–857. https://doi.org/10.1037/pspp0000221

Judge, T. A., Bono, J. E., Ilies, R., & Gerhardt, M. W. (2002). Personality and leadership: A qualitative and quantitative review. *Journal of Applied Psychology, 87*(4), 765–780. https://doi.org/10.1037/0021-9010.87.4.765

Kolditz, T., Gill, L., & Brown, R. P. (2021). *Leadership reckoning: Can higher education develop the leaders we need?* Monocle Press.

Landis, B., Jachimowicz, J. M., Wang, D. J., & Krause, R. W. (2022). Revisiting extraversion and leadership emergence: A social network churn perspective. *Journal of Personality and Social Psychology, 123*(4), 811–829. https://doi.org/10.1037/pspp0000410

McCall, M. W. (2010). Recasting leadership development. *Industrial and Organizational Psychology-Perspectives on Science and Practice, 3*, 3–19. https://doi.org/10.1111/j.1754-9434.2009.01189.x

McCauley, C. D., Van Velsor, E., & Ruderman, M. N. (2010). Introduction: Our view of leadership development. In E. Van Velsor, C. D. McCauley, & M. N. Ruderman (Eds.), *The Center for Creative Leadership handbook of leadership development* (3rd ed., pp. 1–26). John Wiley & Sons.

Rousseau, D. M. (2006). Is there such a thing as "Evidence-Based Management"? *Academy of Management Review, 31*(2), 256–269. https://doi.org/10.5465/amr.2006.20208679

Tesluk, P. E., & Jacobs, R. R. (1998). Toward an integrated model of work experience. *Personnel Psychology, 51*(2), 321–355. https://doi.org/10.1111/j.1744-6570.1998.tb00728.x

CHAPTER 2

# Developmental Systems

## The Problems with Leadership Development Programs

Organizations—large corporations in particular—are major consumers of leader development programs. There are way too many leadership development consultancies to count, but one estimate is that more than USD$160B is spent on leadership development in the US alone and over USD$360B globally (Westfall, 2019). That is a considerable outlay of financial resources, especially when the return on that investment is questionable. In interviews with more than 500 senior executives, McKinsey researchers found that approximately two-thirds of the respondents identified leadership development as their most pressing concern (Gurdjian et al., 2014). Additional research reported in that article indicated that fewer than 10 percent of senior managers think that their companies develop global leaders effectively, and approximately one-third of US companies admit that they do not have adequate numbers of leaders with the right capabilities. The lack of evidence to support the effectiveness of leadership development in for-profit organizations and corporations is unsettling, to say the least.

I once had a conversation with the late (and great) Dr. David Campbell of the Center for Creative Leadership about what we know about leadership development programs and their effectiveness. This anecdote—although not grounded in science but worth repeating—may help


D. V. Day, *Developing Leaders and Leadership*,
https://doi.org/10.1007/978-3-031-59068-9_2

illuminate some of the challenges associated with such programs. Dr. Campbell's perspective, based on decades of personal experience working with developing leaders including many senior leaders, was that leadership development programs have three possible outcomes, two of which are bad. What we think (or hope) happens is that someone goes off to a leadership program, learn a great deal about themselves, acquire new ways of thinking and acting as a leader, which are implemented to great success back on the job. A win–win all-around success scenario!

A second possibility is that after a meaningful, and perhaps transformative, program experience a participant returns to the job, tries to implement what was learned in the program, and everyone around them (especially the boss) observes all these new ideas and behaviors and basically does not like them one bit. "We want the old you before you went to that d*mn program" is a common litany. The result is that the participant reverts to their old ways and the investment in their development is lost. The third possibility is the worst of all. The participant returns after a meaningful program experience and tries to implement the new mindsets and skills, others do not like these new ways, the participant gets frustrated, looks for a new position at a different organization, finds one, and quits.

This raises the difficult question about what are the potential unintended consequences of sending someone to a leadership or leader development program? What we hope will happen is not necessarily what happens. It could be considered another example of the folly of rewarding A while hoping for B (Kerr, 1975). The organization rewards good managerial performance by sending someone to a leadership development program hoping that they will become a more effective leader. But it is also a truism that sending a changed person back to an unchanged system is often an exercise in futility.

Another major consumer of developmental programs for aspiring leaders are business schools. A significant component of the MBA curriculum in business schools is focused on developing their professional students to be more effective leaders. Despite that importance and the investments made in leadership development programs in business schools, research suggests that the programs generally are not evidence-based (Leroy et al., 2022). Interviews with academic directors ($N$ = 60) of leadership centers at "top business schools" indicated that "the selection of programs does not always align with scientific recommendations nor do schools always engage in high-quality program evaluation"

(p. 5). Challenges to promoting greater evidence-based practices in these (mainly) leader development programs include (a) overly broad definitions of leadership and its development, (b) underdeveloped and underappreciated knowledge base for leader development, (c) alternative organizational reasons competing with evidence-based practice, and (d) lack of quality of external monitoring for leader development programs.

One response to the data suggesting that leader development programs in organizations and business schools do not walk the evidence-based talk is to improve the foundation of evidence on which the program is based. But that does not address a fundamental limitation with a programs-based focus when it comes to leadership development. A major problem with program approaches to the complex challenge of developing leaders and leadership is that they are episodic and tend to be relatively short term. This may be due at least in part to a misplaced application of a training mindset and related practices to a phenomenon (i.e., leadership) that is much more complex and idiosyncratic for a typical training program. What is meant by idiosyncratic is that people developing as leaders start at different places and change in different ways. The typical leadership training program does not take that into account.

Leadership training and leadership development initiatives are different albeit complementary approaches. Organizations still tend to think about training "solutions" to very complex leadership problems that require much more long-term and individualized investments (Day et al., 2021). The relevant distinction between leadership training and development will be addressed directly in Chapter 3 when the topic turns to individual leader development. Another important concern is that leader development programs are often goal-driven: What is it that someone wants to achieve? Developmental systems are more about the processes that lead to those outcomes (Clear, 2018).

## Systems Thinking and Developmental Systems

A different response to the challenges of evidence-based leadership development is to engage in more systems thinking. According to one MIT professor who teaches a course on the topic, systems thinking refers to thinking about something as a system, understanding all the components comprised by the system, and the relationships between them (Crawley, 2022). Systems thinking is not new as it can be traced back to Aristotle and pre-Socratic philosophy. It is also the case that an influential general systems theory presented in the 1920s focused on natural and biological systems (Bertalanffy, 1972). What I will focus on is a bit more contemporary and focused on the open systems theory of organizations (Katz & Kahn, 1978) in motivating design thinking and the design of leader and leadership development systems.

A defining the difference between an open and a closed system is that the former has permeable boundaries and interacts with the environment. An open system is involved in cyclical events grounded in transforming inputs to throughputs (or transformed resources) to outputs (Katz & Kahn, 1978). Indeed, one of the essential characteristics of an open system is that it comprises *cycles of events*. It is not a single, stand-alone event but a cycle of repeating events. Translating this perspective to developing leaders and leadership, a typical leadership program is a single, non-cyclical event whereas a developmental system is based on an ongoing cycle of transforming energy into learning that is practiced in the environment, with feedback about that practice episode returned as input to the system. A related event cycle that will be discussed later in the chapter pertains to assessment, challenge, and support.

The cycle of repeating events in developmental systems operates in two ways. One cycle involves the transfer of developmental "energy" or motivation into skills and self-views, which compose the outputs that are released into the environment in the form of leadership behaviors and sensemaking filters. These are the foundations for practice that drive leader development in the form of experiential learning through doing. The experience in experiential learning is the so-called life gym where leadership is practiced (i.e., everyday life). From this practice comes feedback. Did things go well or not so well? What was learned from practicing a leadership skill or mindset? Information is imported from the practice environment or experience, which forms the basis of inputs back to the system for the next cycle of development. This *feedback mechanism* is one of the core characteristics of an open system according to Katz and Kahn (1978), in which "energy" often in the form of new information is fed back to the system.

An example might help illustrate how this developmental cycle works. A developing leader (Ellen) decides that she would like to be more empathic. Perhaps some assessment data (information) suggested that she might be more effective as a leader if she was more empathic. In learning about empathy, Ellen finds out through some background reading that active listening is considered an important skill in becoming more empathic (Rogers & Farson, 1957). She further researches the concept of active listening and learns that it is based on a series of steps or phases, the first two being (1) pay attention to the other person by removing distractions and using positive body language, and (2) suspend judgment and be open-minded (Center for Creative Leadership, 2019a). This learning process denotes the throughput or transformation process part of development.

Ellen decides to practice these basic steps of active listening the next time a friend or colleague confides in her about a problem or asks for advice. When such an opportunity occurs, instead of giving advice or engaging in a conversation, the focus is on paying attention to what the other is saying and suspending judgment, and being as open-minded as possible. The interaction goes very well in that the feedback that Ellen receives is that the other person felt heard, understood, and accepted, which could be considered as indicators not only of active listening but also empathy. Based on this positive feedback, Ellen decides to further enhance her active listening skills by learning about additional steps in the process and practicing them in future episodes. Figure 2.1 provides a simple schematic of this developmental cycle.

Another hallmark characteristic of open systems in *equifinality*, which suggests that a system (in this case, involving a developing leader) can

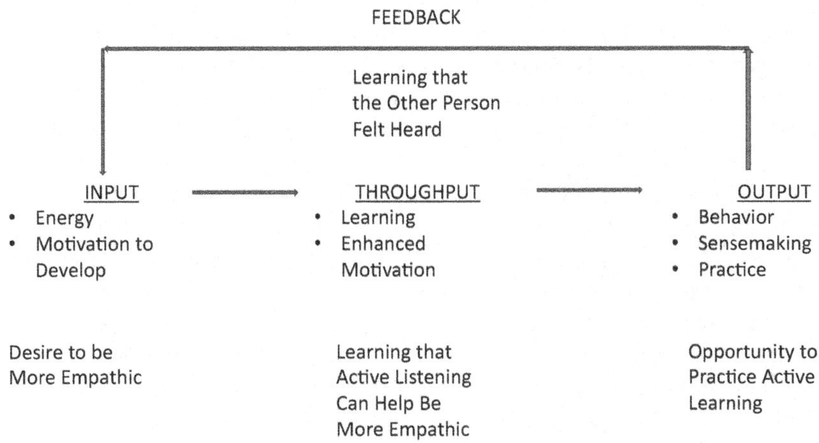


**Fig. 2.1** Cycle of leader development Focused on Empathy and active listening

reach the same final state from differing initial conditions and by a variety of paths (Katz & Kahn, 1978). This is an important principle in developmental systems because individuals start at different places and change in different ways in their respective developmental journeys (more formally called developmental trajectories). It is also the case that the focus of the development differs across individuals because of individual differences in leadership strengths and weaknesses. Two different individuals could choose very different skills or mindsets to work on to become better leaders. Ellen focused on empathy and operationalized it through active listening practice. Pat might choose to focus on being more extroverted given their highly introverted personality. As will be discussed in Chapter 3, this choice about what to work on is something that differentiates leader development from leadership training. Training assumes that individuals all start pretty much at the same place and change in the same way over the course of the intervention. These assumptions do not hold when the focus is development because it is assumed that individuals start at different developmental levels and have different developmental trajectories for a given skill or self-view.

## Assessment, Challenge, and Support

Another type of cycle involves the developmental building blocks of assessment, challenge, and support. As discussed in Chapter 1, these components are important factors in using experience for development. Any experience can be made more developmental to the extent that it includes aspects of assessment, challenge, and support (McCauley et al., 2010). Each of these components will be considered in depth in the following sections. But it is first helpful to consider how they would operate as cycles of events that are characteristic of an open system. Obtaining assessment data on what someone is like (e.g., personality, values, skill strengths, and weaknesses) is a starting place for many developmental experiences. This approach can also be termed assessment for development and can either be part of a larger initiative or a stand-alone practice. Assuming the motivation to develop is present, this data or information is used to set challenges that ideally put someone outside of their comfort zone. Acting in ways that go against what we are like is not easy, which is why including support as part of that event cycle is an important design feature of the system. Support can take the form of feedback, which as depicted in Fig. 2.1, serves as the mechanism providing input for the next developmental cycle.

Although this cycle of assessment, challenge, and support does not map perfectly onto the open systems cycle of input, throughput, and output, it helps illustrate how these components can be mutually reinforcing when considered as a system. Assessment data can help someone decide on an appropriate developmental target and the more specific challenge to undertake. Challenges by definition are challenging and can be better accomplished with support. Evidence supports this position. Research on middle- and senior-level managers ($N = 60$) involved in experientially based leader development (DeRue & Wellman, 2009) found that there was a point of diminishing returns whereby when a challenge became too difficult (i.e., putting someone in way over their head) the learning and development plateaued. This did not occur, however, when the developing leader had support in the form of access to feedback. In those cases, development continued even as the challenge became extremely difficult. In this case, feedback provided support; but feedback can also provide inputs to future cycles of developmental events as a type of interpersonal assessment. In this way (and others) these systems components of assessment, challenge, and support are not just sequenced in a linear manner but can be reciprocal and mutually reinforcing. The next sections provide more detail about the various forms of assessment, challenge, and support.

### *Assessment*

Assessments provide data about what someone is like. These kinds of structured (and sometimes unstructured) appraisals can take various forms. The information that is conveyed from an assessment can be about pretty much anything but tend to focus on constructs such as personality, values, skills (i.e., KSAs), or even self-views such as leadership self-efficacy or leader identity. There are structured measures for these constructs, which are discussed in more detail later in the chapter. Unstructured assessments come in the form of feedback from others, observational data about one's performance in a particular leadership domain or leadership episode, or other kinds of self-reflective processes that do not have a psychometric foundation (i.e., evidence of reliability and validity).

Assessments, when chosen well and used appropriately, can help enhance leader self-awareness, which has been proposed as a cornerstone of effective leadership (Chon & Sitkin, 2021; Kraemer, 2011). Assessments are also important because they form the foundation for system evaluation. If poor assessments are used (i.e., those assessments lacking sound measurement properties) it will inevitably lead to a poor evaluation of whether (or to what degree) the system is performing as designed. Assessments provide the data as to what is expected to change in individuals and collectives who are developing within the larger system.

Not all assessments are created equal. When it comes to structured assessments, these are usually in the form of self-report kinds of questionnaires. An exception might be skills inventories; however, research has used self-report measures of leadership skills in research on leader development (e.g., Miscenko et al., 2017). Other research has used ratings from others such as leadership coaches to assess skills and their development (e.g., Day & Sin, 2011; Kragt & Day, 2020). The kinds of assessments that provide the best quality data have known psychometric properties, such as reliability and validity.

*Reliability* refers to the consistency of the measure either internally across measurement items or as a whole instrument over time. The latter form of reliability is called test–retest reliability and generally is not appropriate in developmental studies because change over time is expected. It is not unreliability but actual changes in the focal construct that are of interest. The former type of reliability is called internal consistency reliability that assesses the consistency of measurements across components (usually items) in the assessment instrument.

*Validity* could be an entire volume on its own given the complexity of the concept and how its evidence is established. Given that this is not intended as a technical treatment of the construct, the description will be brief and to the point. The primary kind of validity that is of interest in leader development assessments is construct validity or how well the assessment measures the construct that it claims to measure.

The point about not all assessments being created equal applies to differences in their respective psychometric properties. Measures used in research studies almost always have these kinds of reliability and validity properties reported, but those measures found in many popular press books do not. It is also the case that many consultancies provide skimpy or no evidence regarding the psychometric properties of their assessment instruments. As a result, the interpretation of scores that are derived from measures lacking identified and acceptable psychometric properties is equivocal. Does the assessment score really mean what the author(s) claim it to mean? Assessments with equivocal interpretations generally have poor validity.

There are also differences in the cost of assessments, sometimes even measuring purportedly the same thing. A good example of this is with personality. You can find high-quality measures of the Big Five personality factors for free online or you could pay a consultant as much as hundreds or thousands of dollars for essentially the same or similar assessment. Consultancies often create their own propriety assessment instruments that they bundle with their intervention programs. One of the most well-established approaches to leader development is the assessment for development approach, so there is nothing wrong with that practice. It is just that money is needlessly spent on proprietary assessments, and many of these proprietary assessments have questionable or unknown psychometric properties.

In assessment for development programs, participants complete self-assessments about their personality, which are summarized in reports that are used for feedback and often as the foundation for a personalized leader development plan. Such a plan usually includes self-assessment data, and sometimes ratings provided by others, in choosing where to focus development and what activities to help achieve the proposed change. Developmental focus is important because it is like goals. If you have too many goals, you really have no meaningful goals (Clear, 2018). If you attempt to develop too many leadership capabilities at once, you will experience little or no developmental progress. The imperative is to focus one's energy otherwise it will be diluted, and no lasting changes will occur. All things equal, the person who focuses on fewer things goes further in terms of development than the person distracted by many.

*Personality*

Although assessments can and do take many forms focused on myriad personal characteristics and skills, personality assessments are frequently used in leader development initiatives (including programs). Personality assessments provide important data about what someone is like but also help reinforce points about individual differences. Personality refers to individual preferences and tendencies about behavior. Personality factors also reflect personal values. For example, if someone is extraverted, they tend to consider being sociable and outgoing as virtues (i.e., positive values). An introvert would likely see things quite differently, valuing a more refrained approach in social interactions. Recognizing that one's personality may be different in many ways to another's personality is the gateway to appreciating individual differences in human behavior.

Personality is also used extensively in leader development because of the underlying assumption that who you are determines to some extent how you lead. Specifically, personality shapes one's preferred leadership style (i.e., how one prefers to behave as a leader), and that leadership style predicts things like follower attitudes and team functions, which in turn, predicts performance and other outcomes (Hogan & Kaiser, 2005). There is both a theoretical and an empirical link between individual personality and leadership (Judge & Bono, 2000; Judge et al., 2002).

The list of possible personality inventories to use in leader development is extensive. As an aside, they are called inventories and not personality tests because test items have right and wrong answers. Inventories have no right or wrong answers just as there is no right or wrong personality. Leader development vendors often have favorites when it comes to personality assessment perhaps because of proprietary reasons (i.e., $$), training certification, or personal philosophy. One of the reasons for the extensive list of personality assessments is that there are so many personality traits. An advance in personality theory in the late twentieth century helped to provide valuable insight as to what the core factors or dimensions of personality are. This led to the five-factor model of personality, also called the Big Five, comprising the factors of Extraversion, Agreeableness, Conscientiousness, Neuroticism, and Openness to Experience (Goldberg, 1990). A brief description of each of these Big Five factors is presented in Table 2.1.

One of the most significant contributions of the Big Five is that the research underlying this model shows how just about any given trait can be mapped onto one of these five factors. That brought about a resurgence in the interest in personality in organizational behavior, generally, and leadership, more specifically. This personality model along with methodological advancements in meta-analysis allowed researchers to draw better-supported conclusions about the relationship between personality and leadership across studies, combining traits into the Big Five factors and correcting for sampling error (i.e., differences in sample sizes across studies) in estimating effect sizes (e.g., Judge et al., 2002).

**Table 2.1** Big five personality factors and subdomain facets

| *Personality factor and description* | *Subdomain facets and descriptions* |
|---|---|
| **Extraversion**: Level of engagement with the external world. Extraverts enjoy being with people, have high energy levels, and tend to experience positive emotions. Introverts at the low end of the scale tend to be quiet, low-key, and disengaged from the social world | • Friendliness: Value connections with other people<br>• Gregariousness: Enjoy the company of others<br>• Assertiveness: Speak out, take charge, and direct others' activities<br>• Activity Level: Vigorous, active, and busy lives versus more relaxed and leisurely<br>• Excitement-Seeking: Bored without high levels of external stimulation<br>• Cheerfulness: Experiences positive moods and emotions |
| **Agreeableness**: Individual differences in tendencies/preferences for cooperation and social harmony. Agreeable individuals value getting along with others. Disagreeable individuals place less value on getting along and tend to be skeptical of others' motives | • Trust: Assumes most people are fair, honest, and have good intentions<br>• Morality: Act without pretense or manipulation in dealing with others<br>• Altruism: Tends to find helping other people to be intrinsically rewarding<br>• Cooperation: Dislike conflict and confrontations<br>• Modesty: Do not claim to be superior to others<br>• Sympathy: Tenderhearted and compassionate |
| **Conscientiousness**: Individual differences in how we control, regulate, and direct impulses. Highly conscientious individuals tend to be organized, dutiful, and rule oriented. Those with low conscientiousness tend to be more spontaneous, free-spirited, and impulsive | • Self-Efficacy: Confidence in one's ability to accomplish things<br>• Orderliness: Well-organized, routine-oriented, and enjoy schedules<br>• Dutifulness: Strength of a person's sense of duty and obligation<br>• Achievement-Striving: Work hard to achieve excellence and be recognized as successful<br>• Self-Discipline: Degree of willpower and persistence<br>• Cautiousness: Tendency to think through various possibilities before acting |

(continued)

**Table 2.1** (continued)

| *Personality factor and description* | *Subdomain facets and descriptions* |
|---|---|
| **Neuroticism**: The tendency to experience negative emotions such as anxiety, anger, or depression. At the low end of the scale is emotional stability (as the factor is sometimes called), which is characterized as being less emotionally reactive, calmer, and free from persistent negative emotions | • Anxiety: Feelings of imminent danger and generally fearful<br>• Anger: Tendency to be angry and enraged when things do not go one's way<br>• Depression: Tendency to feel sad, dejected, and discouraged<br>• Self-Consciousness: Being sensitive about what others think of them<br>• Vulnerability: Feeling strong cravings and urges that are difficult to resist |
| **Openness to Experience**: Cognitive style differences that distinguish imaginative, intellectually curious, and creative people from down-to-earth, conventional people, who value tradition and are less open to change | • Imagination: Tendency to fantasize and create a richer, more interesting world<br>• Artistic Interests: Being absorbed in art and nature, with strong aesthetic interests<br>• Emotionality: Having access and awareness of own feelings<br>• Adventurousness: Eager to try new activities and experience different things<br>• Intellect: Enjoys playing with ideas and are open-minded to new ideas<br>• Liberalism: Readiness to challenge authority, convention, and traditional values |

*Note* Descriptions adapted from the IPIP feedback report

From this research establishing the five-factor personality model, more robust inferences can now be made on the empirical relationships between personality and a whole host of outcomes, including leadership. Assessments may not be couched in the Big Five; however, those that are grounded in this personality model have some of the strongest evidence behind them. One such Big Five assessment is the International Personality Item Pool (IPIP) representation of the NEO PI-R™, which can be completed online for free and provides a detailed feedback report on the results (https://www.personalitytest.net/ipip/index.html). This assessment is highly recommended (either short or long forms) as it offers an evidence-based personality assessment without having to pay for that assessment or the corresponding feedback report. The feedback provided is based on large-sample international norms (one reason why the assessment is free) and provides feedback on the marker facets for each of the Big Five factors. The facet subdomains are presented in Table 2.1.

There are a few points to consider when using personality assessments in leader development. First, there is no right or wrong personality. Someone might feel that a certain personality orientation is limiting them as a leader, which is good data to work with in terms of designing an experiential challenge for development. Second, extremes in personality are "watch out for" indicators because they point to a certain inflexibility in behavioral tendencies. Being at the lowest or highest decile on any personality factor or facet indicates strong behavioral tendencies in that domain. Third, which is related to the previous point, strengths can become weaknesses when taken to the extreme. For example, being extraverted is generally a positive personality trait in the leadership domain; however, if someone is highly extroverted it might indicate a potential problem in giving others necessary airtime in group discussions. That suggests practicing one's listening skills might be helpful in mitigating the potential tendency to dominate conversations with others.

One limitation with more scholarly assessments such as the IPIP and the Big Five in general is terminology. Labels such as Neuroticism, Openness to Experience, and Conscientiousness can sound too academic for many practicing managers and aspiring leaders. Some of these labels (including some facet labels) come with preconceived notions about their value. How could something like Neuroticism ever be a good thing? The answer is that there are situations where being emotionally reactive is functional and being overly calm and emotionally stable a negative (others might think you do not care about the issue).

An alternative, free online personality assessment called PrinciplesYou (https://principlesyou.com/) was designed to be psychometrically sound while also using more accessible terminology than most Big Five assessments. It was developed by Wharton psychologists Dr. Adam Grant and Dr. Brian Little, and sponsored by Bridgewater founder and investor Ray Dalio, whose book *Principles* (Dalio, 2017) was the impetus behind the development of the assessment. There is a detailed feedback report provided (again, free of charge) organized around different personality archetypes. It is a rigorous and accessible personality assessment. Another feature is that there is an option to complete the PrinciplesUs online assessment to enhance not only self-awareness but also a better understanding of what others on your team or organization are like, which makes it appropriate for collective leadership development applications.

This has been a lengthy section on personality assessment, which reflects the relative emphasis placed on enhancing self-awareness of one's behavioral tendencies (i.e., personality) as part of leader development. An important reminder is to choose personality assessments with care and consideration of their psychometric evidence because there are many poorly developed inventories in the field. *Caveat emptor* (buyer beware)!

*Leadership Skills and Competencies*

Next to the difficulties in trying to define leadership accurately is identifying what are the most appropriate skills and competencies to develop. There is no universal list of leadership skills and competencies, or if there is, it is likely way too extensive a list to be useful in development interventions. For this and other reasons, many organizations develop their own list of skills that leaders need to master. When these skills are bundled into higher level aggregations, they can be called leadership competencies. A representation of the relationship between leadership skills and competencies is depicted in a leadership competency model.

Any competency model is based on a theory of performance (Boyatzis, 2008). When the focus is on leadership competencies the model should be based on the prevailing theory of leadership. To be of value, a leadership competency model should be concise, distinct, and locally relevant. A leadership competency model should be something that individuals can remember. It should not be a generic set of leadership-related competencies used by other organizations. A sound leadership competency model is grounded in the shared values held by members of the collective in question.

Leadership competency models are widely used in organizations but not universally endorsed. A debate in the academic literature about this issue summarized the pros and cons of using competency models to develop leaders and leadership (Hollenbeck et al., 2006). Without going into the details of this debate, my perspective on the value of leadership competency models has evolved. For many years I was a skeptic, but now have a better appreciation of how a well-designed and relevant competency model can add value to a developmental system. If the model is not too extensive or otherwise confusing, it can provide a shared language around this fuzzy leadership concept in an organization.

As example, we have designed a leadership competency model at the Kravis Leadership Institute (KLI) that not only offers a shared leadership language but serves as a theoretical foundation for assessments and other practices in our development system designed for undergraduate students who are emerging leaders in the early phases of their respective leadership journeys. The three top-level leadership competencies are Courage, Creativity, and Collaboration. The model proposes that leading courageously, leading creatively, and leading collaboratively are the core components of Responsible Leadership, which is central to the mission of Claremont McKenna College. That mission, in part, is to prepare its students for thoughtful and productive lives and responsible leadership in business, government, and the professions. For each leadership competency there are three core capabilities (See Fig. 2.2).

This is not the one and only correct leadership competency model; rather, it is the right one for the context and culture of Claremont McKenna College. An advantage of having just three core leadership competencies of Courage, Creativity, and Collaboration is that it offers a concise approach to understanding responsible leadership in our college context. It is easy to remember three leadership competencies. In comparison, the Doerr Institute for New Leaders at Rice University has a

**Fig. 2.2** Kravis Leadership Institute (KLI) leadership competency model

model with 21 core leader competencies organized into five themes of (1) Knowing Yourself, (2) Controlling Yourself, (3) Growing and Flourishing, (4) Being Aware of Others, and (5) Working with Others (Kolditz et al., 2021). That leadership competency model is the right one for that university context.

Many organizations of all types (corporate, military, nonprofit, educational) have developed their own leadership competency models; however, most are tightly held as proprietary intellectual property and are not publicly available. That is unfortunate because science relies on transparency. But those for-profit organizations often consider their leadership competencies and investments in developing those competencies to be a source of competitive advantage in their respective industries. Despite its naysayers, the practice of competency modeling is widespread in organizations. The arguments summarizing the reasons for basing leader and leadership development on a context-specific leadership competency model can be found in a scholarly article on meeting the competency needs of global leaders (Brownell, 2006).

An important and relevant question is how such competencies and supporting capabilities are assessed. One approach would be to have performance metrics for each of these features in the leadership competency model, which would require intense investments in measurement development. It is also probably misguided because we would not want every participant in the development system to manifest leadership competencies in the exact same way. That would be unrealistic and probably counterproductive to developing effective leadership. A different approach is based on a self-assessment approach that is part of the KLI Leadership Development Plan for students (contact this Author to request a copy). The self-assessment is loosely based on the Campbell Leadership Descriptor™ (Campbell, 2019) in which participants rate each leadership attribute as to how descriptive it is of them as a leader, a good leader in general, and a poor leader in general. Average scores are created across attributes and perspectives to help participants gain a deeper understanding of how they think about leadership and how each attribute is related to each target perspective (i.e., self as leader, good leader, poor leader). The goal is to help build self-awareness around leadership and its components. A visual depiction of the full KLI Leadership Competency Model including leadership attributes is presented in Fig. 2.3 and Table 2.2 presents this full competency model in outline form. To be clear, our self-assessment is based on the KLI Leadership Competency

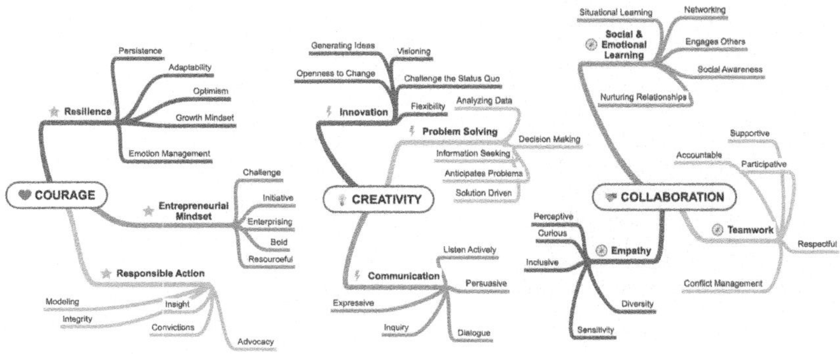


**Fig. 2.3** KLI Leadership Competency Model with capabilities and assessment attributes

Model and Development Plan and not on the competencies assessed with the Campbell Leadership Descriptor™.

*Self-views*

The self has played a pivotal role in shaping the field of psychology going back to the late nineteenth century (James, 1890). Various self-related topics, which collectively can be termed self-views, have a robust foundation of theory and research in contemporary psychology (Leary & Tangney, 2011). Self-views also are relevant and important in understanding leader development processes (Day & Dragoni, 2015; Day et al., 2009). How one thinks of the self, which is reflected in one's self-concept, is something that changes and develops potentially over the entire lifespan. The extent to which someone identifies as a leader (*leader identity*); is aware of their values, behavioral tendencies, and strengths and weaknesses (*self-awareness*); and has confidence to act as a leader when needed (*leadership self-efficacy*) are considered proximal or leading indicators of leader development (Day & Dragoni). Chapter 4 delves into more of the theory and research around leader self-views in leader development. This section provides an overview of how such self-views can be assessed.

Common across all three leader self-views is that they are measured typically as self-appraisals. That is, the developing leader completes self-ratings on the focal construct (although slightly different with self-awareness). It may seem undesirable to use self-ratings of these constructs

**Table 2.2** KLI Leadership Competency Model with assessment attributes in outline form

1. Courage
    1.1. Resilience
        1.1.1. Persistence
        1.1.2. Adaptability
        1.1.3. Growth mindset
        1.1.4. Optimism
        1.1.5. Emotion management
    1.2. Entrepreneurial Mindset
        1.2.1. Enterprising
        1.2.2. Resourceful
        1.2.3. Initiative
        1.2.4. Bold
        1.2.5. Challenge
    1.3. Responsible action
        1.3.2. Insight
        1.3.3. Modeling
        1.3.4. Integrity
        1.3.5. Convictions
        1.3.6. Advocacy
2. Creativity
    2.1. Innovation
        2.1.1. Generating ideas
        2.1.2. Openness to change
        2.1.3. Visioning
        2.1.4. Challenge the status quo
        2.1.5. Flexibility
    2.2. Communication
        2.2.1. Expressive
        2.2.2. Listen actively
        2.2.3. Persuasive
        2.2.4. Inquiry
        2.2.5. Dialogue
    2.3. Problem solving
        2.3.1. Information seeking
        2.3.2. Analyzing data
        2.3.3. Anticipates problems
        2.3.4. Decision making
        2.3.5. Solution driven

(continued)

**Table 2.2** (continued)

3. Collaboration
    3.1. Empathy
        3.1.1. Perceptive
        3.1.2. Curious
        3.1.3. Diversity
        3.1.4. Inclusive
        3.1.5. Sensitivity
    3.2. Social & emotional learning
        3.2.1. Social awareness
        3.2.2. Engages others
        3.2.3. Networking
        3.2.4. Nurturing relationships
        3.2.5. Situational learning
    3.3. Teamwork
        3.3.1. Participative
        3.3.2. Accountable
        3.3.3. Supportive
        3.3.4. Respectful
        3.3.5. Conflict management

as they might be influenced by unwanted influences such as a social desirability bias; however, this ignores the reality that the self is the best judge of these self-views (doh!). It is also the case that many constructs in psychological research such as personality are based on self-ratings. Extensive research has demonstrated that when used appropriately and based on sound psychometric evidence self-appraisal ratings can provide useful data for research as well as practice.

One of the first measures developed to assess ***leader identity*** was published in a dissertation nearly 20 years ago (Hiller, 2005). Internalizing a leader identity is important because "...coming to see oneself as a leader and seizing more and more opportunities to behave accordingly" (Ibarra, 2015), p. 4) is central to owning one's development (see First Principles in Chapter 1). The core marker items in this leader identity measure are (1) *I am a leader*, (2) *I see myself as a leader*, (3) *I describe myself to others as a "leader,"* and (4) *I prefer to be seen by others as a leader.* The participant rates these items on a five-point Likert-type scale (1 = *rarely or never* to 5 = *always*) in terms of how consistently they describe and see themselves as a leader. These items in one form or another have been used in numerous leader development studies. Although the items might seem a bit redundant, this redundancy enhances the internal consistency reliability of the measure. Internal consistency reliability estimates (Cronbach's alpha) have indicated generally good reliability with estimates above the recommended standard of 0.80.

Another measure of leader identity has been developed and implemented by researchers at Rice University. This is a more extensive measure comprising several different identity dimensions. Researchers from the Doerr Institute at Rice use this measure to track changes in leader identity of their students over four years at college. They also do comparative research with the measure, examining differences in leader identity changes and comparing students who have received leadership coaching and those who have not received coaching. The results (see Kolditz et al., 2021, Chapter 3) suggest that certain leader development interventions such as leadership coaching are effective at enhancing the development of leader identity in students. This provides a prime example of a best practice in terms of how sound measures form the background of an evaluation strategy generating evidence to discern to what extent changes are occurring that are consistent with the objectives of the developmental system.

The origins of self-efficacy in psychology can be traced to the influential social cognitive theory with a particular emphasis on the study of behavioral change (Bandura, 1977). There are a variety of ways in which ***leadership self-efficacy*** (LSE) has been measured in research studies. A recent review of the LSE concept and available measures suggests two general approaches to measurement that vary by level of specificity (Dwyer, 2019). The more frequently used approach is relatively narrow and based on leadership task, behavior, and skill-based scales. A second more general type of measure assesses the confidence of the respondent for performing effectively in an overall leader role.

A third type of self-view that is common to many leader development approaches is ***self-awareness***. The concept has been conceptualized in various ways and measurement is not as straightforward as with the self-views of leader identity and LSE. The term is self-descriptive at least on the surface. Enhancing leader self-awareness is about using different practices and processes to realize a deeper awareness of the self. It is also focused on enhancing an understanding of the effect of one's actions on others. In this manner, self-awareness comes down to the accuracy of self-perceptions that can be measured by comparing self-ratings to ratings provided by others on the same items or dimensions. The results of research using this congruence approach found that high performing managers demonstrated better self-awareness as compared with other managers across four independent data sets (Church, 1997).

A comprehensive review of the self-awareness literature suggests that it is very rich in that there are various ways in which self-awareness has been conceptualized and studied (Chon & Sitkin, 2021). Clear guidance around measurement issues was not addressed in this review, but it highlighted that self-reflection processes are often encouraged as ways to enhance self-awareness. Relatedly, the process of writing about one's emotional experiences—often called journaling—has been shown to help alleviate stress and enhance meta-awareness of mental processes (Pennebaker, 1997). Journaling is also widely used in counseling psychology as a means of helping individuals connect their internal processes with their external realities (Hubbs & Brand, 2005). In this manner, it is also valuable as a leader development practice to enhance self-awareness.

Assessments in leader development systems can and do take many different forms and involve a wide range of leadership-related constructs. The focus of this section has been on assessments used for providing information about individual personality, self-assessments of skills and competencies, as well as self-views. This is just the tip of the proverbial iceberg when it comes to what types of assessments can be used in leadership development systems. One overarching comment or warning is the reminder that assessment instruments are not all created equal. There are a lot of bad (i.e., non-evidence-based) assessment practices used in leader development. Learn how to tell the differences between an assessment with acceptable psychometric properties from those that are just a waste of time and money no matter how much fun and insight they promise.

### *Challenge*

A second component to consider in designing a developmental system is a challenge. In encouraging the use of experiences in developing leaders and leadership, it is understood that not every experience has sufficient challenge to motivate development. Choosing challenging experiences that force someone to leave their comfort zone goes against much of human nature that desires comfortable and safe ways of thinking and acting. But the reality is that no one develops when they are comfortable.

In the more popular press domain, James Clear (2018) proposes what he calls the "Goldilocks Zone" (pp. 232–233), which involves working on challenges of just manageable difficulty. He even quantifies that by stating that this Zone is roughly four percent beyond one's current ability. How one can metric that so precisely in everyday experiences is unclear but the point is a valuable one—it is best to take on challenging experiences, but not such that someone feels deeply in over their head (Kegan, 1994). Taking on smallish challenges on a regular basis and having the dedication and persistence to regularly practice such challenges is better than trying to take on big hairy audacious ones if the goal is to develop as a leader.

Dr. Theo Dawson also uses the term Goldilocks Zone in her developmental work. Learning goals need to be "just right" to optimize learning processes that support experience-based development. From her perspective, the Goldilocks Zone is the range in which a learning task is just challenging enough to support optimal learning. This is a well-recognized concept in the developmental psychology literature stretching back to early in the twentieth century. The notion of a *zone of proximal development* suggest that a task must be within the developmental reach of someone with minimal support from others (called scaffolding) to help an individual move to a higher level of functioning (Vygotsky, 1978). The Goldilocks Zone certainly has a more inviting ring to it!

Researchers have attempted to quantify the level of challenge in various aspects of managerial work. The result was a self-assessment instrument called the *Developmental Challenge Profile* (McCauley et al., 1994). The core developmental challenges embedded to various degrees in managerial work were in the form of (1) job transitions, (2) creating change, (3) taking on higher levels of responsibility, and (4) non-authority relationships. The latter three domains were based on task characteristics. Thus, development challenges could be designed into ongoing managerial work by having someone take on a change assignment, accepting greater responsibility, and including non-authority relationships (i.e., influencing others where there is no formal supervisory power). Research on the instrument development is especially notable given the care taken to establish the underlying psychometric properties of the *Developmental Challenge Profile*.

The types of challenges embedded in work experiences is likely to differ depending on the organizational level of the developing individual as well as by career stage. Research examining the early career challenges of recent MBA graduates ($N = 55$) used a semi-structured interview methodology to identify the most common challenges (Benjamin & O'Reilly, 2011). Challenges were embedded in three types of early career transitions (role, business, and personal) that centered around (1) managing and motivating subordinates, (2) managing relationships with peers and bosses, (3) developing a leadership mindset, and (4) coping with setbacks and disappointments. Combined with the earlier qualitative research of Harvard professor Dr. Linda Hill on a similar topic (Hill, 2003), the results offer a realistic preview of the kinds of early career challenges that young professional managers are likely to face. Advanced knowledge of what to expect in terms of experiential challenges can help prepare an aspiring leader to leverage such experiences for development. It is also advisable for early career leaders to develop support mechanisms such as ready access to feedback as research has found that having access to support can enhance development even with very challenging experiences (DeRue & Wellman, 2009).

One additional research article on using global work experiences to develop executive leaders ($N = 234$) is worth mentioning in the context of challenge (Dragoni et al., 2014). Global work experiences are those job assignments that require a leader to transcend national boundaries to develop their strategic thinking. The researchers found that those leaders assigned to a country with a culture that is very different from their own country's culture (i.e., culturally distant) were found to develop higher levels of strategic thinking competency. The greater the cultural distance in the job assignment the greater the developmental stretch that was shown to moderate the relationship between a global job assignment and the development of strategic thinking competency. For example, an American with a global assignment in Canada or Australia would experience less of a stretch than if assigned to China or the Middle East. Of course, the DeRue and Wellman (2009) research findings also point to the potentially important role of support in helping developing leaders manage assignments with greater levels of challenge associated with cultural distance.

### *Support*

Developmental support takes many different forms (McCauley et al., 2010); however, the most common source of support is feedback. As noted by researchers, access to feedback (i.e., support) helps individuals develop even in highly challenging situations (DeRue & Wellman, 2009). Without such support, a plateau can occur in which development stalls as the experience reaches a certain level of challenge. Without access to feedback, an experience becomes overwhelming instead of developmental at high levels of challenge.

Feedback generally takes either a positive or negative valence. Positive feedback can provide reinforcement for trying new behaviors, getting out of one's comfort zone, and/or accomplishing a developmental goal. Negative reinforcement is also very beneficial because it provides informational inputs within the development system (in this case, to a developing leader) about a gap between experienced and desired behaviors and outcomes. Katz and Kahn (1978) observed that negative feedback is the simplest form of informational input that is found in all systems (p. 26):

> Informational feedback of a negative kind enables the system to correct its deviations from course.... If there is no corrective device to get the system back on its course, it will expend too much energy or it will ingest too much energic input and no longer continue as a system.

In other words, negative feedback is not just nice to have, but is essential to maintaining the system's integrity.

Just like there are differences in the developmental potential of experiences, not all feedback is developmentally useful. Providing a general or generic "well done" or "better luck next time" (or worse in terms of personal criticism) does not provide much in the way of informational input to help the system (i.e., individual) maintain or correct its course. One form of feedback that helps to provide concrete, objective, and useful feedback is based on the Situation-Behavior-Impact (SBI) model (Center for Creative Leadership, 2019b). In essence, this model provides a way to frame feedback that reduces defensiveness in the recipient and enhance learning by focusing on behavior.

In the SBI feedback model, Step 1 captures the situation (e.g., "the team meeting we had in the conference room yesterday"), Step 2 describes the behavior (e.g., "you suggested that we revise our client proposal to include an additional support feature"), and Step 3 explains the impact (e.g., "I thought that was a very creative idea that enhanced the overall value of our proposed service"). The impact needs to be framed in terms of its effects on the feedback giver—and not anyone else—to enhance the objectivity of the feedback. Using SBI feedback and encouraging others to frame their feedback in these ways can help avoid common mistakes in feedback processes such as judging a person rather than describing behaviors, being too vague or general, speaking for others, or including a veiled threat about what will happen if they do not change. It is also a mistake to try and sandwich negative feedback between two pieces of positive feedback (i.e., a "crap sandwich"). It is a mistake because it can be confusing. Which of the three pieces of feedback should the recipient focus on?

It is recommended that in designing and implementing a developmental system it is best to be proactive about seeking feedback from others (Ashford & Cummings, 1983). Research on feedback seeking behavior has shown that individuals tend to hold back in seeking feedback from others unless the issue is important or novel, or there is an acute fear of failure (Ashford, 1986). An effective leader development system is one that could be considered a feedback intensive experience. Instead of waiting (or hoping) for feedback, a responsible owner of one's development as a leader seeks and encourages feedback from others. An even better design would include a brief overview of SBI feedback and encourage feedback givers to frame their feedback using that model.

## Implications of Understanding Development as a System

This chapter began with the assertion that programs intended to develop leaders and leadership are limited and limiting. Programs are limited because they are bounded, episodic events that tend to take place over a relatively short period of time (days, possibly weeks). The research evidence on expert performance indicates episodic types of programs are insufficient to motivate long-lasting change in individuals or collectives. Programs are limiting because they tend to be "one off" kinds of events that do not incorporate systems principles or systems design thinking. Programs are also commodities—often very expensive products—in the marketplace of leadership development. More often attention is given to marketing rather than rigorous, evidence-based practices that are integrated into a developmental system.

To be considered a system, there needs to be some attention given to the flow of developmental resources and an understanding how these resources in the form of energy (e.g., attention, motivation) are transformed into new ways of thinking and acting that serve as outputs to the environment. Another way of framing this output step is that it takes transformed resources to the developmental "life gym" and are tried out or practiced. Information in the form of feedback serves as inputs back to the developmental system to prime the next cycle of input-transformation-output.

A hallmark of any open system is the notion of systems as cycles of events in which "the pattern of activities of the energy exchange has a cyclical character" (Katz & Kahn, 1978, p. 24). Open systems also have permeable boundaries that are open to environmental influences. Programs tend to have impermeable boundaries and for the most part are closed off from the external environment. One of the primary reasons that leader development programs fail is that the program designers do not consider the culture (i.e., interpersonal environment) in which the intervention is delivered (Westfall, 2019). The assumption seems to be that the development program operates in a vacuum and is immune to outside influences. Nothing could be farther from the truth. Sending a changed person back into an unchanged system tends to be an exercise in futility. A systems perspective incorporates environmental influence into the design and delivery of leader development interventions.

Another major aspect of considering development from a systems perspective is the principle of equifinality. According to this open systems principle, a system such as a developing leader can reach the same end state from different starting points and by a variety of developmental pathways. People start at different places and change in different ways in their respective developmental journeys to becoming a leader. Compare this with a typical training program, including leadership training. There is an implicit assumption that is just the opposite of a development approach in that people start pretty much at the same place and reach the same final state through identical developmental pathways (Day et al., 2021). Most leader development programs tend to be designed based on the principles of training rather than those found in the thinking around open systems theory. This distinction between leadership training and development will be addressed in more detail in the next chapter.

Another consideration in adopting a systems perspective in leader development are the interrelated factors of assessment, challenge, and support. Leading researchers and practitioners in leader development suggest that any experience can be made more developmental to the extent that these aspects of assessment, challenge, and support are available (McCauley et al., 2010). It is not an either/or proposition when it comes to using ongoing experience for development but more of a continuum. The most developmental experiences embed all three components, but sometimes it is only possible to include two of them (e.g., challenge and support). The omission of assessment does not render the experience developmentally meaningless, just less impactful than an experience that includes all three components.

This chapter reviewed recommendations about enhancing the value of challenge and support through recognized practices such as using challenges that are within a "sweet spot" or Goldilocks Zone in terms of difficulty and designing supportive feedback around the principles of SBI. Perhaps one of the most important decisions is around assessments. Self-assessment instruments and inventories are another commodity in the leader development marketplace and need to be chosen with care. My recommendation is to focus on those assessment instruments with documented psychometric evidence (e.g., sound reliability and validity). Assessment is about measurement. We should care about the quality of those measures because they are also the backbone of system evaluation. If a vendor cannot provide or refuses to share such data, that is a gigantic red flag about what you are being asked to buy. In further advancing the science of developing leaders and leadership there should be an emphasis on using scientifically developed assessments with documented high-quality psychometric evidence.

## Chapter Summary

- Developmental systems thinking offers an alternative to the limited and limiting program approach to developing leaders and leadership.
- A hallmark of open systems theory is that systems are based on cycles of events and are open to the environment. Programs tend to be non-cyclical events and closed to environmental influences.
- In using experience for development, integrating components of assessment, challenge, and support enhances the developmental impact of those experiences.
- Assessments can take many forms, but often leader developmental interventions use personality assessments, measures of skills and competencies (including self-assessments of these attributes), and more recently, self-views in the form of leader identity, leadership self-efficacy, and self-awareness.
- It is highly recommended that in choosing assessments for a development system priority be given to those instruments with the highest quality psychometric evidence.

- The challenge requires getting out of one's comfort zone, but not by too much otherwise it can be overwhelming. Some have referred to this sweet spot as the Goldilocks Zone or in the developmental psychology literature the Zone of Proximal Development.
- Support can take myriad forms, but one of the most helpful forms is that of feedback. There are better and worse ways to give and receive feedback. One process recommendation is to use a Situation-Behavior-Impact (SBI) approach to help make the feedback about another's actions objective and not a value judgment about the person.
- Feedback serves as informational input into the developmental system, enhancing the cyclical nature of development as proposed by open systems theory.
- One of the strongest implications of systems thinking to developing leaders and leadership is that it is ongoing, continuous, and open to the external environment as compared with a single-shot episode that is walled off from environmental influences rendering it more of a closed system.

## References

Ashford, S. J. (1986). Feedback-seeking in individual adaptation: A resource perspective. *Academy of Management Journal, 29*, 465–486. https://doi.org/10.5465/256219

Ashford, S. J., & Cummings, L. L. (1983). Feedback as an individual resource: Personal strategies of creating information. *Organizational Behavior and Human Performance, 32*(3), 370–398. https://doi.org/10.1016/0030-5073(83)90156-3

Bandura, A. (1977). Self-efficacy: Toward a unifying theory of behavioral change. *Psychological Review, 84*(2), 191–215. https://doi.org/10.1037/0033-295X.84.2.191

Benjamin, B., & O'Reilly, C. (2011). Becoming a leader: Early career challenges faced by MBA graduates. *Academy of Management Learning & Education, 10*(3), 452–472. https://doi.org/10.5465/amle.2011.0002

Bertalanffy, L. (1972). The history and status of General Systems Theory. *Academy of Management Journal, 15*(4), 407–426. https://doi.org/10.5465/255139

Boyatzis, R. E. (2008). Competencies in the 21st century. *Journal of Management Development, 27*(1), 5–12. https://doi.org/10.1108/02621710810840730

Brownell, J. (2006). Meeting the competency needs of global leaders: A partnership approach. *Human Resource Management, 45*(3), 309–336. https://doi.org/10.1002/hrm.20115

Campbell, D. (2019). *Campbell leadership descriptor: Facilitator's guide*. CCL Press.

Center for Creative Leadership. (2019a). *Active listening: Improve your ability to listen and lead* (2nd ed.). Author.

Center for Creative Leadership. (2019b). *Feedback that works: How to build and deliver your message* (2nd ed.). Author.

Chon, D., & Sitkin, S. B. (2021). Disentangling the process and content of self-awareness: A review, critical assessment, and synthesis. *Academy of Management Annals, 15*(2), 607–651. https://doi.org/10.5465/annals.2018.0079

Church, A. H. (1997). Managerial self-awareness in high-performing individuals in organizations. *Journal of Applied Psychology, 82*(2), 281–292. https://doi.org/10.1037/0021-9010.82.2.281

Clear, J. (2018). *Atomic habits: An easy and proven way to build good habits and break bad ones*. Avery.

Crawley, E. (2022). Ask an MIT professor: What is system thinking and why is it important? *MIT Open Learning*. Retrieved July 23, 2023, from https://openlearning.mit.edu/news/ask-mit-professor-what-system-thinking-and-why-it-important

Dalio, R. (2017). *Principles*. Simon & Schuster.

Day, D., Bastardoz, N., Bisbey, T., Reyes, D., & Salas, E. (2021). Unlocking human potential through leadership training and development initiatives. *Behavioral Science & Policy, 7*(1), 41–54. https://doi.org/10.1177/237946152100700105

Day, D. V., & Dragoni, L. (2015). Leadership development: An outcome-oriented review based on time and levels of analyses. *Annual Review of Organizational Psychology and Organizational Behavior, 2*, 133–156. https://doi.org/10.1146/annurev-orgpsych-032414-111328

Day, D. V., Harrison, M. M., & Halpin, S. M. (2009). *An integrative approach to leader development: Connecting adult development, identity, and expertise*. Psychology Press.

Day, D. V., & Sin, H. P. (2011). Longitudinal tests of an integrative model of leader development: Charting and understanding developmental trajectories. *The Leadership Quarterly, 22*(3), 545–560. https://doi.org/10.1016/j.leaqua.2011.04.011

DeRue, D. S., & Wellman, N. (2009). Developing leaders via experience: The role of developmental challenge, learning orientation, and feedback availability. *Journal of Applied Psychology, 94*(4), 859–875. https://doi.org/10.1037/a0015317

Dragoni, L., Oh, I. S., Tesluk, P. E., Moore, O. A., VanKatwyk, P., & Hazucha, J. (2014). Developing leaders' strategic thinking through global work experience: The moderating role of cultural distance. *Journal of Applied Psychology, 99*(5), 867–882. https://doi.org/10.1037/a0036628

Dwyer, L. P. (2019). Leadership self-efficacy: Review and leader development implications. *Journal of Management Development, 38*(8), 637–650. https://doi.org/10.1108/JMD-03-2019-0073

Goldberg, L. R. (1990). An alternative "description of personality": The Big-Five factor structure. *Journal of Personality and Social Psychology, 59*(6), 1216–1229. https://doi.org/10.1037/0022-3514.59.6.1216

Gurdjian, P., Halbeisen, T., & Lane, K. (2014). Why leadership-development programs fail. *McKinsey Quarterly*. Retrieved July 23, 2023, from https://www.mckinsey.com/featured-insights/leadership/why-leadership-development-programs-fail

Hill, L. (2003). *Becoming a manager: How new managers master the challenges of leadership* (2nd ed.). Harvard Busiess School Press.

Hiller, N. J. (2005). *An examination of leadership beliefs and leadership self-identity: Constructs, correlates, and outcomes* (Publication Number 3202503), Pennsylvania State University. University Park, PA. https://www.proquest.com/docview/305451315?pq-origsite=gscholar&fromopenview=true

Hogan, R., & Kaiser, R. B. (2005). What we know about leadership. *Review of General Psychology, 9*(2), 169–180. https://doi.org/10.1037/1089-2680.9.2.169

Hollenbeck, G. P., McCall, M. W., & Silzer, R. F. (2006). Leadership competency models. *The Leadership Quarterly, 17*(4), 398–413. https://doi.org/10.1016/j.leaqua.2006.04.003

Hubbs, D. L., & Brand, C. F. (2005). The paper mirror: Understanding reflective journaling. *Journal of Experiential Education, 28*(1), 60–71. https://doi.org/10.1177/105382590502800107

Ibarra, H. (2015). *Act like a leader, think like a leader*. Harvard Business Review Press.

James, W. (1890). The consciousness of self. In W. James (Ed.), *The principles of psychology* (Vol. 1, pp. 291–401). Henry Holt and Co. https://doi.org/10.1037/10538-010

Judge, T. A., & Bono, J. E. (2000). Five-factor model of personality and transformational leadership. *Journal of Applied Psychology, 85*(5), 751–765. https://doi.org/10.1037/0021-9010.85.5.751

Judge, T. A., Bono, J. E., Ilies, R., & Gerhardt, M. W. (2002). Personality and leadership: A qualitative and quantitative review. *Journal of Applied Psychology, 87*(4), 765–780. https://doi.org/10.1037/0021-9010.87.4.765

Katz, D., & Kahn, R. L. (1978). *The social psychology of organizations* (2nd ed.). Wiley.

Kegan, R. (1994). *In over our heads: The mental demands of modern life*. Harvard University Press.

Kerr, S. (1975). On the folly of rewarding A, while hoping for B. *Academy of Management Journal, 18*(4), 769–783. https://doi.org/10.5465/255378

Kolditz, T., Gill, L., & Brown, R. P. (2021). *Leadership reckoning: Can higher education develop the leaders we need?* Monocle Press.

Kraemer, H. M. J. (2011). *From values to action: The four principles of values-based leadership*. Jossey-Bass.

Kragt, D., & Day, D. V. (2020). Predicting leadership competency development and promotion among high-potential executives: The role of leader identity. *Frontiers in Psychology, 11*, 1816. https://doi.org/10.3389/fpsyg.2020.01816

Leary, M. R., & Tangney, J. P. (Eds.). (2011). *Handbook of self and identity* (2nd ed.). The Guilford Press.

Leroy, H. L., Anisman-Razin, M., Avolio, B. J., Bresman, H., Bunderson, J. S., Burris, E. R., Claeys, J., Detert, J. R., Dragoni, L., Giessner, S. R., Kniffin, K. M., Kolditz, T., Petriglieri, G., Pettit, N. C., Sitkin, S. B., Van Quaquebeke, N., & Vongswasdi, P. (2022). Walking our evidence-based talk: The case of leadership development in business schools. *Journal of Leadership & Organizational Studies, 29*(1), 5–32. https://doi.org/10.1177/15480518211062563

McCauley, C. D., Ruderman, M. N., Ohlott, P. J., & Morrow, J. E. (1994). Assessing the developmental components of managerial jobs. *Journal of Applied Psychology, 79*(4), 544–560. https://doi.org/10.1037/0021-9010.79.4.544

McCauley, C. D., Van Velsor, E., & Ruderman, M. N. (2010). Introduction: Our view of leadership development. In E. Van Velsor, C. D. McCauley, & M. N. Ruderman (Eds.), *The Center for Creative Leadership handbook of leadership development* (3rd ed., pp. 1–26). John Wiley & Sons.

Miscenko, D., Guenter, H., & Day, D. V. (2017). Am I a leader? Examining leader identity development over time. *The Leadership Quarterly, 28*, 605–620. https://doi.org/10.1016/j.leaqua.2017.01.004

Pennebaker, J. W. (1997). Writing about emotional experiences as a therapeutic process. *Psychological Science, 8*(3), 162–166. https://doi.org/10.1111/j.1467-9280.1997.tb00403.x

Rogers, C. R., & Farson, R. E. (1957). *Active listening*. The University of Chicago.

Vygotsky, L. (1978). *Mind in society: The development of higher psychological processes*. Harvard University Press.
Westfall, C. (2019). Leadership development is a $366 billion industry: Here's why most programs don't work. *Forbes*. Retrieved July 23, 2023, from https://www.forbes.com/sites/chriswestfall/2019/06/20/leadership-development-why-most-programs-dont-work/?sh=12052d9d61de

CHAPTER 3

# Individual Leader Development

## Leadership and Leader Development

The history of leadership has assumed a heroic, romanticized, and leader-centric perspective. In the scholarly literature, it has been referred to as the romance of leadership (Meindl et al., 1985). We tend to hold overly positive, even idealistic notions of a leader even to the point of attributing positive organizational outcomes to the efforts of visible leaders even when such causal claims are dubious (Meindl & Ehrlich, 1987). This excessive positivity might be considered as mainly a Western fixture (i.e., remnants of the Lone Range or Marlborough Man cultures in the US); however, one can point to the powerful “Big Man” leaders on the African continent, the samurais of Japan, and even the emperors of China as examples of these leader-centric personifications of leadership. As for the latter, in traditional Chinese political theory, the emperor was considered the “Son of Heaven” alluding to a very positive and even other worldly conceptions of leaders. Some scholars have opined more recently on the excessive positivity in leadership theory and research that continues to romanticize leadership unnecessarily (Alvesson & Einola, 2019). Some of these ideas have spilled over and influenced thinking around leadership development as well.

How this translates to leader development is that a commonly held expectation (often tacit) is focusing on developing individual leaders will inherently result in better leadership. Chapter 1 elaborated on how



D. V. Day, *Developing Leaders and Leadership*,
https://doi.org/10.1007/978-3-031-59068-9_3

leader development differs from more collective leadership development and therefore it will not be repeated here. A related issue that was not addressed previously is the so-called leadership pipeline, which is central to many talent management and succession planning strategies. Essentially, the pipeline is a roster of high-potential leaders that are considered to be ready or nearly ready for more responsible leadership roles (Charan et al., 2011; Conger & Fulmer, 2003). The thinking is that having a well-populated pipeline of leaders who can step up and into leadership roles ensures a more effective future of organizational leadership. Two problems are that it confuses a developed leader with effective leadership and that it is often based on a high-potential strategy for development.

Something to always remember is that leadership is a process and not a position. To be an effective leader means being able to work effectively with others. It is not a human capital issue as much as a social capital one. As a reminder from Chapter 1, human capital refers to those intrapersonal knowledge, skills, and abilities (KSAs) that a leader takes from one situation to another. Social capital is about the leadership resources created between people in a more networked fashion. In this sense, leadership resides between people and is not resident in any single individual leader or pipeline of leaders. This point tends to get glossed over when the focus is mainly on preparing to meet the future leadership needs of an organization by "filling the leadership pipeline" (Kaiser, 2005).

## High-Potential Leadership Programs

An assumption and practice that underpins much of leadership development, especially in corporate organizations, is that of identifying and investing in high-potential leaders. The thinking goes that it does not make good financial sense to try and develop everyone as a leader given that organizations are structured like pyramids with fewer and fewer leadership positions at higher organizational levels. Of course, this confuses positions with leadership processes; however, that is not the only potential problem with a high-potential leadership development strategy. It also assumes that leadership potential is a rare commodity in organizations and that organizational decision-makers are good at identifying potential that is differentiated from good job performance. That assumption has historically been difficult to prove, with performance tending to dominate the views of those deciding who to designate as high-potential leaders (Day,

2007). It is a critically important designation because high potentials—also called hi-pos—command the lion's share of developmental resources. If someone is not considered to be a hi-po it is unlikely that they will go very far as organizational leaders in their respective careers. It is also the case that companies have proven to be generally bad at identifying leadership potential (Zenger & Folkman, 2017).

Measurement has been a major problem with the leadership pipeline and high-potential strategies. What kind of evidence is available to show that leadership potential can be measured distinctly from role performance? If such measures and data are available, they tend to be protected as proprietary intellectual property. Fortunately, there is at least one recent peer-reviewed publication providing the kinds of results needed that show how performance and potential each explain unique amounts of variance in high-potential decisions. These data are based on over 9,700 employees in a global multinational organization (PepsiCo) using measures of leadership potential developed in-house in the talent management function of the organization (Church et al., 2021). Results indicated that the observed correlation between assessed potential and performance was statistically significant but relatively modest ($\rho = 0.18$, $p < 0.01$). More interesting were the results showing that performance and assessed potential explained more variance in ratings of designated potential as well as actual promotions than either of these measures alone. The incremental pseudo-R2 values that can be taken as estimates of incremental validity were 0.074 for designated potential and 0.036 for promotions. These estimates may seem modest but were statistically significant and practically meaningful given the high levels of profit-and-loss (P&L) responsibility associated with many high-level leadership roles.

### *Challenges to High-Potential Leader Development Programs*

The field needs more studies like the PepsiCo one published by Church et al. (2021) in advancing an evidence-based science of leader development. What the PepsiCo study illustrates is that leadership potential can be differentiated from job performance, but there needs to be serious investment in developing psychometrically sound measures of potential in organizations for this to happen. Asking members of senior leadership to judge the potential of others as prospective leaders is risky and likely to fall prey to any number of biases, especially a "similar-to-me" or affinity form of cognitive bias. A more popular term nowadays is unconscious bias, in that certain cognitive heuristics or shortcuts are used in decision-making. These shortcuts are made relatively automatically and without awareness or much cognitive effort. In the realm of leader potential, those candidates who remind us of ourselves tend to be seen in a positive light, even without an awareness of this bias occurring. In this way, organizational decision-makers tend to perpetuate the demographic profile of the current members of senior leadership.

Having psychometrically sound measures of leadership potential can help overcome the kinds of institutional biases that can work against organizational members who are unlike the current senior leadership team. Although there has been research interest in measuring leadership potential in general (Spreitzer et al., 1997), the PepsiCo study is the only published study I am aware of that has rigorously examined how to identify leadership potential within a single organization and has linked assessments of potential to relevant career outcomes such as promotions.

High-potential leadership programs are ubiquitous but have distinct limitations. One is that they perpetuate an elitist approach to leadership and leader development. The assumption is that there are relatively few individuals who have sufficient leadership potential worth the investment, typically those considered to be in the top five percent of all employees (Zenger & Folkman, 2017). What about the other 95% of employees? Are these the "no-pos" (i.e., no leadership potential)? Where else would so much value be wasted by focusing on so few?

An alternative, more egalitarian approach has emerged in the so-called Deliberately Development Organization (DDO) (Kegan & Lahey, 2016). Although the DDO approach is uncommon, there are exemplar organizations such as Bridgewater Associates that have built entire cultures around the idea that people development (including leader development) is everyone's business and not just those in the HR or Talent Management functions. As the authors of the DDO volume uncover, being a DDO does not just coexist with conventional success as an organization, or merely contribute to that success, but can be the cause of what makes a successful company successful (p. 198). However it requires a radically different way of thinking about leadership talent and human potential and how it is developed. Rather than focusing on a small percent of purportedly elite high-potential leaders, the DDO approach recognizes that everyone has the potential to be a better leader, and something that organizations need these days is a broader and deeper capacity for creating effective leadership, especially in such dynamic and uncertain times.

John Gardner (1990) provided an apt summary perspective. He argued that "leadership gifts" (p. xix) are widely distributed in the human population but greatly untapped as a potential resource. He estimated that for every leader there are probably many others with the same leadership potential who have never led or considered leading. Why is this the case? Why, indeed. One thing is certain and that is we cannot continue to waste such massive amounts of leadership potential going forward. We have a better understanding today of how much society needs what these individuals with untapped leadership potential can contribute. That is why investing in every individual to become a better leader is needed so that when a leadership moment arrives, they are willing and able to exercise effective leadership.

## Leadership Training

Although this volume is about developing leaders and leadership, a traditional approach to enhancing leadership capabilities is through training. But be clear that leader(ship) development and leadership training are not interchangeable intervention approaches in terms of their goals or their processes (Day et al., 2021). In terms of goals, leadership training strives to bring all participants up to some minimal level of standard related to a given KSA. It also tends to assume that participants all start at the same place and change the same way over time. Training tends to downplay individual differences in providing participants with pretty much the same experience. Training also tends to be more structured than development interventions. There is usually a standard protocol that the training intervention follows. In short, training is usually much more structured than development and less individualized.

A summary of the differences between leadership training and development follows. Training is structured around a set of systematic learning objectives designed to enhance specific job-relevant KSAs with the goal of improving job-related performance as a leader. A more specific goal of leadership training is to provide an individual with new knowledge, add skills to the leader's repertoire, and establish the attitudes necessary to learn and apply the knowledge and skills on the job. Leader development expands a person's capacity to be effective in leadership roles and processes, even as responsibilities and circumstances change. The goal of leadership development is to enhance an individual's and the organization's capacity to address challenges with no known or agreed-upon solution.

Besides being more structured than development, training is also relatively short term with a standardized teaching protocol that is identical across participants. Leadership training also tends to be conducted in a classroom. By design, leader development is tailored more to an individual's strengths and weaknesses and focuses on using ongoing work and life experiences to facilitate practice outside of a classroom. Leadership training is focused on providing proven solutions to known problems whereas leader development is focused on expanding the capacity if individuals to learn their way out of complex adaptive challenges that have never been previously experienced.

Leadership training and development can be used in complementary ways. One example is with SBI feedback. As discussed in Chapter 2, SBI stands for situation, behavior, impact and is a preferred means for feedback giving that focuses on concrete, observable behaviors that have had an impact on the person providing the feedback (and not beyond that person). SBI feedback can be learned through a training module in a classroom to give participants an overview understanding of the technique. There might also be role playing or other forms of classroom-based practice to further enhance the training effects. Development kicks in with the use of SBI feedback in the real world. Training professionals refer to this as a transfer of training (Kirkpatrick & Kirkpatrick, 2006); however, in the world of development, this would be framed just as practice or, in systems terms, exporting transformed knowledge and skills into an environmental output.

Could an individual learn the basics of SBI feedback without engaging in training? Absolutely. Much of the same material could be learned independently through watching a video, reading a summary of SBI feedback, or having someone outside of a classroom explain it as a preferred mode of giving and receiving feedback. Training and development can be designed to complement each other, but they do not need to be always used in that manner. Much of what occurs in leader development is unstructured and individualized, with the thinking being that if someone owns their development (First Principle #1) then they will determine what they need to develop and not be subject to a strict, regimented training program.

### *Is Leadership Training Effective?*

This raises an important question: Does leadership training work? How do we know whether it works? What is the evidence? Researchers have attempted to answer these and other questions about leadership training using a set of accepted quantitative review techniques called meta-analyses (Lacerenza et al., 2017).

One way to understand the benefits of meta-analyses is to compare it with more traditional narrative review procedures. Traditionally, researchers would engage in a review of a particular area of study by reading all the relevant research that is considered part of the topic domain and in a narrative manner, outline what was learned, and summarize the major contributions in the field. There are several problems with this approach.

First, individual biases can affect the review. A researcher chooses to highlight certain studies and downplay others. Often, the criteria for these choices are not made explicit. Second, not all studies are created equal. Some have better designs than others, but another important issue is sampling error. That is, studies based on a small number of participants are likely to yield non-representative findings because the small sample is not representative of the population. A major advantage of meta-analyses is that they correct for sampling error by weighting the effects of each study by its respective sample size. In this manner, the results of a meta-analysis are better balanced and less likely to be skewed by one or more studies with relatively small (and therefore unrepresentative) samples.

#### *Understanding Meta-Analysis*

A non-technical explanation of meta-analysis is that it aggregates effect sizes for similar relationships (e.g., correlations between the same or similar variables) across studies, corrects for sampling error and possibly other artifacts such as measurement error (unreliability), and provides sample-weighted, population-level effect size estimates. These are considered to be population effects to the extent that researchers can document including all published and unpublished effect sizes available. As population effects, any non-zero effect size would be considered statistically significant; however, confidence intervals can be constructed around the effect size estimates based on the variability of the effects to determine whether the 95% confidence interval excludes zero (Borenstein et al.,

2021). If so, researchers can conclude with relative certainty that the true effect size is non-zero.

Meta-analysis also provides a point estimate of the overall corrected effect size between two variables. Note that the effect sizes can be reported in any number of formats (correlation, *t*-test, chi-square, *d* statistic) but need to be converted to a common metric. It is also the case that meta-analysis provides only bivariate effect sizes (i.e., relationship strength between two variables), although there are some published efforts suggesting that it is possible to estimate multivariate path models (e.g., structural equation models) using meta-analytic results (Viswesvaran & Ones, 1995). However the real value of meta-analysis is to provide a more accurate estimate of the relationship between two constructs of interest.

Meta-analysis is a quantitative review procedure, but there are still many judgment calls made in accumulating effects across studies. For example, there are usually differences in how a predictor variable (x) is operationalized or measured. Can it be assumed that different operationalizations or different measurements represent the same underlying construct? This type of judgment call needs to be clearly identified and explained in the research write-up so that other researchers could replicate the data coding process if desired. There are statistical procedures that can be used to understand how well this was done by examining the heterogeneity of effect sizes to determine whether there are any systematic differences in effects across different measurement approaches. If so, that might suggest there are different underlying constructs at play. These procedures are beyond the scope of this non-technical explanation of meta-analysis (see Borenstein et al., 2021, for a more comprehensive treatment of the topic).

Suffice it to say that meta-analysis is now an accepted set of quantitative review techniques; however, there are remaining limitations. Something that meta-analysis cannot correct for is the quality of the primary data. There is the saying "garbage in, garbage out." If all the primary studies are flawed (e.g., using non-causal, self-report data) then there is no way that meta-analysis can fix things such that causal claims can be made. The resulting effect size estimate is correlational and not causal.

### *Four Levels of Training Criteria*

Turning attention back to leadership training, one question of interest is what has meta-analysis contributed to our scientific understanding of leadership training? One question that it can address is whether there are meaningful (i.e., non-zero) relationships between different forms of leadership training and relevant outcomes. What is a relevant outcome in training research? One framework that has been widely adopted posits four levels of training criteria (Kirkpatrick, 1959; Kirkpatrick & Kirkpatrick, 2006): (1) reactions, (2) learning, (3) behavior, and (4) results. These are criteria that can be used in the evaluation of any training program and not just leadership training.

*Reactions* refer to the attitudes or feelings that participants have about the training program. To what extent was the training experience an engaging or enjoyable one or considered to be relevant to one's job situation? This is considered the lowest (i.e., most superficial) level of training criteria (i.e., level 1), and is often referred to as "smile sheets" among training professionals. *Learning* is at the next highest level (level 2). This criterion assesses the extent to which participants learn the intended knowledge, acquire relevant skills, or otherwise internalize the focal training targets. *Behavior* (level 3) refers to the degree that what is acquired through training is used back on the job. This training criterion is sometimes also referred to as transfer of training. *Results* (level 4) can refer to the extent that the targeted outcomes occur because of the training or whether there is a broader, organizational effect associated with the training.

Although the levels of training criteria framework provided by Kirkpatrick (1959) is widely used, it is not without criticism. Specifically, researchers have questioned the generalizability of these four levels, the extent to which the levels are causally linked, and whether the levels are positively correlated (Alliger & Janak, 1989). The framework remains a useful one, although with limitations.

### *Meta-analysis of Leadership Training Effects*

The Kirkpatrick (1959) levels of training criteria framework was applied to better understand the potential effects of leadership training. One question that meta-analysis can help answer is whether leadership training works—is it effective? These effects can be defined in terms of the four levels of training criteria of reactions, learning, behavior, and results. Furthermore, different factors can be examined across studies to determine whether there are moderating influences. Are there discernable training design factors that are associated with stronger or weaker effects across the various outcome levels?

Researchers addressed this and other questions by examining the effects of leadership training across 335 independent studies from the years 1951–2014 (Lacerenza et al., 2017). In addressing the overarching question of whether leadership training matters, meta-analytic results indicated that leadership training is associated with a 20%–30% increase in learning, on-the-job leadership behaviors, and positive organizational outcomes. Overall, leadership training was not associated with reactions; however, there were relatively few studies identified using reactions criteria ($k = 7$). More importantly, it is probably various aspects involved in the delivery of leadership training that matter more when it comes to participant reactions than just participating in leadership training.

Lacerenza et al. (2017) identified several significant between-study moderators, examining associations between 15 different contextual variables and learning, on-the-job leadership behaviors, and organizational-level outcomes. One of the strongest effects of learning and transfer to on-the-job behavior was that a needs analysis was conducted. A needs analysis is a systematic procedure to identify and define the KSAs associated with leadership effectiveness in an organization and identify the people who need them (Day et al., 2021). A needs analysis is considered a best practice in training and the meta-analytic results support this recommendation. Stronger effects for learning and transfer were found when the training was based on needs analysis. Although a needs analysis is recommended for improving the effects of leadership training, a needs analysis is not something that is normally conducted prior to leader development. That is only one factor that differentiates leadership training from development.

### *Leadership Training as Complement to Leader Development Initiatives*

There are no large-scale meta-analyses summarizing the literature on best practices in leader development. This makes it more difficult to evaluate the evidence supporting effective leader development interventions relative to the leadership training evidence and underscores major differences between training and development approaches to leadership. Whereas a training approach looks to use techniques such as needs analysis to identify what KSAs are needed more broadly in an organization (or at a particular organizational level or function), development approaches are inherently more individualized.

Choosing what to focus on to enhance the capacity for effectiveness in leadership roles and processes is endemic to a development approach. Using needs analysis and other procedures to determine what KSAs need to be acquired among organizational leaders (or aspiring leaders) and then designing a protocol that is delivered in a structured and standardized way is the hallmark of training. As noted, development and training initiatives can be considered complementary endeavors; however, they work from different assumptions and are implemented in very different ways.

Some of the problems noted regarding leadership programs probably can be traced to an underlying training mindset on the part of the design team. In many leadership programs, participants go through the experience engaging in pretty much the same activities in the same sequence with the goal being to bring about pretty much the same results. There is a focus on structure and standardization of experience with a training mindset. The approach is controlled mainly by the program facilitators.

With developmental initiatives there is (or should be) more participant control over what is to be developed, how it is to be developed, and how to best use ongoing experiences to develop as a leader. There are roles for facilitators, coaches, and even mentors in enhancing the developmental experience, but it is much more participant-driven than what it typically found in leadership training. Harken back to the First Principle #1 about owning one's development. No one can make anyone develop as a leader. The drive to become a better leader needs to come from within an individual who wants to be a more effective leader.

## Developing Leadership Skills

This section takes a practical look at how our First Principle #1 can play out in development. The focus is on developing leadership skills and competencies taking a true development approach rather than one that is grounded in training principles. A "true development" approach uses ongoing, everyday experiences to develop specific skill(s)—but the fewer the better, as will be explained—over time. This type of development occurs in the "life gym" whereby participants either look for opportunities to put into practice some transformed knowledge or proactively design an experience where this can happen. Think of this in systems terms in which initial energy in the form of motivation to develop is directed at learning or transformation, which is returned to the environment as output (practice), and feedback about the practice experience serves as input into the next developmental event cycle.

Two important open systems principles are central to this type of development: (1) systems as cycles of events, and (2) negative feedback (Katz & Kahn, 1978). A third principle that is central to the approach is equifinality, which posits a given end state can be reached by many potential pathways. This reinforces the point made earlier that in developmental systems people start at different places and change in different ways to get to the long-term objective of creating enhanced leadership capacity (i.e., leadership development).

### *Leadership Competency Models*

For this development system to work effectively it helps to have some sort of map of the territory where that territory is the local understanding of leadership. This is where a well-designed and locally relevant leadership competency model is useful. Although it has been said that a map is not the territory (Korzybski, 1995), sometimes a map can be helpful in understanding the territory. I know I used to get lost more often before the days of Google maps!

The map in this example is the competency model. Just as there are good maps and bad maps (and many in-between quality maps), the same could be said for leadership competency models. The better competency models clearly and concisely map what leadership is thought to be in the local context. To be useful the model (i.e., map) needs to be accurate, representative of the local territory and not a different territory, and offers guidance on how to get from point A to point B (i.e., how to develop).

A leadership competency model introduced in Chapter 2 is one developed and used by the Kravis Leadership Institute (KLI) at Claremont McKenna College (see Figs. 2.2 and 2.3). At the most general level are the leadership competencies of Courage, Creativity, and Collaboration. Each of these competencies comprises three unique capabilities (more specific than competencies), and each of these capabilities comprises five somewhat unique leadership skills or attributes. Note that there is a hierarchy of generality built into the competency model from a very specific, micro-skill to a basic or mini-level capability, to a general leadership competency or meta-skill. An important question therefore is if someone wishes to develop greater levels of courage or creativity or collaboration, what is the best way to do that?

It might be tempting to go out into the world and attempt to be courageous. That sounds inspiring, but what would that look like? How does one practice leadership courage? The answer refers us back to our map or leadership competency model. What do we mean by leadership courage? According the KLI leadership competency model courage is composed of *responsible action* (i.e., courage to act in accordance with one's values), *resilience* (i.e., courage to bounce back and learn from setbacks), and *entrepreneurial mindset* (i.e., courage to take risks and act boldly). Each capability has five more specific skills or attributes that define it. Rather than trying to address something relatively macro like a competency directly, what are some more micro actions that can be taken that go against what is typical or normal behavior for the individual (i.e., something out of one's comfort zone) but also in that sweet spot called the Goldilocks Zone (Clear, 2018)? This requires some further mapping to break down the micro-skills into actionable behavior.

Breaking down the model is a much-needed step in the development process. Our experience with young leaders at KLI (i.e., college students) is that they get stuck trying to figure out ways to practice their leadership. Some believe they first need a leadership position (wrong!) or put themselves in a situation where they need to be *the* leader (wrong again!). What they need to do is think in terms of smaller, more manageable things that they can do regardless of holding a leadership position or trying to be the leader. Relevant research that is helpful in this regard focuses on personality change rather than leadership *per se* (Hudson et al., 2019).

It turns out that personality can be changed but it takes more than just wanting to change, there needs to be follow-through. That follow-through it about doing relatively small, easily implemented behaviors that support or otherwise reinforce the desired change in a particular personality trait. This is not all that different from what happens in a formal leader development intervention. There is usually some type of personality assessment, a participant makes a commitment to change something about their personality (i.e., their behavioral tendencies or action preferences), and then puts together some sort of development plan that outlines the actions that will be taken to support the change.

Hudson et al. (2019) provide an extensive set of developmental challenges that were used to guide participants involved in a personality change study. These challenges were linked to each of the Big Five factors of personality of conscientiousness (C), openness to experience (O), extraversion (E), agreeableness (A), and emotional stability (S) or the converse of neuroticism. Scaling procedures were conducted to also assign a difficulty level to each challenge (1–10 with 10 being the most difficult).

The findings from this study indicated that engaging in small challenges on a regular basis helped to change individual personality; however, the difficulty of the challenge was not a statistically significant factor associated with that change. Individuals did not need to take on big challenges. Rather, embracing smaller behavioral challenges in the so-called Goldilocks Zone were what appeared to drive change. Furthermore, the number of challenges completed was related to the amount of personality change. The take-away is that one does not need to engage in big, difficult challenges to change personality. Completing many smaller challenges consistently over time was associated with significant changes in personality factors.

### *Leadership Skill Mapping*

How does this pertain to leadership and development? It was noted previously that what we are like is often how we lead (Hogan & Kaiser, 2005). Leadership style is very much a function of individual personality. What was done to help students practice their leadership was to use the challenges provided by Hudson et al. (2019) in identifying leadership skills that were similar to a respective Big Five personality factor. Maps of these relationships is provided for courage (Fig. 3.1), creativity (Fig. 3.2), and collaboration (Fig. 3.3).

Moving from the outside of a figure to the inner most central aspects illustrates example challenges listed with the personality factor and difficulty level, linking with micro-skills (sometimes more than one skill is linked to the challenge), with the skills defining a mini-skill or capability, and the capabilities defining the macro-level leadership competency. The maps are represented in tabular form in Table 3.1. The table is more legible but does not capture the big picture interrelatedness of some of the attributes and respective challenges. That is why both the skill map diagrams and the table are presented.

The skill maps were created using SimpleMind mapping software (https://simplemind.eu/). How would a participant use this sort of map? In essence, it is working from the macro-level competency down

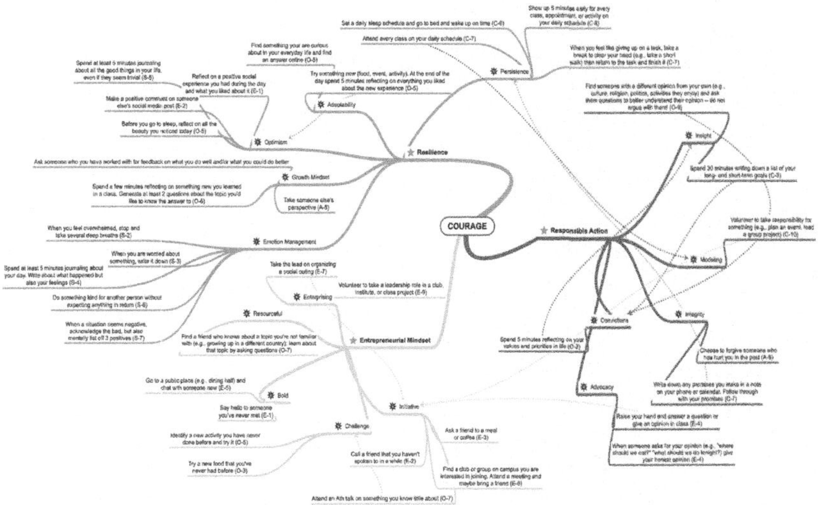


**Fig. 3.1** Courage skill map

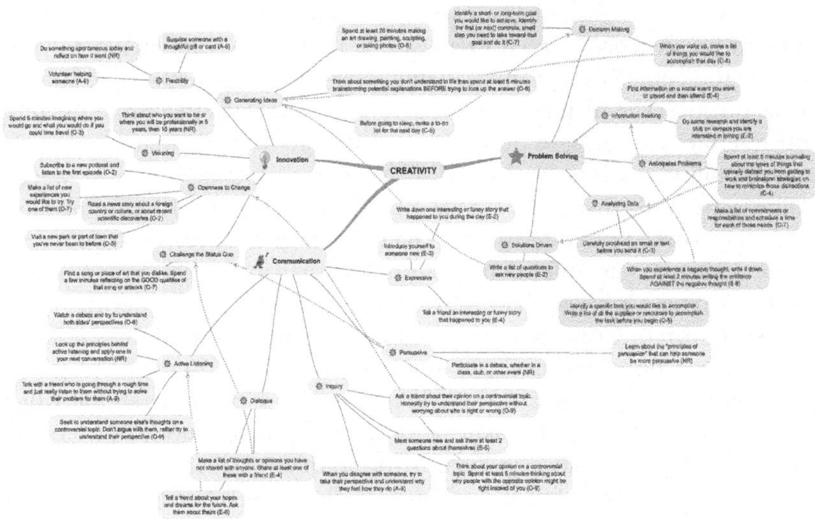


**Fig. 3.2** Creativity skill map

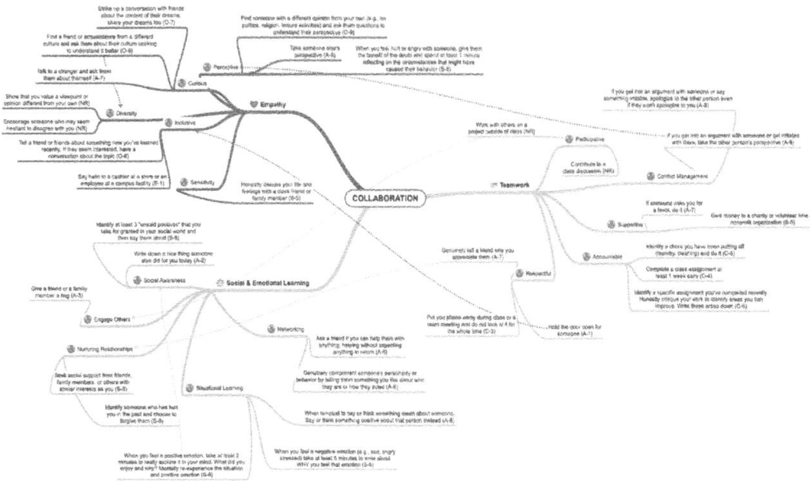


**Fig. 3.3** Collaboration skill map

to the micro-level skills that a participant wants to practice and improve. Students are instructed to choose just one leadership competency to work on over the course of a given academic year (two semesters). The student works through the map choosing capabilities and skills that are most relevant to either choosing or designing a challenge to implement. Follow-up accountability is done by having all participants complete a bi-weekly online activity form that is visible to all members of KLI summarizing what they worked on in terms of a challenge over the previous two weeks.

For example, assume that a student participant chooses to work on developing Courage. The next decision would be to decide which mini-skill form of Courage is most relevant or interesting to the student—responsible action, resilience, or entrepreneurial mindset? If the participant chooses responsible action, that requires a decision about which more specific (micro-level) skill to develop—insight, modeling, convictions, integrity, or advocacy. Each of these micro-skills has one or more challenges associated with it and each challenge is related to a different Big Five personality factor. Most challenges also have a difficulty level associated with it from ratings provided by Hudson et al. (2019). A participant would be encouraged to choose a more manageable, less difficult challenge to implement initially, moving to more difficult challenges

**Table 3.1** Competency skill maps with capabilities, attributes, and challenges

| *Competency (Macro Skill)* | *Capability (Mini Skill)* | *Attribute (Micro Skill)* | *Behavioral challenge* |
|---|---|---|---|
| Courage | Responsible action | Insight | • Find someone with a different opinion based on culture, religion, politics, or activities they enjoy and ask them questions to better understand their opinion—but do not argue with them! (O-9)<br>• Spend 30 minutes writing down a list of your long- and short-term goals (C-3) |
| | | Modeling | • Volunteer to take responsibility for something (e.g., plan an event, lead a group project) (C-10) |
| | | Integrity | • Choose to forgive someone who has hurt you in the past (A-9)<br>• Write down any promises you make in a note on your phone or calendar. Follow through with your promises (C-7) |
| | | Convictions | • Spend 5 minutes reflecting on your values and priorities in life (O-2_ |
| | | Advocacy | • Raise your hand to answer a question or give your opinion in class (E-4)<br>• When someone asks for your opinion give your honest opinion (E-4) |
| | Entrepreneurial mindset | Resourceful | • Find a friend who knows about a topic you're not familiar with (e.g., growing up in a different country); learn about that topic by asking questions (O-7) |
| | | Initiative | • Attend a talk on something you know little about (O-7)<br>• Call a friend that you haven't spoken to in a while (E-2)<br>• Ask a friend to a meal or coffee (E-3)<br>• Find a club or group on campus you are interested in joining. Attend a meeting and maybe bring a friend (E-6) |
| | | Bold | • Say hello to someone you've never met (E-1)<br>• Go to a public place (e.g., dining hall) and chat with someone new (E-5) |

(continued)

**Table 3.1** (continued)

| *Competency (Macro Skill)* | *Capability (Mini Skill)* | *Attribute (Micro Skill)* | *Behavioral challenge* |
|---|---|---|---|
| | | Challenge | • Identify a new activity you have never done before and try it (O-5)<br>• Try a new food that you've never had before (O-3) |
| | | Enterprising | • Take the lead on organizing a social outing (E-7)<br>• Volunteer to take a leadership role in a club, institute, or class project (E-9) |
| | Resilience | Persistence | • Attend every class on your daily schedule (C-7)<br>• Set a daily sleep schedule and go to bed and wake up on time (C-8)<br>• Show up 5 minutes early for every class, appointment, or activity on your daily schedule (C-8)<br>• When you feel like giving up on a task, take a break to clear your head (e.g., take a short walk) then return to the task and finish it (C-7) |
| | | Adaptability | • Find something you are curious about in your everyday life and find an answer online (O-5)<br>• Try something new (e.g., food, event, activity). At the end of the day spend 5 minutes reflecting on everything you liked about the new experience (O-5) |
| | | Optimism | • Before you sleep, reflect on all the beauty you noticed today (O-5)<br>• Reflect on a positive social experience you had during the day and what you liked about it (E-1)<br>• Make a positive comment on someone else's social media post (E-2)<br>• Spend at least 5 minutes journaling about all the good things in your life, even if they seem trivial (S-5) |
| | | Growth mindset | • Ask someone who you have worked with for feedback on what you do well and/or what you could do better (NR)<br>• Spend a few minutes reflecting on something new you learned in a class. Generate at least 2 questions about the topic (O-6)<br>• Take someone else's perspective (A-8) |

| *Competency (Macro Skill)* | *Capability (Mini Skill)* | *Attribute (Micro Skill)* | *Behavioral challenge* |
|---|---|---|---|
| | | Emotion management | • When you feel overwhelmed, stop and take several deep breaths (S-2)<br>• When you are worried about something, write it down (S-3)<br>• Spend at least 5 minutes journaling about your day. Write about what happened but also your feelings (S-4)<br>• When a situation seems negative, acknowledge the bad, but also mentally list off 3 positives (S-7)<br>• Do something kind for another person without expecting anything in return (S-6) |
| Creativity | Problem-solving | Information seeking | • Find information on a social event you want to attend and then attend it (E-4)<br>• Do some research and identify a club on campus you are interested in joining (E-2) |
| | | Analyzing data | • Carefully proofread an email or text before you send it (C-3)<br>• When you experience a negative thought, write it down. Spend at least 2 minutes writing the evidence AGAINST the negative thought (S-8) |
| | | Anticipates problems | • Spend at least 5 minutes journaling about the types of things that typically distract you from getting to work and brainstorm strategies on how to minimize those distractions (C-4)<br>• Make a list of commitments or responsibilities and schedule a time for each of those needs (C-7) |
| | | Decision making | • Identify a short- or long-term goal you would like to achieve. Identify the first (or next) concrete, small step you need to take toward that goal and do it (C-7)<br>• When you wake up, make a list of things you would like to accomplish that day (C-4) |
| | | Solutions driven | • Write a list of questions to ask new people (E-2)<br>• Identify a specific task you would like to accomplish. Write a list of all the resources needed to accomplish the task before you begin (C-5) |

(continued)

**Table 3.1** (continued)

| *Competency (Macro Skill)* | *Capability (Mini Skill)* | *Attribute (Micro Skill)* | *Behavioral challenge* |
|---|---|---|---|
| | Communication | Active listening | • Watch a debate and try to understand both sides' perspectives (O-6)<br>• Talk with a friend who is going through a rough time and really listen to them without trying to solve their problem (A-9)<br>• Look up the principles behind active listening and apply one in your next conversation (NR)<br>• Seek to understand someone else's thoughts on a controversial topic. Don't argue with them, rather try to understand their perspective (O-9) |
| | | Expressive | • Tell a friend an interesting or funny story that happened to you (E-4)<br>• Introduce yourself to someone new (E-3)<br>• Write down one interesting or funny story that happened to you during the day (E-2) |
| | | Persuasive | • Participate in a debate, whether in a class, club, or other event (not rated)<br>• Investigate the "principles of persuasion" that can help someone be more persuasive (NR) |
| | | Inquiry | • Ask a friend about their opinion on a controversial topic. Honestly try to understand their perspective without worrying about who is right or wrong (O-9)<br>• Meet someone new and ask them at least 2 questions about themselves (E-5)<br>• When you disagree with someone, try to take their perspective and understand why they feel how they do (A-8)<br>• Think about your opinion on a controversial topic. Spend at least 5 minutes thinking about why people with the opposite opinion might be right instead of you (O-9) |

| *Competency (Macro Skill)* | *Capability (Mini Skill)* | *Attribute (Micro Skill)* | *Behavioral challenge* |
|---|---|---|---|
| | | Dialogue | • Make a list of thoughts or opinions you have not shared with anyone. Share at least one of these with a friend (E-4)<br>• Tell a friend about your hopes and dreams for the future. Ask them about theirs (E-6) |
| | Innovation | Openness to change | • Read a news story about a foreign country/culture or recent science discoveries (O-2)<br>• Subscribe to a new podcast and listen to the first episode (O-2)<br>• Make a list of new experiences you would like to try. Try one of them (O-7)<br>• Visit a park or part of town that you've never been to before (O-5) |
| | | Generating ideas | • Spend at least 20 minutes making an art drawing, painting, sculpting, or taking photos (O-5)<br>• Think about something you don't understand in life then spend at least 5 minutes brainstorming potential explanations BEFORE trying to look up the answer (O-6)<br>• Before going to sleep, make a to-do list for the next day (C-5) |
| | | Visioning | • Spend 5 minutes imagining where you would go and what you would do it you could time travel (O-3)<br>• Think about who you want to be or where you will be professionally in 5 years, then 10 years (NR) |
| | | Challenge the status quo | • Find a song or piece of art that you dislike. Spend a few minutes reflecting on the GOOD qualities of that song or artwork (O-7) |
| | | Flexibility | • Do something spontaneous today and reflect on how it went (NR)<br>• Volunteer helping someone (A-6)<br>• Surprise someone with a thoughtful gift or card (A-5) |
| Collaboration | Teamwork | Participative | • Contribute to a class discussion (NR)<br>• Work with others on a project outside of class (NR) |

(continued)

**Table 3.1** (continued)

| *Competency (Macro Skill)* | *Capability (Mini Skill)* | *Attribute (Micro Skill)* | *Behavioral challenge* |
|---|---|---|---|
| | | Accountable | • Complete a class assignment at least 1 week early (C-4)<br>• Identify a specific assignment you've completed recently. Honestly critique your work to identify areas one can improve. Write these areas down (C-6)<br>• Identify a chore you have been putting off (e.g., laundry, cleaning) and do it (C-5) |
| | | Supportive | • If someone asks you for a favor, do it (A-7)<br>• Give money to a charity or volunteer time at a nonprofit organization (S-5) |
| | | Respectful | • Put your phone away during class or a team meeting and do not look at it for the whole time (C-3)<br>• Hold the door open for someone (A-1)<br>• Genuinely tell a friend why you appreciate them (A-7) |
| | | Conflict management | • If you get into an argument with someone or say something irritable, apologize to the other person even if they won't apologize to you (A-8)<br>• If you get into an argument with someone or get irritated with them, take the other person's perspective (A-9) |
| | Social & emotional learning | Engage others | • Give a friend or family member a hug (A-3) |
| | | Social awareness | • Write down a nice think someone else did for you today (A-2)<br>• Identify at least 3 "unsaid positives" that you take for granted in your social world and say them aloud (S-6) |

| *Competency (Macro Skill)* | *Capability (Mini Skill)* | *Attribute (Micro Skill)* | *Behavioral challenge* |
|---|---|---|---|
| | | Networking | • Ask a friend if you can help them with anything without expecting anything in return (A-6)<br>• Genuinely compliment someone's personality or behavior by telling them something you like about who they are or how they acted (A-6) |
| | | Nurturing relationships | • Seek social support from friends, family members, or others with similar interests as you (S-8)<br>• Identify someone who has hurt you in the past and choose to forgive them (S-9) |
| | | Situational learning | • When tempted to say or think something mean about someone, say or think somethings positive about that person instead (S-8)<br>• When you feel a negative emotion (e.g., sad, angry stressed) take at least 5 minutes to write about WHY you feel that emotion (S-5)<br>• When you feel a positive emotion, take at least 2 minutes to really explore it in your mind. What did you enjoy and why? Mentally re-experience the situation and positive emotion (S-6) |
| | Empathy | Perceptive | • Take someone else's perspective (A-8)<br>• Find someone with a different opinion from your own (e.g., on politics, religion, leisure activities) and ask them questions to understand their perspective (O-9)<br>• When you feel hurt or angry with someone, give them the benefit of the doubt and spend at least 1 minute reflecting on the circumstances that might have caused their behavior (S-8) |

(continued)

**Table 3.1** (continued)

| *Competency (Macro Skill)* | *Capability (Mini Skill)* | *Attribute (Micro Skill)* | *Behavioral challenge* |
|---|---|---|---|
| | | Curious | • Strike up a conversation with friends about the content of their dreams; share your dreams too (O-7)<br>• Find a friend or acquaintance from a different culture and ask them about their culture seeking to understand it better (O-8)<br>• Talk to a stranger and ask them about themselves (A-7) |
| | | Diversity | • Encourage someone who may seem hesitant to disagree with you (NR)<br>• Show that you value a viewpoint or opinion different from your own (NR) |
| | | Inclusive | • Say hello to a cashier at a store or an employee at a campus facility (E-1)<br>• Tell a friend or friends about something new you've learned recently. If they seem interested, have a conversation about the topic (O-6) |
| | | Sensitivity | • Honestly discuss your life and feelings with a close friend or family member (S-5) |

*Note* Behavioral challenges adapted from Hudson et al. (2019). E = extraversion; A = agreeableness; C = conscientiousness; S = stability; O = openness; Number = difficulty of challenge; Numbers refer to the rated difficulty of the challenge (1–10); NR = challenge not included in Hudson et al. and difficulty not rated over time until there was the sense of sufficient developmental progress and that a different skill or even broader capability should be the focus of subsequent practice. This sense of developmental progress would ideally be linked with feedback or other informational inputs or support that motivate ongoing developmental cycles.

In summary, the goal of a skill map is to break down a macro-level competency that might be difficult to figure out how to practice and develop into smaller, more manageable units. What matters most (and this is based on the Hudson et al., 2019 research) is not doing something audacious one time to develop, but engaging in smaller, less demanding challenges that are implemented repeatedly. This aligns with First Principle #2 that development takes dedicated work/practice over a relatively long period of time to make lasting changes. Do not expect miracles!

A final point about this approach to leader development through focusing on micro-skills: The validity of the approach is an extrapolation from the findings of the Hudson et al. (2019) study about personality change. Those authors found that focusing on regular implementation of small challenges had measurable effects on changing individual personality. Although personality and leadership style are related, they are not identical. For that reason, research is ongoing to collect evidence about changes in the development of leadership skills and competencies from student participants across the number of semesters and years that they are engaged with the developmental system.

## Personal Trajectories of Development

When studying individual development in general and leader development more specifically, change is a core construct. Change is not always positive or linear, but change implies tracking something of interest that does vary in terms of level, frequency, or strength over time. Historically, change has been difficult to measure and model rigorously. Early efforts to quantitatively study change were so dismal and fraught with errors that researchers who wanted to study change were advised to frame their questions in other ways (Cronbach & Furby, 1970). Until the mid- to late-1980s when appropriate statistical procedures were developed and tested (with much thanks to advances in available computing power) the field was a mess. Until that time, "the technical literature on the measurement change was awash with broken promises, erroneous half-truths, and name-calling" (Singer & Willet, 2003, p. 3). Fortunately, times change (pun intended).

To study development and change appropriately, researchers need longitudinal data. Cross-sectional data that is collected only once just will not do. Even with two "waves" of data or measurement periods, it is not truly longitudinal research (Day, 2011) because the only possible change form is linear. One definition of longitudinal research offered in the organizational sciences is "research emphasizing the study of change and containing a minimum of three repeated observations (although more is better) on at least one of the substantive constructs of interest" (Ployhart & Vandenberg, 2010, p. 97). Developmental psychologists have identified the methodological requirements of any study of change as being (1) multiple waves of data (three or more measurement periods), (2) a meaningful metric for time, and (3) an outcome variable that changes systematically (Singer & Willet, 2003, p. 4).

## *Latent Growth Modeling Research*

One approach that has emerged as especially useful in understanding leader development processes is that of individual growth models or latent growth modeling (Day & Lance, 2004). This is a powerful analytical tool for charting and understanding individual trajectories of development. A few relevant examples will be briefly reviewed next. The focus is on non-technical explanations of the studies and their respective methodologies that highlight major empirical findings from research. Readers interested in additional background on how to estimate growth models using random coefficient modeling are referred to this primer (Bliese & Ployhart, 2002) and a somewhat more technical treatment (Raudenbush, 2001). Most major statistical software packages such as R, Stata, and MPlus are equipped to analyze longitudinal data using growth modeling techniques.

### *Research with College Students*

One of the first studies to take an individual growth modeling approach to understanding longitudinal leader development was conducted with college students ($N = 1315$) engaged in a course on leadership and team building in which one component was a team-based action learning project ($k = 205$) (Day & Sin, 2011). One of the objectives of the course and the use of action learning projects was to develop participants as leaders.

Action learning involves a learning-by-doing approach in which a team project is used to deliver results (action) that would be considered to have a meaningful impact on the local community while also focusing on the development (learning) of participants (Marquardt et al., 1998; Revans, 1982). It is a widely recognized approach to leader and leadership development. There were four waves of data collection across a 13-week period. The developmental trajectories of participants were estimated using two classes of growth modeling techniques: Random coefficient modeling and growth mixture modeling.

Study results suggested there were differences in the initial leadership effectiveness levels across participants as well as differences in the shape or form of their personal trajectories. The overall trajectory was J-shaped indicating overall initial declines in rated leader effectiveness across participants followed by a positive slope. It was predicted that adopting a leader identity would serve as a within-person, time-varying covariate of leadership effectiveness (supported) and that goal orientation would serve as a between-person, cross-level moderator of the personal change trajectories (partially supported).

The results of growth mixture modeling analyses revealed two distinct latent classes of developmental trajectories that could be distinguished empirically. The dominant class followed the overall J-shaped trajectory; however, a smaller class of approximately 10% of the participants was found to have an overall positive and linear longitudinal trajectory. Although results could not clearly explain why these two classes of participants tended to have different developmental experiences as reflected in their respective trajectories, there was some evidence to suggest that the adult development processes of selection, optimization, and compensation (Baltes, 1997) played a formative role.

The issues of leader identity and adult development that emerged as potentially significant explanations of longitudinal development will be explored in more detail in Chapters 4 and 5, respectively. This research provides a proof of concept of sorts that applying growth modeling techniques to the study of leader development can help provide valuable insights into longitudinal development processes as well as tests of potential explanatory factors associated with individual differences in personal trajectories of development.

*Research with Professional Graduate Students*

Another study adopting even more sophisticated growth modeling procedures examined the interrelationship between leader identity development and changes in self-rated leadership skills (Miscenko et al., 2017). The trajectories of leader identity and skill development were studied over the course of a seven-week leader development program with a sample of Dutch graduate students ($N = 98$). It was hypothesized that changes in self-perceived leadership skills would be associated with changes in leader identity. Using latent growth curve modeling and latent change score analyses as the primary analytical approaches, the researchers analyzed longitudinal data across seven measurement points. As in the Day and Sin (2011) study, results suggested that leader identity developed in a J-shaped pattern. Furthermore, as hypothesized, changes in leader identity were associated with, and potentially shaped by, changes in leadership skills over time.

This study is notable for incorporating both leaders self-views as well as leadership skills as proximal outcomes of a leader development intervention as proposed by (Day & Dragoni, 2015). Something else worth mentioning is that although the sample size was relatively modest (fewer than 100 participants), measuring change across seven distinct waves ($k = 7$) added to the statistical power of the study. In longitudinal designs, statistical power is a function of both the number of participants ($N$) and the number of measurement waves ($k$) included in the study.

*Research with Military Cadets*

Charting and understanding the trajectories of leader identity and leadership self-efficacy development was the focus of a study of Canadian military cadets ($N = 240$) engaged in a six-week leadership development program (Kwok et al., 2021). Of interest was whether latent growth modeling procedures could detect any systematic changes in these leadership self-views across the program using four waves of measurement data ($k = 4$) and whether these changes could be predicted by individual differences in learning goal orientation (i.e., focus on mastery rather than performance) and affective motivation to lead (i.e., liking to lead).

Leader identity demonstrated an unconditional overall trajectory (i.e., no random effects in the model) that was positive but followed a quadratic shape with slowing growth at higher levels. Participants higher and lower on learning goal orientation developed equally on leader identity, albeit via different trajectories (i.e., demonstrating equifinality). Conditional results for leader efficacy demonstrated that participants lower on affective motivation to lead (i.e., lower levels of liking to lead) exhibited greater changes to their leader efficacy, which was further moderated by learning goal orientation. Leadership self-views in the forms of leader identity, leadership self-efficacy, and leader self-awareness are conceptualized as leading or proximal indicators of leader development (Day & Dragoni, 2015) and will be the focus of Chapter 5. The results from the Kwok et al. (2021) study demonstrate that not only are there underlying positive trajectories of development for two of these leadership self-views, but that the aspects of these trajectories (e.g., intercepts and slopes) can be predicted using between-person individual difference factors.

*Research with Senior Executives*

A final trajectory analysis study that will be summarized here focused on high-potential executives ($N = 80$) working for a multinational conglomerate who were selected to participate in a five-month quasi-residential leader development program (Kragt & Day, 2020). The focus of the research was based on the prediction that distinct leadership competencies (as rated independently by leadership coaches) differ in their development trajectories over time. Across four waves of data collection ($k = 4$), significant differences in the initial levels and the changes in eight distinct leadership competencies were found. It was also shown that the self-view of leader identity predicted the development of certain—but not all—leadership competencies (i.e., identity was a time-varying covariate of some leadership competencies). Evidence was also presented demonstrating that developing certain leadership competencies predicted career advancement (i.e., job promotion).

A notable feature of this study was that the participants were senior executives with considerable amounts of leadership experience. It might be expected that as experienced leaders there would be a ceiling effect for leader identity (all participants would rate their respective leader identity strongly). Although there was noted restriction of range on this variable, leader identity was still predictive of a set of leadership competencies as rated by others (i.e., coaches). This extends previous findings on the leader identity self-view beyond emerging student leaders to other more experienced leadership populations.

### *Summary of Latent Growth Modeling Research in Leader Development*

This chapter section highlighted four studies that adopted an individual trajectory analysis to the study of leader development. As implemented through various growth modeling techniques, results indicate that leader development can be tracked successfully, providing insights into the process of development (i.e., underlying trajectories) rather than just a pre- and post-test of whether any change occurred. Growth modeling also allows for testing time-varying covariates (i.e., constructs that change along with the focal construct of interest) as well as individual difference predictors of these personal trajectories.

One caution is that drawing causal inferences from these kinds of personal trajectory data is challenging. The gold standard for making causal inferences is a randomized experiment in which participants are randomly assigned to different treatment and control conditions. As noted by Raudenbush (2001, p. 522):

> The problem of causal inference for time-varying treatments, assuming no randomization, is extraordinarily challenging. It is a cutting-edge issue on which progress is being made, but methodological workers in this area have not yet achieved a consensus on the best ways to proceed.

Even more than 20 years later, drawing causal inferences from non-experimental data with no randomization is still extraordinarily challenging. But the good news is that huge advances have been made in terms of modeling change effectively and that most of the "name calling" referenced by Singer and Willet (2003, p. 3) has ceased.

## Implications of Individual Leader Development

This chapter focused on individual leader development, pointing out that developing leaders does not inevitably develop leadership. That is because leadership is a process involving more than an individual leader. It is about enhancing the process of working with others to achieve some shared goal or objective. That said, we know a lot more about leader development than leadership development. The latter will be the focus of both Chapters 6 and 7.

In the emerging science of leader development, we have learned a lot over the past two decades about how individuals develop as leaders. Advances in computing power and statistical modeling techniques allow researchers to study change—which is central to development—in rigorous and accepted ways. Researchers have helped to provide evidence supporting the proposition that both self-views and KSAs are relevant leading or proximal indicators that individual development is occurring. More long-term development focuses on the operating system of the individual leaders in terms of mental complexity, dynamic skill, and other deeper level lagging or distal outcomes.

Something that has not been addressed in much detail is about typical intervention practices to help facilitate leader development. Much of the focus of this volume is about using the so-called life gym to practice leadership behaviors on a regular basis in a meaningful context of one's everyday life. However there are more structured interventions that are often used, especially as part of leader development programs. These often require considerable resources to implement without much evidence to support the investments. One way to think about this is to use the gym membership analogy again. One can buy a gym membership, have access to all kinds of different equipment, and be in a context where others are also present to work out…or…one can use the gym of life. Rather than taking a lift, use the stairs. Instead of using a chest press machine do push-ups. Instead of running on a treadmill, run outside on a road or trail. Instead of riding a stationary bike, ride a real bike. You get the idea. Much of what is commoditized in leadership development are these kinds of special gym machines. But such specialized equipment is unnecessary to develop one's leadership capacity if the motivation and discipline to develop as a leader are present.

### *Scaling and Individualizing Interventions*

There are two underlying and somewhat competing factors or dimensions to consider regarding developmental interventions: (1) scalability, and (2) individualization. Scalability refers to how the process or practice can be grown to accommodate numerous participants. One of the benefits of leadership training is that it can be scaled for large numbers of participants. On the other hand, leadership coaching is less scalable because of the costs involved. That said, there are claims that leadership coaching can be relatively scalable and cost effective in university settings (Kolditz et al., 2021). Individualization refers to how tailored the intervention is to the needs of a specific individual. Here is where leadership training falls short because by design training assumes that people pretty much start at the same place, change in the same way, and finish at the same end point. Coaching is highly individualized, which is one of its greatest benefits in leader development.

*Mentoring*

Mentoring is another highly individualized developmental practice. Unfortunately, there is little research focused on mentoring and leader development outcomes. A multidisciplinary meta-analysis of mentoring effects found positive effects comparing mentored versus unmentored individuals on skills and competency development across 13 unique samples and over 2,000 individuals (Eby et al., 2008). The skills involved included socialization, communication skills, problem-solving skills, work knowledge, and goal setting ability. The magnitude of the effect size was relatively small (sample-weighted correlation of 0.11, with a 95% confidence interval ranging from 0.07 to 0.16, excluding zero).

*Coaching*

What is overlooked in mentoring is that there are no training or certification standards for being a mentor. As a result, there is potentially large variability when it comes to the effectiveness of individual mentors. With coaching, there are certification standards imposed and monitored by the International Coaching Federation. Using a certified leadership coach ensures some standardization and level of expertise that is not found with mentoring. Although it is tempting to think of a leadership coach as a type of personal trainer there are important differences. A leadership coach asks good, insightful questions to prompt reflection and behavioral change on the part of the participant. Some have called this "humble inquiry" (Kolditz et al., 2021, p. 43) in which the focus is to uncover underlying individual assumptions, beliefs, and motivations by asking questions. A good leadership coach does not give specific routines or schedules or exhort a participant to work harder as would a personal trainer. But coaching is not personal therapy either, although there may be some similar underlying skill sets of a leadership coach and a therapist. Both are focused on helping an individual cope and adjust with life demands, often based on personal discovery through self-reflection.

*Multisource Feedback*
Another relatively common leader development practice is 360-degree or multisource feedback. This involves gathering ratings from different sources or perspectives (e.g., self, peer, subordinate, supervisor) and presenting these summarized ratings to the participant. The developmental target is enhancing self-awareness and facilitating behavioral change. Because of the large amount of data presented to a participant, which may not be consistent across different rating sources, it can feel overwhelming and confusing without professional guidance on how to interpret a 360-degree feedback report (Day, 2000). It is also the case that meta-analysis of the leadership training literature suggests that 360-degree feedback may not provide much additional predictive validity as compared with providing feedback from a single source (Lacerenza et al., 2017). In an earlier publication, I provided a summary of selected practices in leader development (e.g., 360-degree feedback, coaching, mentoring, networking, job assignments, and action learning) and refer interested readers to that article (Day, 2000).

One take-away from this discussion of leader development interventions is that many of the "bells and whistles" associated with pricey developmental programs probably are unnecessary. It is not so much what access there is to special developmental equipment as it is engaging in manageable stretch assignments on a regular basis. Using the overarching First Principles presented in Chapter 1 of using experience for development and including aspects of assessment, challenge, and support to enhance the effects of developmental experiences can offer a great deal of potential impact without an exorbitant price tag. This puts much of the onus for development on the actor or developing leader, but the philosophy reflected in this volume suggests that this should not be a problem. A place to begin with this philosophy should be by understanding leadership self-views, which will be the focus of the next chapter.

## Chapter Summary

- Developing leaders is not equivalent to developing leadership. A leader needs to put into action what has been learned and that needs to be done in an interpersonal context (i.e., with others such as followers) to enhance effective leadership.

- A common approach to leader development in corporate organizations is the leadership pipeline in which there is a roster of possible individuals to take on more responsible leadership roles if needed. The leadership pipeline is a prime example of confusing a leader with leadership, and positions with processes.
- High-potential leadership programs focus development investments on a small proportion of employees (usually five percent or fewer). There is an underlying assumption that leadership potential is not widely distributed in the population so there is a great need to be able to identify this potential. Organizations have not generally been good at spotting leadership potential, but a published example from PepsiCo provides an exception to this general rule (Church et al., 2021).
- A more egalitarian approach to developing leaders can be found in Deliberately Developmental Organizations (DDOs), which make people development everyone's job. By investing in developing the potential of all employees—including their leadership potential—an organization has enhanced capacity to achieve its business goals. DDOs believe this is a must-have and not just a nice-to-have approach.
- Leadership training and leader development are different but potentially complementary approaches to enhancing the leadership capacity of individuals. Training tends to be highly structured and focused on providing proven solutions to known problems. Leader development is less structured and more individualized than training and focuses on enhancing the capacity of individuals to learn their way out of novel adaptive challenges.
- Meta-analysis has been used to estimate whether leadership training is effective across training criterion levels of: (1) reactions, (2) learning, (3) behavior, and (4) results. Meta-analytic results indicated that leadership training is associated with a 20–30 percent increase in learning, on-the-job leadership behaviors, and positive organizational outcomes, thus answering the question affirmatively as to whether leadership training is effective. Certain boundary conditions (or between-study moderators) such as a needs analysis being conducted were shown to strengthen the results of leadership training.

- Leadership skill development is an important part of leader development. Rather than trying to develop relatively large, complex competencies directly, it is recommended that participants "drill down" on a competency model to the smallest, micro-level skills and then choose or devise challenges to address these more manageable developmental targets.
- There is an emerging literature in the leader development field that is focused on using personal trajectories of development to chart and understand change over time. Adopting these rigorous and accepted techniques for modeling development provides insight not only into the form of developmental trajectories but the kinds of factors that can predict or shape how change unfolds over time.
- A final point in this chapter is that the type of intervention used is less important than choosing relevant and manageable challenges and implementing them regularly in the so-called life gym.

## References


Alliger, G. M., & Janak, E. A. (1989). Kirkpatrick's levels of training criteria: Thirty years later. *Personnel Psychology, 42*(2), 331–342. https://doi.org/10.1111/.1744-6570.1989.tb00661.x

Alvesson, M., & Einola, K. (2019). Warning for excessive positivity: Authentic leadership and other traps in leadership studies. *The Leadership Quarterly, 30*(4), 383–395. https://doi.org/10.1016/j.leaqua.2019.04.001

Baltes, P. B. (1997). On the incomplete architecture of human ontogeny—Selection, optimization, and compensation as foundation of developmental theory. *American Psychologist, 52*(4), 366–380. https://doi.org/10.1037/0003-066x.52.4.366

Bliese, P. D., & Ployhart, R. E. (2002). Growth modeling using random coefficient models: Model building, testing, and illustrations. *Organizational Research Methods, 5*(4), 362–387. https://doi.org/10.1177/109442802237116

Borenstein, M., Hedges, L. V., Higgins, J. P. T., & Rothstein, H. R. (2021). *Introduction to meta-analysis*. John Wiley & Sons.

Charan, R., Drotter, S., & Noel, J. L. (2011). *The leadership pipeline: How to build the leadership powered company*. John Wiley & Sons.

Church, A. H., Guidry, B. W., Dickey, J. A., & Scrivani, J. A. (2021). Is there potential in assessing for high potential? Evaluating the relationship between performance ratings, leadership assessment data, designated high-potential

status and promotion outcomes in a global organization. *The Leadership Quarterly, 32*(5), 101516. https://doi.org/10.1016/j.leaqua.2021.101516
Clear, J. (2018). *Atomic habits: An easy and proven way to build good habits and break bad ones*. Avery.
Conger, J. A., & Fulmer, R. M. (2003). Developing your leadership pipeline. *Harvard Business Review, 81*(12), 76–84, 125.
Cronbach, L. J., & Furby, L. (1970). How we should measure "change"—or should we? *Psychological Bulletin, 74*(1), 68–80. https://doi.org/10.1037/h0029382
Day, D., Bastardoz, N., Bisbey, T., Reyes, D., & Salas, E. (2021). Unlocking human potential through leadership training and development initiatives. *Behavioral Science & Policy, 7*(1), 41–54. https://doi.org/10.1177/237946152100700105
Day, D. V. (2000). Leadership development: A review in context. *The Leadership Quarterly, 11*(4), 581–613. https://doi.org/10.1016/S1048-9843(00)00061-8
Day, D. V. (2007). *Developing leadership talent: A guide to succession planning and leadership development*. Society for Human Resource Management Foundation.
Day, D. V. (2011). Integrative perspectives on longitudinal investigations of leader development: From childhood through adulthood. *The Leadership Quarterly, 22*(3), 561–571. https://doi.org/10.1016/j.leaqua.2011.04.012
Day, D. V., & Dragoni, L. (2015). Leadership development: An outcome-oriented review based on time and levels of analyses. *Annual Review of Organizational Psychology and Organizational Behavior, 2*, 133–156. https://doi.org/10.1146/annurev-orgpsych-032414-111328
Day, D. V., & Lance, C. E. (2004). Understanding the development of leadership complexity through latent growth modeling. In D. V. Day, S. J. Zaccaro, & S. M. Halpin (Eds.), *Leader development for transforming organizations: Growing leaders for tomorrow* (pp. 41–69). Lawrence Erlbaum Associates.
Day, D. V., & Sin, H. P. (2011). Longitudinal tests of an integrative model of leader development: Charting and understanding developmental trajectories. *The Leadership Quarterly, 22*(3), 545–560. https://doi.org/10.1016/j.leaqua.2011.04.011
Eby, L. T., Allen, T. D., Evans, S. C., Ng, T., & DuBois, D. L. (2008). Does mentoring matter? A multidisciplinary meta-analysis comparing mentored and non-mentored individuals. *Journal of Vocational Behavior, 72*(2), 254–267. https://doi.org/10.1016/j.jvb.2007.04.005
Hogan, R., & Kaiser, R. B. (2005). What we know about leadership. *Review of General Psychology, 9*(2), 169–180. https://doi.org/10.1037/1089-2680.9.2.169

Hudson, N. W., Briley, D. A., Chopik, W. J., & Derringer, J. (2019). You have to follow through: Attaining behavioral change goals predicts volitional personality change. *Journal of Personality and Social Psychology, 117*(4), 839–857. https://doi.org//https://doi.org/10.1037/pspp0000221

Kaiser, R. B. (Ed.). (2005). *Filling the leadership pipeline*. Center for Creative Leadership.

Katz, D., & Kahn, R. L. (1978). *The social psychology of organizations* (2nd ed.). Wiley.

Kegan, R., & Lahey, L. L. (2016). *An everyone culture: Becoming a deliberately developmental organization*. Harvard Business Review Press.

Kirkpatrick, D. (1959). Techniques for evaluating training programs. *Journal of the American Society for Training and Development, 13*, 3–9.

Kirkpatrick, D. L., & Kirkpatrick, J. L. (2006). *Evaluating training programs: The four levels* (3rd ed.). Berrett-Koehler.

Kolditz, T., Gill, L., & Brown, R. P. (2021). *Leadership reckoning: Can higher education develop the leaders we need?* Monocle Press.

Korzybski, A. (1995). *Science and sanity: An introduction to non-Aristotelian systems and general semantics* (5th ed.). International Non-Aristotelian Library, Institue of General Semantics.

Kragt, D., & Day, D. V. (2020). Predicting leadership competency development and promotion among high-potential executives: The role of leader identity. *Frontiers in Psychology, 11*, 1816. https://doi.org/10.3389/fpsyg.2020.01816

Kwok, N., Shen, W., & Brown, D. J. (2021). I can, I am: Differential predictors of leader efficacy and identity trajectories in leader development. *The Leadership Quarterly, 32*(5), 101422. https://doi.org/10.1016/j.leaqua.2020.101422

Lacerenza, C. N., Reyes, D. L., Marlow, S. L., Joseph, D. L., & Salas, E. (2017). Leadership training design, delivery, and implementation: A meta-analysis. *Journal of Applied Psychology, 102*(12), 1686–1718. https://doi.org/10.1037/apl0000241.supp

Marquardt, M. J., Leonard, H. S., Freedman, A. M., & Hill, C. C. (1998). *Action learning for developing leaders and organizations: Principles, strategies, and cases*. American Psychological Association.

Meindl, J. R., & Ehrlich, S. B. (1987). The romance of leadership and the evaluation of organizational performance. *Academy of Management Journal, 30*(1), 91–109. https://doi.org/10.2307/255897

Meindl, J. R., Ehrlich, S. B., & Dukerich, J. M. (1985). The romance of leadership. *Administrative Science Quarterly, 30*(1), 78–102. https://doi.org/10.2307/2392813

Miscenko, D., Guenter, H., & Day, D. V. (2017). Am I a leader? Examining leader identity development over time. *The Leadership Quarterly, 28*, 605–620. https://doi.org/10.1016/j.leaqua.2017.01.004
Ployhart, R. E., & Vandenberg, R. J. (2010). Longitudinal research: The theory, design, and analysis of change. *Journal of Management, 36*(1), 94–120. https://doi.org/10.1177/0149206309352110
Raudenbush, S. W. (2001). Comparing personal trajectories and drawing causal inferences from longitudinal data. *Annual Review of Psychology, 52*, 501–525. https://doi.org/10.1146/annurev.psych.52.1.501
Revans, R. W. (1982). What is action learning? *Journal of Management Development, 1*(3), 64–75. https://doi.org/10.1108/eb051529
Singer, J. D., & Willet, J. B. (2003). *Applied longitudinal data analysis: Modeling change and event occurrence*. Oxford University Press.
Spreitzer, G. M., McCall, M. W., & Mahoney, J. D. (1997). Early identification of international executive potential. *Journal of Applied Psychology, 82*(1), 6–29. https://doi.org/10.1037/0021-9010.82.1.6
Viswesvaran, C., & Ones, D. S. (1995). Theory testing: Combining psychometric meta-analysis and structural equation modeling. *Personnel Psychology, 48*(4), 865–885. https://doi.org/10.1111/j.1744-6570.1995.tb01784.x
Zenger, J., & Folkman, J. (2017, February 20). Companies are bad at identifying high-potential employees. *Harvard Business Review*. Retrieved August 18, 2023, from https://hbr.org/2017/02/companies-are-bad-at-identifying-high-potential-employees

CHAPTER 4

# Self-Views and Leader Development

## Time and Leader Development

This may seem like it is stating the obvious, but development takes time. A central question is how much time. The answer, of course, is that it depends. The amount of time to develop leadership-related skills, self-views, and mindsets depends on the focus of development as well as the design of the experiential intervention. It is simply much harder to "move the needle" on certain things relative to others. Learning to act in ways that counter or overcome well-entrenched habits that someone wishes to change likely takes a lot more time compared with acting in ways that are consistent with an established habit, such as building on a strength. It is also the case that developing a specific leadership skill such as charismatic communication could be accomplished in a few days or weeks using a structured training protocol (Antonakis et al., 2011). At the other end of the spectrum, it may take years or decades to reach expert leadership levels through internalizing a leader identity and engaging in regular ongoing practice (Day et al., 2009). Summarizing this perspective, if the focus is on a specific skill, then the time scale for development is likely to be much shorter than if a more Gestalt-like perspective on developing the whole leader is taken (Day, 2014).

The amount of time needed to develop might also depend on the design of the experience. It was noted previously that not all experiences are created equal when it comes to their developmental impact (McCall,



D. V. Day, *Developing Leaders and Leadership*,
https://doi.org/10.1007/978-3-031-59068-9_4

2010; Tesluk & Jacobs, 1998). It would be expected that an experience that includes all three aspects of assessment, challenge, and support (McCauley et al., 2010) would help bring about development in less time than experiences missing one or more of those features.

Having a well-thought-out understanding of the role of time in developmental processes is critical to all three areas of theory, research, and practice. It should be noted that these are interrelated areas of concern in the design, delivery, and scientific understanding of leader development. Time lags occur between the delivery of an intervention and the expected effect. These lags are important concerns for the design and study of change; however, most longitudinal research models do a poor job of incorporating appropriate time lags (Gollob & Reichardt, 1987). A common approach in research is to consider how long one can study a given intervention, then divide that total amount of time by the number of possible measurement waves to come up with an operationalization of the "appropriate" time lags to study (Day, 2014). Such an approach fails to consider the timing of effects and the careful specification of when developmental targets are likely to change.

## Specifying the Timing of Developmental Effects

Researchers have argued for decades that there needs to be better theoretical specification of time in longitudinal research, especially in terms of understanding when effects are hypothesized to occur (Mitchell & James, 2001). This is just another way of saying that time lags are not well understood and usually are not specified with much theoretical guidance. Perhaps it is time (pun intended) to think about things a little differently. Rather than attempting a detailed theoretical specification of time lags, researchers are beginning to realize that more is better when it comes to measurement waves. This ignores the practical concerns associated with measuring something many times; however, there are recent efforts to collect and model intensive longitudinal data (Hamaker & Wichers, 2017). At the most extreme end of the continuum are studies in which data are collected in an ongoing, continuous manner, typically involving controlled laboratory studies involving animals (Collins, 2006). That said, the technological advances made in wearable devices are starting to bring continuous measurement practices into studies with human participants.

When it comes to research involving human participants, including studies of leader development, it is not the case that data are typically collected in such a continuous manner. That said, advances are ongoing in terms of technology that might make this a reality in studying the development of leaders and leadership. Some research exists now that have examined communication patterns in teams using wearable devices (Pentland, 2012). A more popular methodology involves experience sampling and so-called diary studies in which there are "repeated measurements of the same participants as they go about their daily lives, with a focus on assessing variables that fluctuate over the short term" (Fisher & To, 2012, p. 865). Of course, what is short term and what is long(er) term is a matter of subjective judgment. But the more important point is that measuring developmental outcomes as many times as possible in longitudinal research helps to build better understanding of time lags in domains such as leader development. Doing so involves adopting more of an inductive rather than deductive approach to understanding the timing of effects. This has led to the conclusion that "far shorter time lags than those frequently found in the literature are justifiable, and we call for more 'shortitudinal' studies in the future" (Dormann & Griffin, 2015, p. 1).

The advent of intensive longitudinal data has sparked tensions between whether the focus of research should be on studying intraindividual (i.e., within-person) or interindividual (i.e., between-person) variation (Molenaar, 2004). The former is more of an idiographic approach that seeks to first understand change within the individual and the discovery of general principles as secondary. As noted by Collins (2006), "...growth is a phenomenon that occurs within the individual and therefore intraindividual variability is a primary interest in statistical modeling of longitudinal data" (p. 506). It is also the case that intraindividual approaches such as those based on intensive longitudinal data provide a wealth of information about how dynamic processes unfold within individuals over time. Nonetheless, there are statistical techniques that provide multilevel estimates of growth that capture both intraindividual and interindividual variability.

As noted by Hamaker and Wichers (2017), techniques that combine intensive longitudinal data with dynamic multilevel modeling has led to new insights in clinical psychology. These approaches include time-series analyses at the intraindividual level while also considering individual differences at the interpersonal level in the prediction of these intraindividual change parameters. Similar insights are being gleaned from the application of such techniques to leader development. There have been extraordinary advances in the study of developmental models since the call from early proponents to adopt longitudinal methods in the study of intraindividual change (Schaie, 1983).

### *Integrating Longitudinal Research*

In the design and implementation of effective longitudinal research, Collins (2006) has proposed the "seamless integration" (p. 507) of three distinct elements. First is a *theoretical model of change* that provides a clear, concise, but comprehensive statement about the nature of the change phenomenon that is to be observed. Is the expected change pattern linear or curvilinear? What are the best estimates of the expected time lags? The more information that can be presented about the expected nature of the change the better. The second element is the *temporal design* used to study the change phenomenon. This operationalizes the theory of change specified in the first element in terms of the number of measurement waves that would be needed to capture the underlying change with reasonable certainty. A cogent presentation of how a mismatch between the theory of change and the temporal design can lead to erroneous conclusions can be found in the organizational literature (Ployhart & Vandenberg, 2010). The third element is the choice of an appropriate *statistical model of change*. Fortunately, there are numerous choices of statistical approaches to model change that are rigorous, defensible, and provide potentially valuable insights into the many facets of leader development and individual change. As discussed in Chapter 3, latent growth modeling, growth mixture modeling, multilevel change modeling, random coefficients modeling, and latent change score analyses have all been used in the longitudinal study of leader development.

A non-technical treatment of this literature was promised, and I fear that perhaps this is getting too far "in the weeds" for many readers. The basic takeaway here is that we need to be thinking more carefully about the role of time in leader development. Certain things related to the development of leaders and leadership are likely to develop more quickly and others more slowly. As noted in the research on executive leaders, different leadership competencies were found to have different underlying trajectories (Kragt & Day, 2020). At a conceptual level, researchers have made a very general attempt at including time into a multilevel model of the development of leaders and leadership (Day & Dragoni, 2015). At the individual-level developmental interventions are proposed as shaping the capacities that an individual brings to an experience into the proximal—or leading—indicators of development that take the forms of self-views and leadership-related knowledge skills, and abilities (KSAs) (see Chapter 2). With intensive practice over longer time periods, these proximal indicators are further developed into deeper distal—or lagging—indicators of development that are associated with many of the ways in which adult development has been considered theoretically. The next section focuses on these proximal self-view indicators of leader development. Chapter 5 takes a deep dive into the proposed distal indicators of leader development .

## Proximal Indicators of Leader Development

This chapter argues for a more careful consideration of time in leader development. After all, it cannot be reasonably expected that the effects of a developmental intervention occur immediately. But how long is long enough for an effect to occur is the crucial question. A related concern is how long can we expect an effect to continue, which is something hardly ever addressed in the development literature. It can be said with certainty that the effects of any leadership intervention will decay unless there is some transfer to work/life through extended practice or booster sessions provided on what was acquired through an intervention.

An attempt at giving time its due in leader development was offered by Day and Dragoni (2015). Instead of attempting to develop an extensive taxonomy of expected time lags in developing leaders and leadership, the focus was more coarse-grained. Two general categories of effects were proposed. Proximal indicators of development were thought to happen relatively quickly following an intervention whereas distal indicators were thought to take much longer to realize and would occur only after an extensive period of dedicated practice. At the level of the individual leader, the proximal indicators were proposed to be self-views and leadership KSAs. These can be transformed or developed in a matter of hours or days. Distal indicators associated with enhanced mental complexity and the development of dynamic skills happen more slowly over the course of months, years, or even longer.

### *Leadership KSAs*

Leadership KSAs can take myriad forms and in many cases are amenable to training. In one published example that is notable for its experimental design (Antonakis et al., 2011), charisma was taught to middle managers ($N = 34$) across two sessions separated by a few days. The first phase of the intervention lasted five hours and provided participants with an overview of what constitutes effective charismatic communication and charismatic leadership. This overview culminated in individual feedback reports and the creation of tailored development plans on how to implement these principles on the job. Follow-up phone calls of about an hour focused on individual coaching with a discussion on how the participant planned to improve their leadership and especially how they would practice their charisma. This is a good example of how training can be considered more of a developmental intervention given the focus on individualized needs. Three months later the participants were re-rated by coworkers who evaluated the participants prior to training on their charismatic leadership, demonstrating a significant effect of training on leader charisma.

There is an almost infinite list of the types of leadership skills KSAs can be trained and/or developed. One such set of leadership KSAs that has been examined in randomized field experiments involves transformational leadership. This is based on a specific leadership theory proposing that world-class leadership involving performance beyond expectations builds on exchange-related transactional factors (e.g., contingent reward, management by exception) to include transformational leadership behaviors (Bass, 1985). The so-called 4Is of transformational leadership theory are (1) *idealized influence* (serving as a positive role model for followers), (2) *inspirational motivation* (motivation of followers through challenge and providing meaning), (3) *intellectual stimulation* (stimulate follower's efforts to be creative and innovative), and (4) *individualized consideration* (paying attention to each follower's individual needs). Instead of going into all the details and research on transformational leadership theory (see Bass & Riggio, 2006, for a review) three field experiments are reviewed briefly with an eye to understanding the amount of developmental investment in terms of training times and the time lags used in studying the hypothesized outcomes.

### *Field Experiments with Transformational Leadership Theory*

One such field experiment (Barling et al., 1996) was conducted on managers from different bank branches ($k = 20$). The managers in the experimental group ($n = 9$) participated in one day of group training plus four monthly "booster" sessions that consisted of a personal meeting with the lead researcher. Those managers in the control condition ($n = 11$) received no training. The outcomes of interest were employee ratings of transformational leadership behaviors of the bank manager and financial performance of the bank branch (controlling for pre-training measures) five months after training. There was evidence of statistically significant effects of training—otherwise there probably would be no publication!—as was the case in all three of the experiments reviewed here. Of interest here is the lag time between the intervention and the expected effects (five months in the Barling et al. study).

A second field experiment was conducted this time with members of the Israeli Defense Force (Dvir et al., 2002). Of interest were the effects of transformational leadership training on the attitudes and performance of direct followers ($n = 900$) and indirect followers ($n = 724$) of 54 military leaders. Training consisted of a three-day workshop (both training and control conditions, although the training content differed between conditions) followed by a three-hour booster for those in the experimental condition. Outcomes were measured six months after training and indicated the leaders in the experimental group had a more positive impact on direct followers' development and on indirect followers' performance than did the leaders in the control group. Again, the focus here is on the lag time, which was six months.

A third experimental field study (Jacobsen et al., 2022) focused on educational leaders (e.g., school principals) in Denmark ($N = 463$ completing post-training measures). The training consisted of four sessions each eight hours in length of either transformational leadership, transactional leadership, or a combined session and transactional and transformational leadership. This approach is notable because it does not compare experimental training against nothing (i.e., no-treatment control condition) but against transactional leadership, which is thought to be effective at least to some extent in shaping follower performance outcomes. Leader behavior was assessed via self-report three months after training and objective outcomes (e.g., student standardized test performance, student grade point average, student completion rates) two years after the training. The underlying model proposed that the leadership training would affect leadership behavior, which in turn, would increase organizational performance. Causal claims can be made here because of the randomized experimental design. The results were mixed with findings showing higher levels of transformational leadership behavior but lots of inconsistent findings on the organizational outcomes.

Across the four experimental studies reviewed here, the lag times ranged from three months to two years. A pertinent question is whether there might be alternative outcomes worth examining in the context of leader development that might provide other proximal insights into ongoing development. This leads us to a relatively recent addition to the leader development literature of leadership self-views as indicators of development.

### *Provisional and Possible Leadership Self-Views*

Another category of proximal developmental indicators is self-views. These views take the primary forms of leader identity, leader self-awareness, and leadership self-efficacy. Self-views are closely related to the self-concept—how one comes to see and understand the self—that have important influences on individual emotions, cognitions, and behavior. Scholars working in this, and other related areas, have noted that the self is a "unifying construct within psychology and other social and behavioral sciences" (Leary & Tangney, 2011, p. 1).

It may be unifying, but it is not univocal. Leary and Tangney (2011) identified over 260,000 scientific abstracts that included a hyphenated "self" term (e.g., self-concept, self-esteem, self-control, self-efficacy, self-awareness, and apparently lots more!). What is important about the self is that it provides "the mental apparatus that underlies self-reflection" (p. 6). It is this capacity for reflexive thinking that is key to promoting individual development. But the self is not some sort of homunculus that resides within a person and serves as a causal agent; rather, the self is a collection of various concepts that people hold about themselves, provisionally (Ibarra, 1999) and as possibilities (Morf & Mischel, 2011).

In the domain of leader development, self-views are thought to mediate between individual capabilities and more distal individual-level outcomes associated with longer-term adult development (Day & Dragoni, 2015). Self-views have also been proposed as the most malleable aspects of leader development. Research reviewed in the following section suggests that self-views can be intervened on efficiently and effectively, with evidence accruing about how self-views that are more "leader-like" can have very short lag times in terms of linking with developmental outcomes (e.g., Day & Sin, 2011).

*Possible Selves*

One theoretical foundation for incorporating self-views into the leader domain literature is that of possible selves. According to the authors who introduced the term into the psychological literature, possible selves "represent individuals' ideas of what they might become, what they would like to become, and what they are afraid of becoming, and thus provide a conceptual link between cognition and motivation" (Markus & Nurius, 1986, p. 954). The approach underscores an important point that individuals are in a constant state of becoming and that journey is likely to be a lifelong one. How one thinks of the self at age 20 is likely to be quite different from that self-view at age 40 or 60 or any other age (Cross & Markus, 1991).

Of interest and relevance here is the notion of being (or becoming) a leader as one possible self that can be internalized along with other life and work roles (e.g., mom/dad, brother/sister, engineer, architect, and so forth). It might also be something that individuals try out or experiment with provisionally to see before integrating with the self-concept (Ibarra, 1999). What does it mean to think of oneself as a leader, and more importantly, how might that self-view shape behavior and development as a leader? The same questions apply to one's self-awareness manifested in understanding personal strengths and weaknesses, the blind spots that might prevent one from being more effective in leadership roles and processes, as well as the perceived self-confidence to act as an effective leader when needed (i.e., leadership self-efficacy).

What follows is a more detailed treatment of the role of leadership self-views in leader development with a particular focus on the more specific forms of leader identity, leader self-awareness, and leadership self-efficacy. As noted, there is no shortage of self-related constructs, processes, and phenomena in the scholarly literature. In addition to reviewing three leadership self-views, an overarching question to consider is what additional self-related constructs might be helpful in furthering the scientific understanding of the pathways of leader development.

## The Self-in-Leader Development

This section reviews what we know from theory and research on the self as a developmental focus in leader development. Self-related constructs are clearly of interest to researchers in the social and behavioral sciences (Leary & Tangney, 2011) but what, specifically, do these constructs offer to researchers interested in leader development? The short answer is that developing leadership-related self-views are thought to provide valuable insights as to whether longer-term development will likely occur. Individuals with stronger leader identities, deeper self-awareness, and higher levels of leadership self-efficacy have a greater likelihood, *ceteris paribus* or all things equal, of building further competence and demonstrating enhanced effectiveness as a leader relative to individuals holding a weak leader identity, having limited self-awareness, and maintaining lower levels of leadership self-efficacy. The reasons and evidence for these claims are discussed next.

### *Leader Identity*

> The problem of self-identity is not just a problem for the young. It is a problem all the time. Perhaps the problem. It should haunt old age, and when it no longer does it should tell you that you are dead.—Norman Maclean (1992, p. xiii)

The preceding quote comes not from a scholarly book or research article on identity, but a work of nonfiction about the Mann Gulch fire disaster of 1949 (Maclean, 1992) where 13 smokejumpers lost their lives in an epic wildfire in the Montana mountains. Smokejumpers are those rugged souls (now including young women) who are members of a profession

> ...with the aim of taking on at the same time three of the four elements of the universe—air, earth, and fire—and in a simple continuous act dropping out of the sky and landing in a treetop or on the face of a cliff in order to make good on their boast of digging a trench around every fire they landed on by ten o'clock the next morning. (p. 19)

The relevance to leadership and identity was developed in a case study of the Maclean book (Weick, 1993). The framing of the Weick article was around the collapse of sensemaking in organizations and its disastrous consequences. The gist of his analysis is that if as a firefighter you drop your tools to engage in flight rather than to fight a fire then who are you? Identity loss triggers a loss of sensemaking that turns young people who jump out of planes to fight wildfires into victims. Maclean was in a similar fire as a young man but survived. His book is in many ways a search for self-understanding about how that event shaped him and how it could have turned out quite differently. I am unsure whether Maclean was referring to actual physical death or more of a metaphorical one in the opening quote. For our purposes, when identity stops haunting us, it is developmental death that occurs.

Identity is important because it provides for self-understanding but also frames sensemaking processes. Identity reflects what we value in life and therefore informs resource allocation decisions. The most important resource we have is time because it is the only resource available to us that is nonrenewable. What we value is central to our identities and shapes personal decisions about when, where, and how we spend our time. Making room in a multifaceted identity space to value being a leader means that someone will be more likely to invest temporal resources in developing and practicing being a better leader. Identity shapes personal agency when it comes to development, which is codified in First Principle #1 in this volume. Having a weak or nonexistent leader identity translates into fewer personal resources devoted to owning one's development as a leader. Internalizing a leader identity does not inherently make one a leader; however, a tenet of social cognition is that thinking is for doing; social understanding operates in service of social interaction (Fiske, 1992).

In the case of leader identity, it is understanding of the self (i.e., self-understanding or self-awareness) that guides interpersonal interactions around leadership. It is also the case that doing causes thinking. By engaging in leadership behavior and practice, doing leadership reinforces one's thinking of the self as a leader. It provides the open systems feedback loop with new data to initiate the next cycle of development. One can also think about possible thinking-doing-thinking spirals of leader development. The issue of identity-development and efficacy-performance spirals will be taken up later in this chapter.

### *Identity-Development Spirals*

Consistent with the perspective expressed in the opening quote from Maclean (1992), identity is a process of lifelong construction and revision. Leader identity also is dynamic in its development. Day et al.

(2009) proposed that individuals experience positive and negative spirals of leader identity. A positive spiral occurs when someone engages in leadership behavior or attempts a developmental challenge and meets with a positive response. It may be that others grant them leadership status in response to an attempt to establish or claim a leader self-identity (DeRue & Ashford, 2010). The positive response on the part of others reinforces the claim of a leader identity, which should initiate another cycle of energy and information input into the system to transform those resources into skills, mindsets, and/or self-views that are returned to the environment as output in future leadership episodes. This represents a positive or *virtuous cycle* of identity development (see Fig. 4.1a). It does not mean that an individual will inevitably develop further as a leader by engaging in another input–throughput–output cycle; however, it is more likely to occur given the positive reinforcement that is received. Of course, this depends on how important you view reinforcement in terms of behavioral repetition. Most psychologists and economists would acknowledge the importance of reinforcement incentives in encouraging repeated behavior.

But what happens when this same developing leader meets with resistance or rejection when claims of a leader identity are made? One possibility is that this negative experience initiates a negative or *vicious cycle* of identity development whereby an individual begins doubting their abilities to lead and thus eroding an emerging leader identity. If the

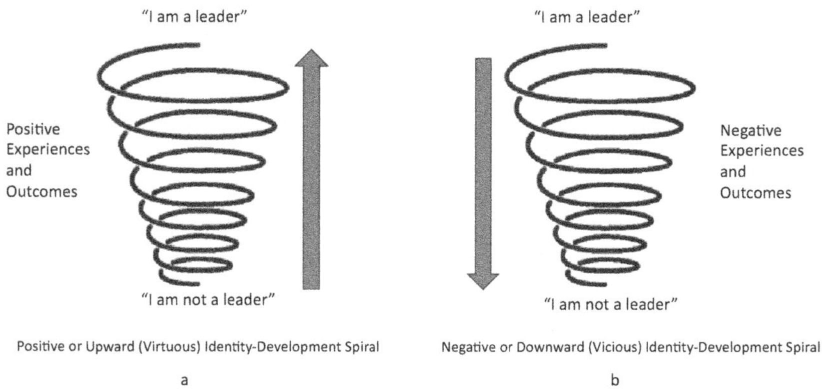


**Fig. 4.1** Identity development spirals

leader continues to have negative experiences when attempting to lead or initiate developmental challenges, it could lead to the unfortunate result of completely abandoning a leader identity ("I am not a leader;" see Fig. 4.1b). The individual in question may experience a type of learned helplessness in which they come to believe that they do not have what it takes to be an effective leader. That is most unfortunate because it represents a loss of leadership potential to an organization or the world at large. Of course, those who endorse a high-potential perspective on leadership potential would likely just shake their heads and say something like: "I told you that some people just do not have what it takes to be a leader."

A negative vicious spiral is not inevitable. There are individual differences that matter. One example is personal resilience. Researchers define resilience as "positive adaptation in the context of significant adversity" (Masten et al., 2009, p. 117). An individual persists despite obstacles and setbacks to achieving what they want. Consider it something of a test as to how important or how valued something like being a leader is to an individual. To what extent is being or becoming a leader a core value that translates into a leader identity? Putting it into more everyday vernacular, some people want it more than others and are willing to go through quite a bit of pain to build and maintain a leader identity.

Other individual differences may come into play as well, such as developmental self-efficacy in which an individual believes that despite the obstacles they can develop into an effective leader (Murphy & Johnson, 2016). This approach to understanding leader identity development spirals has a foundation in theorizing on efficacy-performance spirals in organizations (Lindsley et al., 1995). Leadership self-efficacy will be addressed later in this chapter as one of the leadership self-views that serves as a proximal indicator that longer-term development is occurring.

*Identity- Versus Outcome-Based Change*

A potentially helpful way of thinking about the role of identity in motivating change in the pursuit of being a more effective leader is whether the forces for change are being driven internally or externally. This difference has been articulated in the guise of habits by Clear (2018), in which *identity-based habits* are differentiated from *outcome-based habits*. What lies in between identity (deep level) and outcomes (surface level) are processes (mid-level).

Much of the performance change literature focuses on outcome-based approaches following goal-setting principles and processes. Research has shown that goal setting is effective at improving performance, especially when goals are specific and challenging rather than easy or do your best (Locke et al., 1981). People often begin a personal change project by identifying what they want to achieve (i.e., the goal). Setting a specific and challenging goal (e.g., quit smoking by a certain date), leads to changes in processes (e.g., reducing the number of cigarettes smoked per day) until the goal is reached and identity is changed (e.g., becoming a nonsmoker). This approach can work and has been shown to work but is it the most effective way to change?

A different approach to change that Clear (2018) calls identity-based works from more of an inside-out framework. First decide on what kind of person you want to be (e.g., nonsmoker). Internalizing that identity should change processing tendencies, which will lead to the desired outcome. The change starts by deciding on who we want to become, compared with focusing on an outcome to guide the process. Here is how Clear describes it:

> Most people don't consider identity change when they set out to improve. They just think "I want to be skinny (outcome) and if I stick to this diet, then I'll be skinny (process)." They set goals and determine the actions they should take to achieve those goals without considering the beliefs that drive their actions. They never shift the way they look at themselves, and they don't realize that their old identity can sabotage their new plans for change. (p. 32)

Shifting the way someone thinks about the self (i.e., identity change) is thought to work the same way in leader development (see Fig. 4.2a and b). Thinking about oneself as a leader (i.e., identity) changes the processes associated with how you use the big life gym to implement small leadership challenges, which gets one to the outcome of becoming a more effective leader. Of course, there is that little matter of time! But internalizing and valuing a leader identity provides someone with the motivation to implement the processes that result in change—over time. It is also the case that behavior (processes) that are inconsistent with the self (identity) will not stick. This is the essence of that psychological construct called cognitive dissonance (Festinger, 1962). We strive to be consistent in terms of internally held attitudes including identity and behavior.

Identity has been called the self-concept, especially in earlier times. Something that is a potentially important concern when it comes to

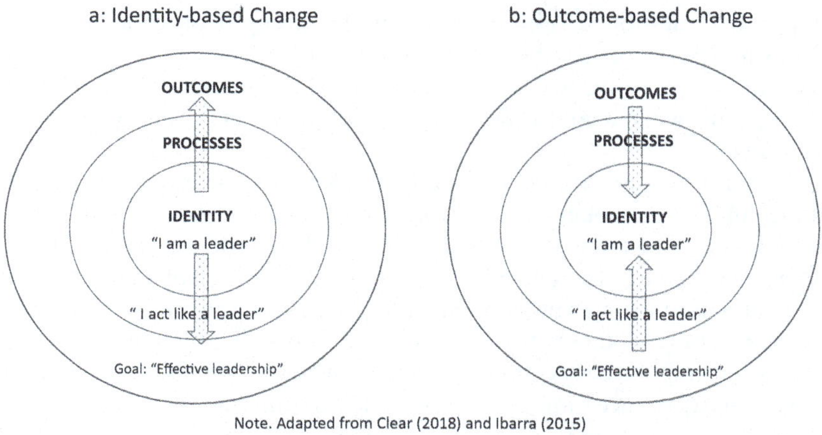


**Fig. 4.2** Two forms of personal change

identity-based change and individual development is the degree of self-concept clarity that one has about the self. It is a structural aspect of the self that is assessing the "extent to which self-beliefs are clearly and confidently defined, internally consistent, and stable" (Campbell et al., 1996, p. 141). These researchers developed and published a 12-item measure that can be used to measure self-concept clarity. Representative items from the scale include "In general, I have a clear sense of who I am and what I am" and "My beliefs about myself often conflict with each other" (reverse scored) (p. 145, Table 1). Researchers at the Doerr Institute for New Leaders at Rice University use the measure (among others) to evaluate individual changes associated with leader development interventions such as leadership coaching. Results of their pre-post data collection show that individual leadership coaching of Rice students significantly increases self-concept clarity and strengthens leader identity (Kolditz et al., 2021, p. 98, Table 3).

Most of the research conducted on leader identity has measured it in terms of identity *strength* such as the degree that someone sees themselves as a leader (see Chapter 3 for specific measurement items). Researchers have demonstrated that leader identity strength operates as a time-varying covariate with changes in leader effectiveness (Day & Sin, 2011), leadership skills (Miscenko et al., 2017), and leadership competency development (Kragt & Day, 2020). A relevant and potentially important question is how malleable is the strength of leader identity? Previous research cited above has shown that leader identity can change over time suggesting it is a dynamic construct; but how often might it change and what would cause it to change have yet to be examined in any detail.

Recent research with college students ($N = 69$) investigated whether there might be frequent changes in leader (and follower) identity that are a function of event strength experienced daily (Nieberle et al., 2023). Strong events are unexpected and emotionally disruptive such as being in a car accident or a family member experiencing a medical emergency; however, some of these strong events can be positive such as presenting well at an important meeting or acing a difficult class exam. The study mixed an experience sampling approach (i.e., gathering intensive longitudinal data focused on intrapersonal change) with longitudinal, multilevel random coefficients modeling in providing evidence to support the assertion that time and context are important considerations when it comes to leader identity development. Strong daily events motivate positive shifts in the leader identities of young adults (i.e., college students), making leadership more salient than followership.

Leader identity strength is an important consideration, but others have suggested that there are potentially additional components of leader identity to consider (Hammond et al., 2017). Other components that have been suggested include *integration* (i.e., how integrated a leader identity is with one's self-concept), level of *inclusiveness* (i.e., is identity conceptualized mainly at individual, relational, or collective levels), and *meaning* (i.e., is leadership about dominance, influence, or shared collaboration). There is a need for more research examining the proposed components of leader identity beyond identity strength.

One study that has examined the development of a leader identity meaning adopted a qualitative, grounded theory approach to study a small group of students ($N = 13$) over the course of their four years in college (Komives et al., 2005). Results suggested that what it means to be a leader changed over time following these general phases: (1) Awareness, (2) Engagement/ Exploration, (3) Leader Identification, (4) Leadership Differentiated, (5) Generativity, and (6) Integration/Synthesis. The meaning of leadership tended to become broader and more inclusive over time, moving from something considered to be rare and exclusive to, as one participant stated, "more of an everyday thing" (p. 607). What subsequent applications of the model developed in this theory-building research indicated was that students come to realize that they do not need to be *the* leader to be *a* leader in their lives (Komives et al., 2006).

In bringing this section on leader identity self-views to a close, it is important to reiterate that thinking of oneself as a leader is likely to motivate acting like a leader, which over time enhances the likelihood of demonstrating effective leadership. When a leader identity is internalized and becomes a clear, strong signal about who someone is in terms of what is valued and what can be expected by others, it is likely to result in more opportunities to practice leadership and implement small challenges in the name of leader development (Ibarra, 2015).

### *Leader Self-Awareness*

Another relevant leadership self-view concerns respective levels of self-awareness. The origins of self-awareness can be traced to the foundational Delphic maxim of *know thyself* in Greek philosophy. The general construct of self-awareness also has a rich and deep history in the social sciences and psychology especially. Several large-scale reviews have been published that summarize what researchers know about self-awareness at a general level (Carden et al., 2022; Chon & Sitkin, 2021; London et al., 2023). The more specific concern here is that of leader self-awareness in terms of what it means, why is it important to study leader development, and how it is developed (i.e., methods and interventions).

#### *The Trouble With Emotional Intelligence*

Before turning to leader self-awareness, a note on emotional intelligence (EI) is in order. The EI construct has taken the field of leadership and leadership development by storm (or have held it hostage), with more consultancies, certificate providers, and other practitioners working in this space than can be counted. Harkening back to some of the earliest writing on EI, self-awareness was positioned as one of its core components along with self-regulation, motivation, empathy, and social skills (Goleman, 1998). What's not to like? Unfortunately, this is a prime example of over-promising and under-delivering.

Measurement has always been an issue with EI, with many approaches based on self-report measures. Can someone really provide accurate assessments of their respective levels of self-awareness? Can they self-report their level of emotional "intelligence" [sic]? That point aside, claims have been made that EI explains 90% or more of the performance of "star" leaders relative to average leaders (Goleman, 1998, p. 94). No concrete evidence has ever been presented to support this claim. When something seems to be too good to be true it probably is.

It is also the case that most claims for the relationship between EI and leadership effectiveness are conflated by the failure to control for cognitive ability (i.e., intelligence) or Big Five personality factors—both of which have been shown to be robust predictors of leadership (Antonakis, 2003; Joseph et al., 2015). There are many believers in the absolute importance of EI in leadership, but I am not one of them. It is another area where *caveat emptor* is recommended. I think we all need to ask ourselves whether leadership—and leader development—needs EI (Antonakis et al., 2009). My answer is no, but I strongly believe leadership needs to consider leader self-awareness. For that reason, the remainder of this section will focus on the role of leader self-awareness as a proximal indicator of leader development.

*Becoming Self-Aware*

According to Hall (2004), self-awareness along with adaptability are two overarching personal capabilities that help leaders "learn how to learn" new skills and competencies (p. 153). Self-awareness is an important component of effective leadership in that it involves an individual's ability to understand their personal strengths, weaknesses, behavioral tendencies, values, and the impact they have on others in conjunction with participating in leadership roles and processes. Self-awareness arises from the human capacity for self-reflexivity (Wernsing, 2018). Indeed, one of the primary ways of enhancing self-awareness is through self-reflection or introspection and the other is through receiving feedback.

Leader self-awareness is about understanding what you are like as a leader. This can be through formal or informal assessment data that can help guide where to focus learning and development. The notion of leader development being highly individualized is relevant here because the processes that lead to greater leader self-awareness provide one type of assessment data about where to potentially focus development. Formal assessment data can be from personality assessments, value clarification exercises, or other structured mechanisms to help individuals better understand what they are like. Information to enhance self-awareness can also come from feedback, either provided "on the fly" in a more informal manner (e.g., ongoing SBI feedback) or through formal processes such as 360-degree feedback.

Why is leader self-awareness important? Why it is critical to know thyself as a leader? Consider the counterfactual of not knowing yourself as a leader or not having self-awareness. Could you still be an effective leader? The answer is probably yes because there are (unfortunately, too many) notable case studies of arrogant and insensitive leaders who would be considered effective by many standards but appear to have little sense of—or interest in –the impact they have on others. But how much more effective could they be if they had greater levels of self-awareness? That is mainly a rhetorical question because it is impossible to know.

The reasons why self-awareness is important relate to personality, values, and others' impressions. Knowing yourself involves knowing what you tend to do (i.e., behavioral tendencies), which are the overt manifestations of personality and values. What is it that you feel most comfortable doing and how might that limit you as a leader? A tenet of leader development is that no one develops when comfortable (First Principle #2). Understanding where that comfort zone resides is needed if one can avoid or overcome it—if one chooses to do so. Values tell you what is most important to you. It is critical to be aware of your values so you understand when you might not be leading in ways that are consistent with those values. Finally, understanding the effect that you have on others is important to being an effective leader because leadership is an interpersonal process. If a leader has little clue about how others are experiencing their leadership, it is easy to be deluded that you are better than others experience you as a leader.

*Leader Hubris*

Ultimately, self-awareness is the antidote to hubris as a leader. As noted in a review of hubristic leadership (Sadler-Smith et al., 2017):

> Hubristic leaders over-estimate significantly their own abilities and believe their performance to be superior to that of others...they make over-confident and over-ambitious judgements and decisions. The fact that hubristic leaders tend to be resistant to criticism, and invulnerable to and contemptuous of the advice of others further compounds the problem. (p. 525)

A hubristic leader believes that they have nothing to learn from new experiences or other people around them. Such leaders are close-minded and are at risk for derailment (i.e., failing as a leader). Across time and cultures, one of the leading factors for leader derailment is having difficulties with interpersonal relationships (Van Velsor & Leslie, 1995). A lack of self-awareness means (among other things) a lack of understanding of the effect someone has on others. Other leading causes of leader derailment that might be due in part to a lack of self-awareness are the inability to build and lead and team and the inability to develop or change.

*Measurement Concerns*

Given that leader self-awareness is proposed as one of the main self-views serving as a proximal indicator of leadership development (Day & Dragoni, 2015), it might be assumed that it is measured well. That is not the case, but it offers opportunities for future researchers. There are three ways in which self-awareness has been measured. The first is through self-report. The situational self-awareness scale (Govern & Marsch, 2001) is a nine-item self-report measure that leaders can use to report on various aspects of self-awareness including public, private, and surroundings awareness. The three items pertaining to private self-consciousness are those most consistent with how self-awareness is conceptualized in leader development (I am conscious of my inner feelings, I am reflective about my life, and I am aware of my innermost thoughts). Although the internal consistency reliability of the measure is marginally acceptable (Cronbach's alpha of 0.70), the bigger concern is about validity. What evidence exists that respondents can and do accurately report on their private self-consciousness? I am unaware of any such evidence or how it would be gathered.

Another way in which leader self-awareness has been measured is through follower ratings of the leader. In one such study (Wernsing, 2018), followers rated their leaders on four self-awareness items (1) Seeks feedback to improve interactions with others, (2) Accurately describes how others view his/her capabilities, (3) Knows when it is time to reevaluate his/her position on important issues, and (4) Shows he/she understands how specific actions impact others. Acceptable internal consistency reliability was demonstrated for the measure (alphas ranging from 0.80 to 0.88 across country cultures) but the more important issue is interrater reliability (i.e., to what extent do different followers rate the leader's self-awareness similarly). Unfortunately, that information is not available. Again, accuracy and validity of these ratings of leader self-awareness is a concern as with the self-report ratings.

The third approach addresses this issue of accuracy by conceptualizing leader self-awareness in terms of self-other rating agreement. There is a rich literature on self-other rating agreement in the leadership field (Fleenor et al., 2010), with the general finding that those leaders who rate themselves similar to how others rate them tend to be more effective as leaders (Church, 1997); however, the findings are more nuanced across specific performance outcomes. There are reviews of the literature on self-other rating agreement in the leader development literature (e.g., Day et al., 2014). The point to remember is that when it comes to using self-awareness as an indicator of leader development, the issue of change or growth is paramount relative to establishing its relationship with effectiveness outcomes.

When it comes to self-views of leaders, understanding changes in self-awareness are important. One area that cries out for more attention is measurement. We need additional measures of leader self-awareness that provide alternatives to self-report ratings (because of potential social desirability biases), others' ratings (unclear on interrater reliability and agreement across raters), and self-other rating agreement (issues associated with using difference scores in research; Fleenor et al., 2010).

### *Leadership Self-efficacy (LSE)*

The notion of self-efficacy—or often referred to in the academic literature as *perceived* self-efficacy—refers to the belief in one's ability to succeed in specific situations, accomplish a specific task, or achieve a goal in a specific performance domain (Bandura, 1997). Self-efficacy is a cornerstone of Bandura's (1977, 2001) social cognitive theory of performance and behavioral change. Something that has been central to social cognitive theory is that self-efficacy is situational rather than generalized. An individual perceives self-efficacy to successfully perform tasks and achieve goals in a specific domain (e.g., leadership) rather than in general. More recently, some researchers have challenged this notion of situational self-efficacy and have developed a general measure of the construct (Chen et al., 2001). The items developed for the measure are presented in Table 4.1 modified to include the referent of a leader.

For our purposes, self-efficacy is exclusive to the leadership domain. It is a person-in-context construct with leadership roles and processes defining that context. Leadership self-efficacy (LSE) refers to the perceived competence one possesses to be effective as a leader, although it

**Table 4.1** General self-efficacy scale adapted for LSE

| | |
|---|---|
| 1. | I will be able to achieve most of the goals that I have set for myself (as a leader) |
| 2. | When facing difficult tasks, I am certain that I will accomplish them (as a leader) |
| 3. | In general, I think that I can obtain outcomes that are important to me (as a leader) |
| 4. | I believe I can succeed at almost any endeavor to which I set my mind (as a leader) |
| 5. | I will be able to successfully overcome many challenges (as a leader) |
| 6. | I am confident that I can perform effectively on many different tasks (as a leader) |
| 7. | Compared to other people, I can do most tasks very well (as a leader) |
| 8. | Even when things are tough, I can perform quite well (as a leader) |

*Note* Table and scale items adapted from Chen et al. (2001)

is noted that it has been defined in different ways by different researchers over the years (Paglis, 2010). Examining the items in the General Self-efficacy Scale (Table 4.1), the measure can be adapted to pertain only to leadership and performance as a leader by simply adding "as a leader" to the end of each item. The same would apply if the directions stated to respond to each with the preface "As a leader…."

LSE is about having agency as a leader; that is, it refers to acts of self-regulation or self-control. Self-regulating human beings—including leaders—have defining qualities of thinking about the future and not just the present, and as actors with personal agency to act on the world (Cervone et al., 2011). Based on Bandura's (1997) conceptualization, there are four general processes through which LSE can influence behavioral outcomes. First, perceived LSE informs decisions about which leadership activities to pursue. Second, after choosing a leadership activity, perceived LSE influences effort and task/goal persistence. Third, perceived LSE regulates emotions with those leaders perceiving high LSE more likely to experience less anxiety in ambiguous or threatening experiences. Fourth, perceived LSE influences the quality of analytical and cognitive performance leading to superior decision-making as a leader.

A meta-analysis examined the relationship between self-efficacy and measures of work performance across 157 independent samples and over 21,000 participants (Stajkovic & Luthans, 1998). Findings suggested robust sample-weighted average correlations in the 0.4 to 0.5 range, although task complexity was identified as a between-study moderator. The moderating effects were such that the relationship between self-efficacy and work performance was strongest at lower levels of task complexity. In terms of leader development implications, this reinforces the recommendation of choosing relatively easy (i.e., low complexity) challenges to motivate development. Nonetheless, an important issue needing additional research attention is that individuals with low levels of LSE may self-select out of leadership activities rather than merely display inferior performance once an activity has begun. LSE is a worthwhile self-view to consider in leader development as it might be predictive of engagement levels in developmental activities. Specifically, those with low LSE levels may find it difficult to own their development and engage in even minor challenges that take them outside of their respective comfort zones.

It was noted that researchers have hypothesized efficacy-performance spirals in which stronger self-efficacy beliefs are thought to motivate higher levels of performance, which further strengthens self-efficacy (Lindsley et al., 1995). This theorizing about the cyclical effects of self-efficacy on performance was addressed empirically across a two-wave field study and a longitudinal three-wave laboratory study (Salanova et al., 2011). The researchers examined how efficacy beliefs reciprocally influence activity engagement (vigor, dedication, and absorption) indirectly through their impact on positive affect (enthusiasm, satisfaction, and comfort) over time. This provides much-needed evidence that perceived self-efficacy is a potentially important concern in leader development, as the findings from these studies suggest a spiraling relationship with engagement through individual emotions. Building stronger LSE with emerging leaders may be especially important in enhancing the engagement of individuals in leadership challenges that contribute to their development as leaders.

One question to consider is the potential intercorrelations among the various leadership self-views. Unfortunately, there are few studies that have addressed this issue. In one longitudinal study of military cadets, researchers found moderately strong correlations ($r = 0.4$ to $0.6$) between leader identity and LSE action and LSE self-regulatory forms (Kwok et al., 2021). This might have been a good opportunity to further examine the possibility of reciprocal or spiraling effects, but that was not the study focus.

It is likely that leader identity, self-awareness, and leadership self-efficacy (LSE) are positively intercorrelated. That is, they may have overlapping effects but are not completely redundant. This provides an opportunity for future researchers to study how these different leader self-views develop as a set over time. Of particular interest is the possibility of leader identity-self-awareness-LSE spirals in which changes in one self-view can be shown to influence changes in the other self-views.

Just a few years ago it would have been something of a pipedream to estimate such effects empirically; however, with the rapid advancements taking place in longitudinal modeling it is now possible. A good example can be found in estimating bivariate change models, where changes in one variable can be shown to relate to subsequence changes in a different variable (Grimm et al., 2012). This modeling approach has been used in at least one leader development study (Miscenko et al., 2017) but should be adopted more widely in studying change to take advantage of sophisticated methodologies and statistical analyses that are available. There is still much to do and learn about the development of leadership self-views.

## Implications of Incorporating Proximal Outcomes in Research and Practice

An important consideration in advancing the science of leader development is paying closer attention to time, time scales, and time lags in development. Not only does the delivery of training and development interventions take different amounts of time but the expected effects can range from almost immediately to years in the future. There is very little known scientifically about the time lags in leader development. Think about it in terms of everyday experience: If you take a couple of aspirins to relieve a headache you might not expect immediate effects—but you wouldn't expect it to take years, either!

One way that has been proposed to get a better handle on time lags is that there are more proximal indicators of expected developmental effects and more distal indicators (Day & Dragoni, 2015). The present chapter is focused on the former. The two categories of indicators are leadership self-views (e.g., leader identity, self-awareness, and LSE) and leadership KSAs and competencies. Historically, there has been mainly attention focused on training and developing leadership skills. The introduction of leadership self-views is a relatively recent addition to the leader development literature but offers a potentially valuable complement to a skills-based perspective on development.

Leadership self-views are grounded in the social cognition maxim of *thinking is for doing* (Fiske, 1992). More specifically, how one thinks of the self is an important precursor to behavior. The point was made that internalizing a leader identity means that the notion of being a leader is valued and as such will guide decisions about resource allocations of one's time. In this manner, holding a leader identity is likely to result in finding more opportunities to practice leadership and implement small challenges in the name of ongoing leader development (Day et al., 2009; Ibarra, 2015).

Research findings indicate that self-views are relatively dynamic and can change over the course of an intervention lasting a few days or weeks (Day & Sin, 2011; Kragt & Day, 2020; Kwok et al., 2021; Miscenko et al., 2017) or even change during the course of a given day when strong events are experienced (Nieberle et al., 2023). Note that the focus is on changes in the respective self-view and not any relationship between self-views on outcomes such as leadership effectiveness. That is perfectly okay in my book (including this book).

Leader development is inherently about change over time. Focusing on changes in self-views through the application of techniques such as longitudinal growth modeling and personal trajectory analysis are helping illuminate how people change in their development as leaders and the kinds of factors that might help shape those trajectories of development. The point is not how these changes ultimately affect leadership performance. That is because (1) there are myriad factors influencing leadership performance and its effectiveness with many outside the control of individual leaders and (2) performance comes about through the application of development and is not an inevitable result of development.

Those are key points to remember as there are innumerable perspectives on how to estimate the return on investment (ROI) for leader and leadership development investments. Our focus in further building a science of developing leaders and leadership is in understanding the developmental processes of change on various indicators of development and not trying to show directly how development influences performance. In leader development, the focal outcome of interest is development and not performance or effectiveness.

Looking ahead to Chapter 5, the focus will be on distal outcomes of leader development. It is in looking at the more long-term effects of leader development that the role of adult development processes comes to the forefront. Long term or distal indicators of development are based on the deep-seated operating principles of a developing leader. More about how this is thought to occur and why it is of importance in fully understanding leader development processes will be taken up in the next chapter.

## Chapter Summary

- Time matters in the scientific study—and practice—of leader development.
- There has been lots written but comparatively little of substance done about better understanding the role of time in leader development.
- An exception to this current state of affairs is the suggestion that researchers consider proximal and distal outcomes of leadership development (Day & Dragoni, 2015).
- Two categories of proximal indicators of leader development are self-views and leadership KSAs and competencies.
- Proximal indicators are helpful in studying leader development because, by definition, they are thought to change relatively quickly and indicate that longer-term development is occurring.
- The leader self-views that have been studied to date are leader identity, self-awareness, and leadership self-efficacy (LSE).
- Leader identity has been most often studied in terms of identity strength with research suggesting that it serves as a time-varying covariate along with leadership skills and competencies in leader development.
- Leader self-awareness refers to the self-understanding of what someone is like as a leader, including personality, values, and impact on others.
- LSE is the self-perceived competence one possesses to be effective as a leader.
- Researchers have conceptualized leader identity development spirals along with self-efficacy-performance spirals. Another way of thinking about spirals is as mutually reinforcing factors of identity and leader development and between LSE and engagement in leadership activities.
- Additional research is needed to better understand the interplay between the various leadership self-views and how they might be mutually reinforcing (i.e., spiraling) in leader development processes.

## References

Antonakis, J. (2003). Why "emotional intelligence" does not predict leadership effectiveness: A comment on Prati, Douglas, Ferris, Ammeter, and Buckley (2003). *The International Journal of Organizational Analysis, 11*(4), 355–361. https://doi.org/10.1108/eb028980

Antonakis, J., Ashkanasy, N. M., & Dasborough, M. T. (2009). Does leadership need emotional intelligence? *The Leadership Quarterly, 20*(2), 247–261. https://doi.org/10.1016/j.leaqua.2009.01.006

Antonakis, J., Fenley, M., & Liechti, S. (2011). Can charisma be taught? Tests of two interventions. *Academy of Management Learning & Education, 10*(3), 374–396. https://doi.org/10.5465/amle.2010.0012

Bandura, A. (1977). Self-efficacy: Toward a unifying thoery of behavioral change. *Psychological Review, 84*(2), 191–215. https://doi.org/10.1037/0033-295X.84.2.191

Bandura, A. (1997). *Self-efficacy: The exercise of control*. Freeman.

Bandura, A. (2001). Social cognitive theory: An agentic perspective. *Annual Review of Psychology, 52*(1), 1–26.

Barling, J., Weber, T., & Kelloway, E. K. (1996). Effects of transformational leadership training on attitudinal and financial outcomes: A field experiment. *Journal of Applied Psychology, 81*(6), 827–832. https://doi.org/10.1037//0021-9010.81.6.827

Bass, B. M. (1985). *Leadership and performance beyond expectations*. The Free Press.

Bass, B. M., & Riggio, R. E. (2006). *Transformational leadership* (2nd ed.). Erlbaum.

Campbell, J. D., Trapnell, P. D., Heine, S. J., Katz, I. M., Lavallee, L. F., & Lehman, D. R. (1996). Self-concept clarity: Measurement, personality correlates, and cultural boundaries. *Journal of Personality and Social Psychology, 70*(1), 141–156. https://doi.org/10.1037/0022-3514.70.1.141

Carden, J., Jones, R. J., & Passmore, J. (2022). Defining self-awareness in the context of adult development: A systematic literature review. *Journal of Management Education, 46*(1), 140–177. https://doi.org/10.1177/1052562921990065

Cervone, D., Mor, N., Orom, H., Shadel, W. G., & Scott, W. D. (2011). Self-efficacy beliefs and the architecture of personality. In K. D. Vohs & R. F. Baumeister (Eds.), *Handbook of self-regulation: Research, theory, and applications* (2nd ed., pp. 461–484). Guilford Press.

Chen, G., Gully, S. M., & Eden, D. (2001). Validation of a new general self-efficacy scale. *Organizational Research Methods, 4*(1), 62–83. https://doi.org/10.1177/109442810141004

Chon, D., & Sitkin, S. B. (2021). Disentangling the process and content of self-awareness: A review, critical assessment, and synthesis. *Academy of Management Annals, 15*(2), 607–651. https://doi.org/10.5465/annals.2018.0079

Church, A. H. (1997). Managerial self-awareness in high-performing individuals in organizations. *Journal of Applied Psychology, 82*(2), 281–292. https://doi.org/10.1037/0021-9010.82.2.281

Clear, J. (2018). *Atomic habits: An easy and proven way to build good habits and break bad ones*. Avery.

Collins, L. M. (2006). Analysis of longitudinal data: The integration of theoretical model, temporal design, and statistical model. *Annual Review of Psychology, 57*, 505–528. https://doi.org/10.1146/annurev.psych.57.102904.190146

Cross, S., & Markus, H. (1991). Possible selves across the life span. *Human Development, 34*(4), 230–255. https://doi.org/10.1159/000277058

Day, D. V. (2014). Time and leadership. In A. J. Shipp & Y. Fried (Eds.), *Time and work: How time impacts groups, organizations and methodological choices* (Vol. 2, pp. 30–52). Psychology Press.

Day, D. V., & Dragoni, L. (2015). Leadership development: An outcome-oriented review based on time and levels of analyses. *Annual Review of Organizational Psychology and Organizational Behavior, 2*, 133–156. https://doi.org/10.1146/annurev-orgpsych-032414-111328

Day, D. V., Fleenor, J. W., Atwater, L. E., Sturm, R. E., & McKee, R. A. (2014). Advances in leader and leadership development: A review of 25 years of research and theory. *The Leadership Quarterly, 25*(1), 63–82. https://doi.org/10.1016/j.leaqua.2013.11.004

Day, D. V., Harrison, M. M., & Halpin, S. M. (2009). *An integrative approach to leader development: Connecting adult development, identity, and expertise*. Psychology Press.

Day, D. V., & Sin, H. P. (2011). Longitudinal tests of an integrative model of leader development: Charting and understanding developmental trajectories. *The Leadership Quarterly, 22*(3), 545–560. https://doi.org/10.1016/j.leaqua.2011.04.011

DeRue, D. S., & Ashford, S. J. (2010). Who will lead and who will follow? A social process of leadership identity construction in organizations. *Academy of Management Review, 35*(4), 627–647. https://doi.org/10.5465/amr.35.4.zok627

Dormann, C., & Griffin, M. A. (2015). Optimal time lags in panel studies. *Psychological Methods, 20*(4), 489. https://doi.org/10.1037/met0000041

Dvir, T., Eden, D., Avolio, B. J., & Shamir, B. (2002). Impact of transformational leadership on follower development and performance: A field experiment. *Academy of Management Journal, 45*(4), 735–744. https://doi.org/10.2307/3069307

Festinger, L. (1962). Cognitive dissonance. *Scientific American, 207*(4), 93–106. https://www.jstor.org/stable/24936719

Fisher, C. D., & To, M. L. (2012). Using experience sampling methodology in organizational behavior. *Journal of Organizational Behavior, 33*(7), 865–877. https://doi.org/10.1002/job.1803

Fiske, S. T. (1992). Thinking is for doing: Portraits of social cognition from daguerreotype to laserphoto. *Journal of Personality and Social Psychology, 63*(6), 877–899. https://doi.org/10.1037/0022-3514.63.6.877

Fleenor, J. W., Smither, J. W., Atwater, L. E., Braddy, P. W., & Sturm, R. E. (2010). Self–other rating agreement in leadership: A review. *The Leadership Quarterly, 21*(6), 1005–1034. https://doi.org/10.1016/j.leaqua.2010.10.006

Goleman, D. (1998, November–December). What makes a leader? *Harvard Business Review*, 93–102.

Gollob, H. F., & Reichardt, C. S. (1987). Taking account of time lags in causal models. *Child Development, 80–92*,. https://doi.org/10.2307/1130293

Govern, J. M., & Marsch, L. A. (2001). Development and validation of the situational self-awareness scale. *Consciousness and Cognition, 10*(3), 366–378. https://doi.org/10.1006/ccog.2001.0506

Grimm, K. J., An, Y., McArdle, J. J., Zonderman, A. B., & Resnick, S. M. (2012). Recent changes leading to subsequent changes: Extensions of multivariate latent difference score models. *Structural Equation Modeling: A Multidisciplinary Journal, 19*(2), 268–292. https://doi.org/10.1080/10705511.2012.659627

Hall, D. T. (2004). Self-awareness, identity, and leader development. In D. V. Day, S. J. Zaccaro, & S. M. Halpin (Eds.), *Leader development for transforming organizations: Growing leaders for tomorrow* (pp. 153–176). Lawrence Erlbaum Associates.

Hamaker, E. L., & Wichers, M. (2017). No time like the present: Discovering the hidden dynamics in intensive longitudinal data. *Current Directions in Psychological Science, 26*(1), 10–15. https://doi.org/10.1177/0963721416666518

Hammond, M. M., Clapp-Smith, R., & Palanski, M. (2017). Beyond (just) the workplace: A theory of leader development across multiple domains. *Academy of Management Review, 42*(3), 481–498. https://doi.org/10.5465/amr.2014.0431

Ibarra, H. (1999). Provisional selves: Experimenting with image and identity in professional adaptation. *Administrative Science Quarterly, 44*(4), 764–791. https://doi.org/10.2307/2667055

Ibarra, H. (2015). *Act like a leader, think like a leader*. Harvard Business Review Press.

Jacobsen, C. B., Andersen, L. B., Bøllingtoft, A., & Eriksen, T. L. M. (2022). Can leadership training improve organizational effectiveness? Evidence from a randomized field experiment on transformational and transactional leadership. *Public Administration Review, 82*(1), 117–131. https://doi.org/10.1111/puar.13356

Joseph, D. L., Jin, J., Newman, D. A., & O'Boyle, E. H. (2015). Why does self-reported emotional intelligence predict job performance? A meta-analytic investigation of mixed EI. *Journal of Applied Psychology, 100*(2), 298–342. https://doi.org/10.1037/a0037681

Kolditz, T., Gill, L., & Brown, R. P. (2021). *Leadership reckoning: Can higher education develop the leaders we need?* Monocle Press.

Komives, S. R., Longerbeam, S. D., Owen, J. E., Mainella, F. C., & Osteen, L. (2006). A leadership identity development model: Applications from a grounded theory. *Journal of College Student Development, 47*(4), 401–418. https://doi.org/10.1353/csd.2006.0048

Komives, S. R., Owen, J. E., Longerbeam, S. D., Mainella, F. C., & Osteen, L. (2005). Developing a leadership identity: A grounded theory. *Journal of College Student Development, 46*(6), 593–611. https://doi.org/10.1353/csd.2005.0061

Kragt, D., & Day, D. V. (2020). Predicting leadership competency development and promotion among high-potential executives: The role of leader identity. *Frontiers in Psychology, 11*, 1816. https://doi.org/10.3389/fpsyg.2020.01816

Kwok, N., Shen, W., & Brown, D. J. (2021). I can, I am: Differential predictors of leader efficacy and identity trajectories in leader development. *The Leadership Quarterly, 32*(5), 101422. https://doi.org/10.1016/j.leaqua.2020.101422

Leary, M. R., & Tangney, J. P. (2011). The self as an organizing construct in the behavioral and social sciences. In M. R. Leary & J. P. Tangney (Eds.), *Handbook of self and identity* (2nd ed., pp. 1–68). Guilford Press.

Lindsley, D. H., Brass, D. J., & Thomas, J. B. (1995). Efficacy-performance spirals: A multilevel perspective. *Academy of Management Review, 20*(3), 645–678. https://doi.org/10.2307/258790

Locke, E. A., Shaw, K. N., Saari, L. M., & Latham, G. P. (1981). Goal setting and task performance: 1969–1980. *Psychological Bulletin, 90*(1), 125–152. https://doi.org/10.1037/0033-2909.90.1.125

London, M., Sessa, V. I., & Shelley, L. A. (2023). Developing self-awareness: Learning processes for self- and interpersonal growth. *Annual Review of Organizational Psychology and Organizational Behavior, 10*, 261–288. https://doi.org/10.1146/annurev-orgpsych-120920-044531

Maclean, N. (1992). *Young men and fire*. University of Chicago Press.

Markus, H., & Nurius, P. (1986). Possible selves. *American Psychologist, 41*(9), 954–969. https://doi.org/10.1037/0003-066X.41.9.954

Masten, A. S., Cutuli, J. J., Herbers, J. E., & Reed, M.-G. J. (2009). Resilience in development. In S. J. Lopez & C. R. Snyder (Eds.), *The Oxford handbook of positive psychology* (2nd ed., pp. 117–131). Oxford University Press.

McCall, M. W. (2010). Recasting leadership development. *Industrial and Organizational Psychology-Perspectives on Science and Practice, 3*, 3–19. https://doi.org/10.1111/j.1754-9434.2009.01189.x

McCauley, C. D., Van Velsor, E., & Ruderman, M. N. (2010). Introduction: Our view of leadership development. In E. Van Velsor, C. D. McCauley, & M. N. Ruderman (Eds.), *The Center for Creative Leadership handbook of leadership development* (3rd ed., pp. 1–26). John Wiley & Sons.

Miscenko, D., Guenter, H., & Day, D. V. (2017). Am I a leader? Examining leader identity development over time. *The Leadership Quarterly, 28*, 605–620. https://doi.org/10.1016/j.leaqua.2017.01.004

Mitchell, T. R., & James, L. R. (2001). Building better theory: Time and the specification of when things happen. *Academy of Management Review, 26*(4), 530–547. https://doi.org/10.2307/3560240

Molenaar, P. C. M. (2004). A manifesto on psychology as idiographic science: Bringing the person back into scientific psychology, this time forever. *Measurement, 2*(4), 201–218. https://doi.org/10.1207/s15366359mea0204_1

Morf, C. C., & Mischel, W. (2011). The self as a psycho-social dynamic processing system: Toward a converging science of selfhood. In M. R. Leary & J. P. Tangney (Eds.), *Handbook of self and identity* (2nd ed., pp. 21–49). The Guilford Press.

Murphy, S. E., & Johnson, S. K. (2016). Leadership and leader developmental self-efficacy: Their role in enhancing leader development efforts. *New Directions for Student Leadership, 2016*(149), 73–84. https://doi.org/10.1002/yd.20163

Nieberle, K. W., Acton, B. P., Braun, S., Lord, R. G., & Fu, Y. (2023). Leader identity on the fly: Intra-personal leader identity dynamics in response to strong events. *Journal of Business and Psychology*. https://doi.org/10.1007/s10869-023-09906-7

Paglis, L. L. (2010). Leadership self-efficacy: Research findings and practical applications. *Journal of Management Development, 29*(9), 771–782. https://doi.org/10.1108/02621711011072487

Pentland, A. S. (2012). The new science of building great teams. *Harvard Business Review, 90*(4), 60–69.

Ployhart, R. E., & Vandenberg, R. J. (2010). Longitudinal research: The theory, design, and analysis of change. *Journal of Management, 36*(1), 94–120. https://doi.org/10.1177/0149206309352110

Sadler-Smith, E., Akstinaite, V., Robinson, G., & Wray, T. (2017). Hubristic leadership: A review. *Leadership, 13*(5), 525–548. https://doi.org/10.1177/1742715016680666

Salanova, M., Llorens, S., & Schaufeli, W. B. (2011). "Yes, I can, I feel good, and I just do it!" On gain cycles and spirals of efficacy beliefs, affect, and engagement. *Applied Psychology, 60*(2), 255–285. https://doi.org/10.1111/j.1464-0597.2010.00435.x

Schaie, K. W. (1983). What can we learn from longitudinal studies of adult development? In K. W. Schaie (Ed.), *Longitudinal studies of adult psychological development* (pp. 1–19). Guilford Press.

Stajkovic, A. D., & Luthans, F. (1998). Self-efficacy and work-related performance: A meta-analysis. *Psychological Bulletin, 124*(2), 240–261. https://doi.org/10.1037/0033-2909.124.2.240

Tesluk, P. E., & Jacobs, R. R. (1998). Toward an integrated model of work experience. *Personnel Psychology, 51*(2), 321–355. https://doi.org/10.1111/j.1744-6570.1998.tb00728.x

Van Velsor, E., & Leslie, J. B. (1995). Why executives derail: Perspectives across time and cultures. *Academy of Management Perspectives, 9*(4), 62–72. https://doi.org/10.5465/ame.1995.9512032194

Weick, K. E. (1993). The collapse of sense making in organizations: The Mann Gulch disaster. *Administrative Science Quarterly, 38*(4), 628–652. https://doi.org/10.2307/2393339

Wernsing, T. (2018). Leader self-awareness and follower psychological empowerment across cultures. In D. Cotter-Lockard (Ed.), *Authentic leadership and followership: International perspectives* (pp. 3–32). Springer International Publishing. https://doi.org/10.1007/978-3-319-65307-5_1

CHAPTER 5

# Considering Adult Development in Leadership Development

## Lifelong Learning and Leader Development

Previous chapters in this volume adopted relatively short-term perspectives on time, focusing on what has been called proximal indicators of leader development. These leading indicators of leader development were proposed in two forms: (1) self-views and (2) leadership knowledge, skills, and abilities (KSAs) and competencies. This implies that a relatively focused investment in developing oneself as a leader through enhancing self-views and leadership KSAs might be sufficient to do the job. That would be very misleading.

Individuals can boost how they perceive and construe the self in relatively short order. Internalizing a leader identity translates practically into making that identity salient—thinking about oneself as a leader chronically in the so-called life gym, which primes someone to act in leader-like ways. Similarly, changes in self-awareness and leadership self-efficacy (LSE) can occur relatively quickly through experience or structured intervention. Someone can learn and apply a particular leadership skill in a matter of hours or days. So why do some researchers claim that developing as a leader is potentially a lifelong endeavor (Day et al., 2009)?

The answer can be partly found in how learning is changing. It has become commonplace to hear discussions of lifelong learning that claim



D. V. Day, *Developing Leaders and Leadership*,
https://doi.org/10.1007/978-3-031-59068-9_5

it is necessary due to the increasing complexity of the world, rapid technological advances, and other related challenges that perhaps have never been experienced before. This is especially the case for leader development. Just as leader development has evolved from a unique event to an ongoing process (Fulmer, 1997), learning is what differentiates those who stop developing as adults as well as leaders as they age. John F. Kennedy once said that leadership and learning are indispensable to each other. This quote was part of remarks he planned for an event in Dallas, Texas on November 22, 1963. He never got the chance to deliver that message.

The relevant point to consider is learning and development are lifelong endeavors without an end state (except when life ends). It is not inevitable that it happens, but development—including leader development—can continue across the lifespan. Learning and development are not interchangeable concepts, nor are they completely independent; however, they come from different theoretical and research-based perspectives. There is learning theory and there is developmental theory, and they are different. One difference between them is that learning occurs over a shorter time scale (i.e., more quickly) than development (Hoyer & Touron, 2002). It has also been proposed that learning is any enduring change in behavior, adaptive or nonadaptive, whereas development is always adaptive (Feldman, 1995). For our purposes learning and development are conceptualized as somewhat different but mutually reinforcing processes. Learning influences the nature and course of adult development, and development influences the processes and products of learning.

So how do people stop learning and developing as adults? That is probably easier to answer than the question of *why* they stop learning and developing. Development is a function of both nature and nurture—shaped by biological and environmental forces. In child and adolescent development there is a relatively equal focus on both sets of causes, with perhaps a bit more emphasis on the biological or maturational forces behind development (Belsky & Pluess, 2009). Once an individual enters young adulthood and beyond, that equation shifts more to nurture and environment than nature and biologically driven development. If anything, development needs to overcome inherent cognitive declines that come with aging. Nonetheless, longitudinal research suggests that having an intellectually engaging lifestyle might buffer against cognitive declines associated with aging (Hultsch et al., 1999). That might be the ticket right there—lifelong learning through ongoing intellectual engagement.

To be clear, lifelong learning is not a process of only gains. It is not just about adding more knowledge or a greater number of skills over time through ongoing learning processes throughout the lifespan. Lifespan development consists of managing the dynamic between gains and losses over time (Baltes, 1987). If development continues into adulthood, and especially into late adulthood, then the gains in the forms of resources and functioning outweigh the losses that are an inevitable part of aging. When those losses begin to outweigh developmental gains, then not only does development cease but it begins a negative spiral. It is important to remember that minimizing losses over the lifespan is as important as maximizing gains. When it comes to managing both developmental gains and losses, personal agency is critical.

### *Personal Agency and Development*

Henry David Thoreau wrote in *Walden* (Thoreau, 1854/2006), "The mass of men [sic] lead lives of quiet desperation. What is called resignation is confirmed desperation." Substitute humankind for men and it applies today as much as it did in the 1800s. Alienation appears to be at record levels. More recently, the late author David Foster Wallace commented on this notion of quiet desperation in somewhat different terms. In a commencement address at Kenyon College (Wallace, 2009), he opined that the value of a liberal arts education was not to teach students to learn how to learn, which he found patronizing. Rather the value of that education is learning what to focus on in your life and choosing to focus on something of value. In his words:

> ...the real, no bullshit value of your liberal arts education is supposed to be about: how to keep from going through your comfortable, prosperous, respectable adult life dead, unconscious, a slave to your head and to your natural default setting of being uniquely, completely, imperially alone day in and day out. (https://fs.blog/david-foster-wallace-this-is-water/, paragraph 12)

The gist of this wonderful essay—and I encourage you to read or listen to it using the URL above—is that we all have a choice and personal agency (some more than others) but often default to the more automatic, unconsidered life. Do you want to be someone going through life on automatic pilot (i.e., leading a life of quiet desperation) or do you want to be someone who elects to see things in a more compassionate way and choosing to invest in their lifelong learning? Foster Wallace called the latter being well-adjusted.

If it is numbers that you want, a more evidence-based perspective suggests that the level of work engagement these days is shockingly low. According to researchers at Gallup Corporation, just 32 percent of US employees are engaged at work; worldwide, 13 percent of employees are engaged (Mann & Harter, 2016). From the perspective of Gallup, being engaged means that employees are involved in, enthusiastic about, and committed to their work and workplace. It is difficult to learn and develop on one's job if disengaged from the work and the organization that provides it. Owning one's development (First Principle #1) is especially critical as an adult and becomes increasingly more important over the lifespan.

A big reason people stop developing as adults is that they are not engaged learners, or stop being so. They stop making choices about what to focus on and therefore what to do and how to be, whether you call that being engaged, well-adjusted, or something else. If one stops challenging oneself and stops trying new behaviors or learning new things, then the kind of developmental death Norman MacLean wrote about is one likely result. Ray Dalio offers a similar life principle and that is *evolve or die* (Dalio, 2017). People can and do develop (i.e., evolve) as leaders in contexts outside of work (Hammond et al., 2017), but most of us spend at least half of our waking hours in some sort of organized work context. That is an important context where we can choose to focus on developing as a leader, or not.

## Leader Development and Expert Performance

This part of the chapter may seem to be getting a bit far afield from time and development; however, it is highly relevant. If we are lucky, we will spend a lot of time as adults. Think about that, because if you are reading this book, you are likely an adult. We will be adults longer than the time we spend as children and more time than we spend as teenagers. For this reason, we need to think more deeply about the how and why (and maybe the what) of leader development in the context of ongoing adult development. Just as the time scale for adult development can be in decades, the same might be said about leader development. What happens to motivate development over such a long period of time, potentially?

The short answer to the preceding question is practice and not just any type of practice, but deliberate practice. You might have come across the adage that it takes 10 years or 10,000 hours of dedicated practice to become an expert in most if not all domains. There is research evidence to support this claim, but it was not done by Malcom Gladwell, he just made it famous through his book *Outliers* (Gladwell, 2008). There is a long-standing science of expertise and expert performance, which is where Gladwell gleaned this deliberate practice finding. The relevance to adult development is that developing expertise takes considerable time and, importantly, a certain kind of *deliberate* practice.

There is a very robust and evidence-based literature on expert performance. There are not just one but two prestigious scholarly handbooks on the topic (Ericsson et al., 2018; Ward et al., 2019). The researcher who is probably best known for developing an evidence-based science of expertise and expert performance is the late Eric Ericsson (e.g., Ericsson et al., 1993). More accessible summaries of his perspective on the role of deliberate practice in the making of an expert are available for interested readers (Ericsson, 2008; Ericsson & Pool, 2016; Ericsson et al., 2007; Parrish, 2023).

### *Understanding Deliberate Practice in Leader Development*

Deliberate practice is just that—deliberate. It is a mindful and structured approach to performance improvement with a very conscious and effortful orientation to skill development. Despite the so-called 10,000-hour rule, it does not mean that anyone can become an expert just with the time investment in deliberate practice. Talent matters, as well. There have been evidence-based criticisms of the notion of developing expertise through deliberate practice (Macnamara et al., 2016); however, it should be no surprise that there are individual differences to consider. Some individuals with greater amounts of raw talent in a specific domain may not need 10 years of deliberate practice to reach expert levels of performance whereas others might need considerably more deliberate practice to reach that same level of expertise. There are individuals with loads of raw talent who do not invest in deliberate practice and thus plateau very early on in terms of skill development.

This perspective on practice does not mean that anyone can become a basketball star and play professionally just through deliberate practice, especially if "vertically challenged." But it does mean that they can acquire very high skill levels in certain domains such as foul shooting or dribbling a basketball developed through an extensive investment of time devoted to deliberate practice. Being an expert basketball player involves developing a wide array of different and interrelated skills. The same might be said of leadership. Looking ahead in the chapter, this is why dynamic skill theory (Fischer, 1980; Fischer & Bidell, 2006) can be useful in understanding leader development through the lens of adult development.

In an extensive review of the expert performance literature, Ericsson et al. (1993) concluded that significant improvements in performance were realized when (1) there was a specific task with a well-defined goal, (2) an individual was motivated to improve, (3) feedback was provided, and (4) there were opportunities for repetition and gradual refinements of performance. But it is also the case that deliberate efforts to improve one's performance beyond the current level require intense concentration and often benefit from problem-solving to find better methods of performing the task.

This brings us to the domain of leadership. Can someone develop to become an expert leader through 10 years or 10,000 hours of deliberate practice? Some have argued that leadership skills are just as amenable to practice as are skills in any other domain (e.g., Lord & Hall, 2005). The development of leadership expertise is indeed very relevant, along with the domains of identity and adult development in the study of leader development (Day et al., 2009). Nonetheless, there still is much to learn about how to practice leadership.

In a review article examining leadership development through the lens of time and levels of analysis, it was proposed that proximal outcomes of leader development would be transformed into more distal outcomes through intensive deliberate practice and support (Day & Dragoni, 2015; see Fig. 5.1 in this volume). It is worth restating that practice without feedback and support is unlikely to result in significant development or changes in expertise levels. The relevant point is that intensive deliberate practice over extended periods of time would likely develop expertise and enhance outcomes associated with adult development.

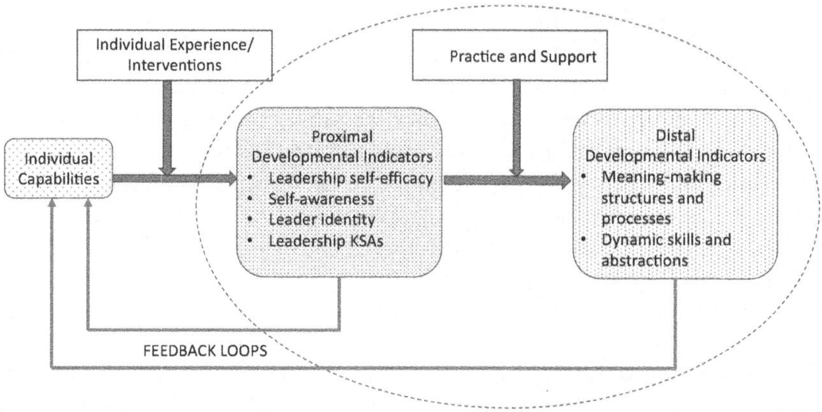


Note: Adapted from Day & Dragoni (2015)

**Fig. 5.1** Individual leader development with proximal to distal outcomes indicated

## Establishing Criteria for Adult Development

Researchers have noted that development in adulthood is different from development in earlier years. In childhood and adolescence, development has been defined as a universal process involving structural transformation progressing toward maturity (Moshman, 2003). This is an inadequate definition of adult development as changes in adulthood are largely attributable to experiences and lack the kind of structural transformation and progression to maturity that define development in earlier years. Rather than concluding that what occurs in adulthood is not development, Moshman proposed that adult development is a different kind of development that requires conceptualization "strict enough to meaningfully distinguish some types of change from others but broad enough to encompass what can be reasonably construed as developmental aspects of change in adulthood" (p. 46).

By relaxing the definitional constraints of structural transformation that are associated with stage models of development in childhood and adolescence, there is a stronger case for development across the lifespan. Three criteria were offered by Moshman (2003) to distinguish adult development from non-developmental change. In his view, adult development involves changes that are (1) qualitative, (2) progressive, and (3) internally directed. On that last point, what he means by internally directed is that it refers to changes that are constructed by an individual rather than caused by the environment in an objective sense. This point is an essential one as we discuss the theoretical perspectives related to constructive-developmental theory as they pertain to leadership (McCauley et al., 2006). In essence, people need to make sense of their experiences, which has been loosely defined as interpreting experience meaningfully (Perry, 1970). This sensemaking process is something that can develop across the lifespan such that experiences are made sense of in deeper and more meaningful ways.

If adults can develop then what is it that develops potentially over the entire lifespan? Here again, Moshman (2003) offers some valuable insights, proposing that what can develop in adulthood are three overarching constructs: (1) identity, (2) morality, and (3) epistemic cognition. These are relatively broad categories and at least one (identity) has been covered in detail in this volume already. But you might be asking: Where is leadership? Researchers in the fields of developmental psychology and lifespan development might be forgiven for overlooking leadership as something that can develop in adulthood given the ever-present disciplinary silos. So how do outcomes related to adult development pertain to leadership?

The point is that these and other outcomes are not leadership skills per se; however, they inform the performance of leadership behaviors and mindsets in myriad ways. Becoming a more highly evolved adult has implications for how that individual engages with others as a leader. This notion of being highly evolved or demonstrating greater development enhances the likelihood—but does not guarantee—that an individual will be a better leader simply by virtue of having higher levels of mental complexity and more sophisticated sensemaking filters. These and other features of adult development will be discussed next as the more distal outcomes of leader development.

## Distal Outcomes in Leader Development

Distal outcomes of leader development are those qualities that are thought to require investment in time and effort (e.g., deliberate practice) to change in substantial and long-lasting ways. The criteria for adult development proposed by Moshman (2003) apply to these distal outcomes. Development should involve qualitative, progressive, and internally directed changes. The focus of this section is on applying these criteria to leadership-related developmental changes. Although Moshman identified identity formation, moral development, and the development of epistemic cognition as three general domains in which development continues through adulthood, at least for some individuals, these domains also are relevant for leader development. Those points of relevance will be highlighted. Following this review, there will be a deeper examination of two categories of human development theory with implications for leader development. Those are constructive-developmental approaches to adult development and dynamic skill theory.

### *Leadership Meaning(s)*

Chapter 4 provided a detailed review of the theory and research on leader identity, why it is important as an indicator of proximal leader development, as well as how it supports the development of leadership KSAs and competencies. Much of the attention on leader identity has focused on *identity strength*. That is, to what extent or degree does someone identify as a leader? Although this focus might tick the box for the criteria of being progressive and internally directed, questions might be raised about whether changes in identity strength represent qualitative changes. Probably not. It is certainly representative of quantitative change, but it is less clear how it would constitute qualitative change.

Much of what developmental psychologists consider to be qualitative changes in development are traceable to progression across identified stages. The kinds of stage-like transformations are more difficult to document in adulthood, although there are some notable exceptions (e.g., Kegan, 1994; Loevinger, 2014). There is no stage model of leader identity strength; however, there may be more to consider in terms of how the *meaning* of leadership changes in adulthood, which has been proposed as another facet of leader identity (Hammond et al., 2017).

As individuals develop as leaders, they find themselves in novel and challenging situations. This is especially the case if an individual is in an organizational position and moving into higher levels of responsibility. It almost goes without saying that more responsibility means more leadership role complexity. This is not what Heifetz would call technical challenges, which are like close-ended problems with an identified correct solution (Heifetz, 1994). Rather, leadership challenges are what he calls adaptive challenges, which are those without an expert or otherwise agreed-upon correct solution. These are the kinds of challenges where the answers are not provided in the proverbial back of the book. Adaptive challenges usually involve people's problems. This focus on people and their problems is surprising to many emerging leaders as they move up the organizational ranks, especially in going from being a single contributor to supervisor and then general manager (Day & Harrison, 2007). Kurt Vonnegut summed things up this way in his book *Piano Player*: "If it weren't for the people… always getting tangled up in the machinery. If it weren't for them, the world would be an engineer's paradise" (Vonnegut, 1952). Indeed!

The focal point is that with complex leadership challenges comes additional pressure to think about these challenges in more complex ways. Remember the social cognition maxim that thinking is for doing. If one thinks about adaptive challenges only in relatively simple terms, then only relatively simple leadership behavior will likely follow. Sometimes this will work, but a leader who thinks in simple terms about the challenges faced, even as those challenges become more complex and ambiguous, will quickly reach their limits of effectiveness.

*Three Leadership Principles as Different Ways of Leading*

An example might be helpful. In his book on rethinking the source of leadership, Drath (2001) argued that there are three general ways to conceptualize and enact leadership: (1) personal ***dominance***, (2) interpersonal ***influence***, and (3) relational ***dialogue***. These match with the criteria for adult development in that these leadership principles involve qualitative, progressive, and internally directed change (Moshman, 2003).

The notion of personal dominance is the first principle we tend to learn about leadership—a kind of might makes the right approach. In adulthood, this could be considered one's force of personality that creates leadership, but one thing is certain that it is unidirectional in flowing from the leader to followers.

The second principle of interpersonal influence transcends but does not replace dominance and takes more of a reciprocal perspective. It is about negotiation and coming to some consensus with at least one other individual. There is a reason why most MBA programs include a course on negotiation. A lot of organizational leadership comes down to the use of effective influence processes.

The third principle, which transcends but does not replace influence, is relational dialogue. This is when a solution is co-created by two or more individuals where the goal is not to influence one another but to use filters such as active listening and perspective taking to better understand where others are coming from. This is a very advanced way of thinking about leadership, but it is especially needed when the application of influence reaches its limits. Instead of regressing to dominance to unstick things—which is the typical result—what is needed is to progress to a more sophisticated leadership approach that better matches with the complexity of the situation.

An important feature of these three leadership principles is if one can think and act using relational dialogue, then it is likely that a leader can also think and act in ways reflecting interpersonal influence and personal dominance when appropriate. After all, if the situation is considered a crisis and the leader has a workable solution, then using personal dominance to implement that solution could be exactly what is needed. But it does not work the other way because there is a type of intransitivity. If all the leader knows is personal dominance, then that leader cannot—presto!—progress to think and act using the more complex leadership principles of influence or dialogue even when needed. This notion of intransitivity in development is a core principle of many developmental theories (Kegan, 1982).

*Development of Leadership Meanings*

The meaning of leadership develops even among young adults across their college years (Komives et al., 2005). Extending this time scale across the entire adult lifespan could mean that profound changes occur in how people "make sense" of leadership. One perspective on this possibility was offered in the proposition of leadership as meaning-making in a community of practice (Drath & Palus, 1994). A summary of the five concepts that represent the core of how this thinking differs from traditional leadership thinking is presented in Table 5.1.

In summary, changes in leadership meaning are conceptualized from a very leader-centric perspective in which a dominant leader acts on followers in a completely unidirectional way (leader to followers) to a process that is more collective and multidirectional with a foundation built on shared meaning-making (or sensemaking). This perspective pre-dates much of the more recent work on shared leadership and offers deeper potential insights about developmental processes involved

**Table 5.1** Changes in leadership meaning

| *From (traditional):* | *To (nontraditional):* |
|---|---|
| Dominant Individual | Participation in a Shared Process |
| (Leader Acting **on** Followers) | (Leader Acting **with** Followers |
| Social Influence | Social Meaning-making |
| Motivation to Act | Frameworks Within Which to Act |
| Authority Figure as Leader | Authority Figure as a Participant in a Leadership Process |
| "How Do I Take Change and Make Things Happen?" | "How Do I Participate in an Effective Leadership Process?" |

*Note* Adapted from Drath and Palus (1994)

in moving from relatively simple and traditional approaches to leadership to thinking about leadership as a resource that is created by and drawn from people engaged in shared work that connects them as a community.

The last concept in the table is perhaps the most powerful in illustrating how the meaning of leadership can be radically different and how it might change over time. My experience working with many emerging leaders (i.e., students or those in early career roles) is that they tend to equate leadership with "taking charge." Think about how that can be construed as personal dominance. Developing a different mindset about leadership as a dynamic process in which multiple people can and do participate. The question leaders ask themselves changes from "how do I exercise my leadership in this situation" to "how can I best participate in leadership in this situation?" As noted, sometimes the best course of action is not to dominate but to listen and reflect. It is also a move from conceptualizing leadership in relatively exclusive terms (how to take change) to more inclusive terms (how can I best participate).

This proposed change or development in perspective regarding the meaning of leadership harkens back to a point made earlier in this volume: Leadership development—as compared with leader development—must involve more than an individual leader. By acknowledging and even embracing nontraditional ways of seeing leadership that are grounded in social sensemaking processes, it is apparent how developing leaders and leadership is informed by adult development. In terms of leader identity formation, what is key to understanding this as adult development is the change in what leadership means as leaders develop.

### *Moral Development*

If morals and morality develop over the lifespan, how do they develop? The study of moral development has a long and rich history, especially when the focus is on children and adolescents. Everyone with children has seen how the framing of right and wrong changes dramatically through the first couple of decades of life. There is even a journal devoted to the topic of moral education (*Journal of Moral Education*) that is billed as an "interdisciplinary forum for the discussion and analysis of moral education and development throughout the lifespan." The concepts of individual morals and morality can sometimes have unintended meanings to those outside of developmental psychology. Specifically, it can be misconstrued as having religious overtones or considered to be grounded in a particular faith-based perspective. It is probably better described as the development of personal ethical philosophies, or as some have called it, character (Cohen & Morse, 2014; Grant, 2023).

Whereas the term ethics has a long history in philosophy it is also termed moral philosophy. I guess there is no getting away from this issue of morality (note that ethics and morals are used interchangeably in this section). It is nonetheless something that has been the focus of philosophers, historically, and later studied by social scientists. In essence, it is the study of right and wrong. Philosophers have debated and, well, philosophized, and what makes something right and good versus wrong and bad for centuries.

#### *Kohlberg's Theory of Moral Development*

Perhaps the most well-known theory of moral development in the social sciences based on the extensive research of Lawrence Kohlberg (1984). This is a "classic" stage model of development comprising six stages representing qualitatively different perspectives on morality. In essence, Kohlberg's theory arranges the six stages sequentially (i.e., there is a universal order of progressive change) into three levels (see Table 5.2). Level 1 is labeled as pre-conventional where the focus is on the self. Level 2 is conventional where the focus is on others. Level 3 is post-conventional where the focus is on ethical principles. Despite the proposition that the higher levels of moral/ethical reasoning develop throughout the lifespan and especially in adulthood, Kohlberg's research found that most adults reason mainly from the perspective of personal usefulness

**Table 5.2** Kohlberg's (1984) Stages of moral/ethical development

| *Level* | *Stage* |
|---|---|
| Pre-Conventional (Focus on the **Self**) | Stage 1: Punishment and Obedience<br>Stage 2: Personal Usefulness |
| Conventional (Focus on **Others**) | Stage 3: Group Conformity<br>Stage 4: Authority and Social Order |
| Post-Conventional (Focus on **Principles**) | Stage 5: Social Contract and Human Rights<br>Stage 6: Universal Ethical Principles and Personal Conscience |

(Stage 2) and that most never progress to the authority and social order frame (Stage 4) or higher.

This is a disheartening finding but could help explain a great deal as to why the apparently intractable issues of abuse of power, conflict-of-interest, individual and organizational corruption, and other ethical problems continue to be ubiquitous in organizations and the world at large. There are clear leadership implications at the heart of ethical development concerns. It would seem likely that few would choose to follow someone who leads from an ethical perspective of punishment and obedience (Stage 1) or personal usefulness (Stage 2); however, political examples of increasing authoritarianism around the world suggest otherwise.

Morals can develop across the lifespan, but such development is not inevitable. The development of morality and ethical reasoning is closely tied to the development of mental complexity in adulthood. A landmark study connecting these topics was conducted by William Perry focusing on young adults in their college years. This led to an influential book on intellectual and ethical development (Perry, 1970). As Perry noted, how people think about and take responsibility for what they know and value changes in major ways from adolescence to young adulthood.

Thinking in sophisticated ways about ethics and ethical behavior involves sophisticated thinking in general (i.e., thinking is for doing). In the business world, it is not just a matter of following the law because the law is far from clear-cut on many issues. Just consider the number of lawyers employed in a typical corporate organization and why that is the case. There are certain ethical principles that lend themselves to training. One example is abuse of power, which is often at the heart of sexual harassment. Most organizations today provide mandatory sexual harassment training to help sensitize employees to identify sexual harassment in the workplace and to be aware of its causes. Knowing about the abuse of power and its various forms does not necessarily mean that an individual will shift their thinking to more sophisticated levels of ethical and moral reasoning; rather, they learn that abuse of power and engaging in *quid pro quo* forms of behavior are problematic and even illegal, and therefore are (in theory) less likely to engage in such behavior. Is it because they come to realize that abusive behavior is morally wrong or is it the fear of getting caught and punished? The difference is indicative of different levels of moral reasoning.

## Ethical Dilemmas

Moral development has a basis in understanding the nature of ethical dilemmas, which are prevalent in leadership contexts. An ethical dilemma occurs when there are two competing decision alternatives, both of which have a foundation in positive values and morality. Accepting one alternative has ethical implications by virtue of rejecting the other alternative. Perhaps a simpler way of expressing this is as a values conflict. There is a decision in which two or more core values are embedded in decision alternatives so that accepting one alternative means rejecting the alternative value.

If these values are all positive (i.e., virtues), it constitutes a type of approach–approach conflict in which a choice needs to be made between two desirable outcomes. But a dilemma occurs because accepting one alternative means rejecting the alternative and both are based on desirable virtues. There is no easy answer to how to handle any ethical dilemma; however, one approach helps an individual become aware of their core values through values clarification exercises (i.e., making an individual's core values explicitly known). At its core, it involves enhancing self-awareness, which is one of the leadership self-views discussed in Chapter 4. Becoming aware of the underlying conditions that create an ethical dilemma is one way of developing more sophisticated levels of ethical reasoning.

A prime example of this kind of ethical dilemma can be found in a conflict-of-interest situation. In such situations, something that might personally benefit one as the leader could (inadvertently) hurt or disadvantage another. Seeing a conflict-of-interest sometimes is difficult because of the so-called blind spots people have when it comes to self-serving behavior (De Cremer & Moore, 2020). Something at the core of these kinds of conflicts is the ability to take others' perspectives beyond one's own. This ability to see issues from multiple perspectives extends beyond ethical dilemmas to decision-making processes more generally. It is tied to the notion of leader complexity.

Creating conditions to help leaders have a more conscious awareness of their core values can be accomplished in relatively short order. One of the proximal outcomes of leader development involves self-awareness. Enhancing this self-view can occur through structured reflection exercises in a classroom-type environment (Newstead et al., 2024). The longer term and more distal outcome of developing sophisticated levels of ethical decision-making occurs as a function of using this awareness regularly over time in the so-called life gym. This involves giving more thought to whether a particular decision presents an ethical dilemma, understanding what values are in conflict, which can help a leader make more effective decisions and be aware of their potential ethical implications. Many leaders try to compromise when faced with an ethical dilemma through decision-making that does not fully embrace (or reject) either value. An attempt is made to drive a decision midway between two competing values. Rarely do such compromises lead to an effective resolution to the dilemma. The goal seems to be to appease the guilty conscience of the decision-maker. Values sometimes come at a cost and becoming a values-based and principled leader often means making difficult (and painful) decisions.

The implications of abuse of power and ethical dilemmas are just two of the more prevalent causes of moral/ethical lapses in leadership. Ethics are complex constructs attesting to the long history of debate and study in the fields of philosophy and the social sciences. Moral and ethical development in adulthood is inherently tied to the underlying complexity of thought processes. Ethics is not just about following rules, at least not at the higher levels of ethical reasoning. As noted, the development of ethical reasoning is closely tied to the development of mental complexity in adulthood. One way that this has been studied—and a domain identified by Moshman (2003) as an indicator of adult development—is through systematic changes in epistemic cognition across the lifespan.

### *Epistemic Cognition and Reflective Judgment*

Epistemic cognition is rooted in epistemology, which is a branch of philosophy that examines the nature of knowledge, how we acquire it, how we come to understand if knowledge is true. When referring to cognition, it boils down to understanding personal epistemological beliefs that are held explicitly or more often implicitly by an individual. Epistemic cognitions are those thoughts and personal beliefs about or relating to knowledge and its acquisition (Greene et al., 2016). It refers to how we think about what we think we know.

Epistemic cognition is relevant to leaders and leadership because it serves as a foundation for problem-solving, especially in solving those problems that are ill-structured (i.e., without a recognized correct answer). Leaders deal a lot in the arena of ill-structured problems. They can be considered adaptive challenges that some scholars have argued require leadership and not a technical solution (Heifetz, 1994). Adaptive challenges are considerably more complex than the typical technical challenge, the latter of which can be solved through the application of technical skills and expertise. As noted previously, adaptive challenges tend to be those involving people, chock full of myriad individual differences and free will.

Epistemic cognition is thought to develop over the lifespan and especially in adulthood. Its development is tied to an underlying concern grounded in mental complexity—which is not the same as intelligence. Rather, mental complexity involves a succession (or progression) of increasingly complex mental logics. Intelligence is more of a fixed trait related to intellectual capacity. One aspect of mental complexity is understanding the causal factors related to knowledge. How do we come to believe that something is true? How do we know what we know or believe what we do? What does one's personal epistemology suggest is true?

#### *Reflective Judgment Model*

A prominent model proposed by developmental psychologists to capture progressive changes in epistemic cognition is the Reflective Judgment Model (King & Kitchener, 1994; Kitchener & King, 1981). The model "describes a developmental progression that occurs…in the ways that people understand the process of knowing and in the corresponding ways that they justify their beliefs about ill-structured problems" (King & Kitchener, p. 13). The developmental progression in reasoning about knowing and how knowledge is acquired is summarized in seven distinct sets of assumptions (see Table 5.3). These assumptions could be called stages, levels, or positions (e.g., Perry, 1970); however, they meet the criteria set forth by Moshman (2003) for adult development by capturing qualitative, progressive, and internally directed changes that occur in the adult years.

The perspective represented by the Reflective Judgment Model will be further discussed in the next section on constructive-developmental approaches to adult development. That is because the notion of mental complexity is central to that class of theories and could also apply to reflective judgment. But one brief example might be helpful. A well-established "error" or cognitive heuristic involves overestimating individual dispositional factors such as personality as the cause of others' behavior. It is so endemic to human perception that it has been labeled the ***fundamental attribution error*** (Jones, 1979). In essence, if I observe you doing something profoundly stupid, I am more likely to think you are profoundly stupid as compared with evaluating possible situational causes for your behavior. As a leader, it is imperative to avoid falling into the fundamental attribution error with followers as it leads to a type of "blame-game." The follower's shortcomings or dispositional flaws are seen as the cause of their faulty behavior when it is as (or more) likely that the individual failure was causally related to aspects of the situation.

The good news is that people can learn to avoid the tendency to fall into this attributional error by deliberative reflecting on the alternative possible explanations for why someone did what they did. What are the alternative possible explanations for their behavior? The practice of trying to identify and understand alternative explanations for a phenomenon is central to the development of epistemic cognition. One means of having a deeper epistemological understanding of the cause of different experiences is to reflect on as many different possible causal explanations as possible. At the most advanced stages of reflective judgment, the attribution of causality for what is known is not an either/or, 100% or nothing proposition but more of a probabilistic judgment of what are the most likely explanations (i.e., causes) for the knowledge at hand.

Recent work has adopted the principles proposed in the Reflective Judgment Model in understanding how to develop more complex levels of leader self-awareness (Newstead et al., 2024). Thus, there is a direct application to developing leaders and leadership through the focus on one

**Table 5.3** Stages in reflective judgment development

| | |
|---|---|
| Pre-reflective thinking | **Stage 1**<br>• What a person believes to be true is true<br>• "I know what I have seen."<br>• No justification is necessary<br>**Stage 2**<br>• A person can know with certainty either directly or via an authority<br>• "If [this authority] says it's true then it must be true."<br>• Justification is via an authority perspective<br>**Stage 3**<br>• In some areas, knowledge is temporarily uncertain<br>• "When there is convincing evidence that everyone says is true then it will be knowledge. Until then it's just a guess."<br>• Justification is based on what feels right now. In other areas, authorities truly know, and knowledge is certain |
| Quasi-reflective thinking | **Stage 4**<br>• Knowledge is generally uncertain because of situational variables<br>• "Some things like the pyramids, we will never know. Who are you going to ask? No one alive now was there."<br>• What we can know and how we justify beliefs is idiosyncratic<br>**Stage 5**<br>• Knowledge is contextual: People know via individual conceptual filters<br>• "Other theories could be as true as the one I believe but based on different evidence."<br>• Justification is context-specific |
| Reflective thinking | **Stage 6**<br>• Knowledge is constructed by comparing evidence and opinion on different sides of an issue or across contexts<br>• "It's very difficult to be 100% sure. There are degrees of certainty. You come to a point where you are sure enough for a personal stance on the issue."<br>• Justification involves explaining such comparisons<br>**Stage 7**<br>• Knowledge is an outcome of an inquiry process that is generalizable across issues<br>• "One can judge an argument by how well thought out it is, what kinds of reasoning and evidence are used to support it, and how consistent the way one argues on a topic as compared with other topics."<br>• Justification is probabilistic, involving the use of evidence and argument to present the most complete or compelling understanding of an issue |

*Note* Adapted from King and Kitchener (2002)

of the core forms of self-views proposed as a proximal indicator of leader development.

## Adult Development Theories

Science has a solid foundation in theory. The most compelling reason for good theory is that it helps explain why things happen, not just that there are data to show that they do happen. Good theory also allows us to predict what is likely to happen even before it is experienced. An overarching criterion for what makes a good theory is that it is falsifiable—it can be shown to be false (Popper, 2005). Theories that cannot be falsified explain everything and nothing simultaneously. Social science theories are "softer" than those coming from the basic sciences; nonetheless, theories must illustrate ways that they can be proven wrong to be considered a good, falsifiable theory. Theories in psychology and other social sciences are continuously being tested and revised. Rather than talking about a theory as if it were an end state, perhaps a better way is to describe it is as theorizing, reflecting the ongoing process of theoretical development and revision (Weick, 1995b). Theories are powerful tools and without theory "we're at sea without a sextant" (Christensen, 2017, p. 17), especially as researchers.

Theory is also important to individual leaders, especially given the proposed focus of using experience to motivate the development of leaders and leadership. But to paraphrase a quote from W. Edwards Deming (Deming, 2018), experience without theory teaches nothing. Theory provides the meaning to understand experience, which is why there can be no learning without theory.

This section provides summaries of two classes of human development theories that include propositions and predictions about adult development. This is notable because until the late twentieth century, the prevailing thought among developmental psychologists was that pretty much everything that could be developed in a person had been developed by around age 20. We now have data—and theory!—to suggest otherwise. People can develop well into later adulthood, but it doesn't mean that such development is inevitable. This is one reason why researchers in human development such as Moshman (2003) argue that what development means in adulthood is different from what it means in earlier years.

The theories reviewed in this next section are two of the most widely known and researched classes of developmental theories that apply to adult development. They offer insights as to potential distal outcomes of leader development. As noted previously, leader development occurs in the context of ongoing adult development. Being a more highly developed adult offers the possibility of being a more highly developed leader; however, the opposite is not necessarily true. Focusing on developing as a leader does not mean that there is any substantive change in the distal indicators of adult development. This section helps to explain why that is the case.

By proposing a set of more distal outcomes in leader development it may inadvertently suggest that there is a developmental endpoint. To be clear: There is no endpoint to development for a living being. But as will be discussed, most adults do not reach the highest stages of development as proposed in these theories. This is problematic, especially as the pace of change accelerates in the world. Put somewhat differently, the level of individual adult complexity does not meet or match with the complexity in the environment. Going forward, the potential complexity gap has serious implications for leader development and the quality of leadership locally and globally.

### *Constructive-Developmental Theories*

Constructive-developmental refers to a group of theories that share certain theoretical assumptions. There is no way to review all the constructive-developmental theories in a concise way and to try and do so would probably be an entire volume on its own. The goal of this section is to give readers a basic understanding of what these theories are about and how they pertain to leadership and leader development.

The term constructive-developmental can be traced back to Robert Kegan (1980) who remains an influential voice in the field of adult development. At its core, the term and approach refer to "the study of the *development* of our *constructing* or meaning-making activity" (p. 373, italics in original). Meaning-making is interchangeable with the term sensemaking (Weick, 1995a), which has more traction in the organizational and social cognition literatures. The key concept is that individuals are not passive recipients of experiential information but actively construct the meaning of their "lived experience," and there are identifiable patterns of these constructions that are shared across individuals.

The basic tenets of constructive-development theory according to Kegan (1980) are presented in Table 5.4. What is central to this theoretical framing is that meaning-making or sensemaking shapes the interpretation of experience, it guides behavior (i.e., thinking is for doing), and there are regularities across individuals in their respective meaning-making systems. These systems of sensemaking reflect qualitative changes across the lifespan, they reflect systematic and progressive changes and are internally directed (Moshman, 2003).

An important question is what facilitates development? At the heart of developmental processes in constructive-developmental theory are *subject–object relations*. What an individual is subject to are implicit assumptions about people and the world. These are implicit frames that an individual tends to *look through*. Surfacing a subjective assumption will make it an object and thus something that an individual can *look at* instead of looking through it. These progressive subject–object transitions drive individual development. The central idea is that by surfacing or making object those deeper assumptions of what is subject over time will result in more complex understandings of the world (Table 5.4).

According to thought leaders in the field (Kegan & Lahey, 2016), development is a "specific, describable, and detectable phenomenon" (p. 77) involving:

- the growth of mindsets or meaning-making logics;
- qualitative advances in abilities to see more deeply and accurately into the self and the world; and

**Table 5.4** Basic tenets of constructive-developmental theory

1. *Human being is meaning-making*: Evolving as a human equates with evolving systems of meaning
2. *Meaning systems shape experience*: Experience is not so much what happens to an individual but what is made of or interpreted about what happens
3. *Meaning systems guide behavior*: Thinking is for doing
4. *A meaning system organizes thinking, feeling, and acting over a wide variety of human functioning*: Meaning systems are ever-present in human functioning, except when in transition to a new system
5. *There are measurable regularities in the underlying structure of meaning-making systems*: There are predictable progressions in meaning-making systems across the lifespan

*Note* Adapted from Kegan (1980)

- the process of successively being able to look at premises and assumptions that were formerly looked through.

This developmental process is about enhancing mental complexity (which is not the same as general intelligence) to understand deeper causal connections about the way the world works and our place in it. When that focus is on knowledge and knowledge acquisition, it becomes apparent how it also can be used to understand the development of epistemic cognition and reflective judgment. The underlying assumptions are virtually the same. And although mental complexity is not a developmental panacea, Kegan and Lahey (2016) argue that "for those at a higher level of mental complexity, a complex world is more manageable" (p. 73).

*Three Plateaus of Adult Development*

Following tradition in developmental psychology, Kegan frames the qualitative and progressive changes in adulthood as stages but also as plateaus. Change is not perfectly linear or continuous but flattens out in distinct plateaus until further development is motivated through more advanced subject–object relations (see Fig. 5.2). The first of these in adulthood is termed the "Socialized Mind" (Stage 3 in the full human development model) that is *dependent* on others to make sense of the world. This is a typical stage at which young adults leave high school and enter college (for those who go that route). Much of the self is defined by the "friend groups" in which an individual is embedded and are used to define themselves.

Progressing to the next plateau, which can take much developmental energy to break away from the previous plateau, leads to the "Self-authoring Mind." The so-called action logic at this plateau works from an *independent* view of the world based on internalized beliefs and values. The final plateau, which research suggests fewer than 1% of the adult population ever achieves, is based on an *interdependent* action logic termed the "Self-transforming Mind." It represents a type of meta-awareness in which the limits of personal authority can be reflected upon. Dialectics, inconsistencies, and paradoxes are synthesized and guide thinking and behavior. If it sounds complex—it is! This might be a big reason why so few people ever fully achieve this final plateau in their development. It is also the case that individuals can be identified as working between different plateaus or stages of development. It is typically not a radical jump from one stage to another, but a longer-term process that

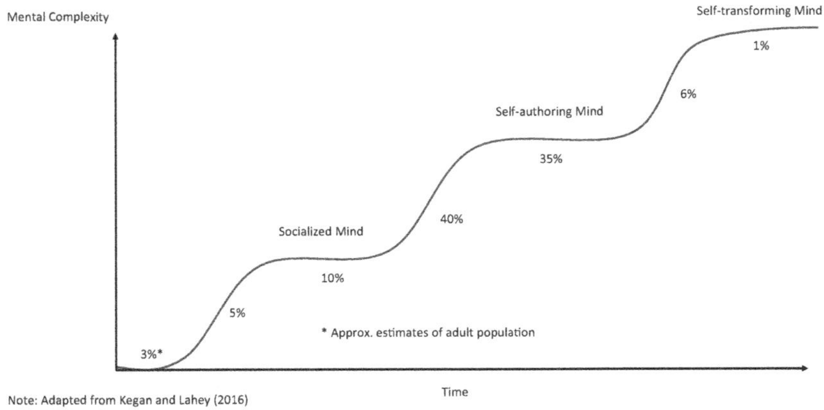


**Fig. 5.2** Three plateaus of adult development

is based on working through increasingly more complex subject–object relations.

A helpful overview of Kegan's constructive-developmental framework can be found in Kegan and Lahey (2016), especially in Chapter 2 ("What Do We Mean by Development?"). A more comprehensive treatment can be found in earlier works (Kegan, 1994). Another viewpoint on these stages of adulthood that is more fully focused on leadership can be found in a Harvard Business Review piece that is one of its most downloaded articles (Rooke & Torbert, 2005). Other researchers working in similar spaces include Jane Loevinger, Bill Torbert, and even Lawrence Kohlbeg (of moral development fame).

A narrative review examined the use of constructive-development theory to advance understanding of leadership, with a particular focus on the proposition that a leader's order of development should play a role in determining leadership effectiveness (McCauley et al., 2006). Overall, the results suggested the evidence was mixed in this regard; however, researchers continue to adopt emerging methodologies and analytic techniques to better understand the relationships between adult development, mental complexity, and leadership role performance (Thornton, 2023).

The next section provides an overview of a different theoretical approach to understanding human development with implications for adult development. Because it differs from constructive-developmental theories in some notable ways, those differences will be featured in terms of their implications for leader development.

### *Dynamic Skill Theory*

There are two aspects of dynamic skill theory that set it apart from constructive-developmental theories. First, the focus of dynamic skill theory is on the individual and not some aggregate or statistical average. Second, human variability is ubiquitous and interesting and should be considered a core construct in that theory. Both aspects are central to the goal of establishing a science of the individual (Rose et al., 2013). This theoretical perspective is grounded in dynamic systems (Thelen & Smith, 1994) with a particular focus on human variability. It is also consistent with the long-standing goal of longitudinal research, which is to gain information about intraindividual or within-person change (Schaie, 1983).

A core assumption of constructive-developmental theory and others that are grounded more explicitly in the Piagetian tradition of development is that individuals at the same stage, level, or position (Perry, 1970) all make sense of their world in similar ways using similar mental frames. This is not the case with dynamic skill theory (Fischer, 1980; Fischer & Bidell, 2006). Development is domain-specific such that an individual might function at a relatively high level in one area of life or skill domain on their own but would need a lot of support to function at a similar level in a different domain.

What is a skill? Perhaps the simplest way of conceptualizing a skill is that it is anything that can be practiced. Research shows that practicing a skill using deliberate practice routines will develop that skill to the point that it can be manifested in relatively automatic ways (i.e., requiring little cognitive effort). What dynamic skill theory postulates is that a skill will be integrated with other developing skills in what is termed a *web of development* (Fischer & Rose, 2001). Rather than thinking about development as a one-dimensional ladder where individuals just go up (or sometimes down) in a linear manner, dynamic skill theory considers development to be an ongoing process of connecting various strands and branches of different skill domains in establishing an integrated web of various connected skills. It is a similar process to what was described in Chapter 3 about more macro-level competencies comprising mini- and micro-level skills and more basic kinds of habits.

There also is no universal stage-like changes that individuals progress across in dynamic skill theory. Rather, development is different for every individual although the underlying processes consist of predictable cycles ranging from establishing simple representations to complex abstractions. One way to think about these cycles is to think of building blocks in which the simple blocks for representations eventually create a new kind of more complex building block to begin the capacity to think abstractly (Fischer, 2008). It is something like progressing from one-dimensional space (separate point and line) to two dimensions (square) to three dimensions (cube).

Dynamic skill theory has been used to explain how reading skill develops among children (e.g., Fischer & Rose, 2001), but it is sufficiently flexible to help understand the development of a complex skill such as leadership in adults. What is important to consider is the skill domain or context. It could be that leadership is entirely based on work or organizational life, or it could link multiple domains that span work, family, and life in general (Hammond et al., 2017).

How does dynamic skill theory help us better understand leader development? It proposes that distal outcomes in development (using this human development theoretical framework) involve more abstract ways of knowing and doing—what some have called leadership action logics (Rooke & Torbert, 2005). Thus, there are some points of connection with advances in mental complexity as a distal outcome that is proposed by constructive-development theories.

## Implications of Considering Adult Development in Leader Development

An overarching belief when considering the longer-term indicators of leader development is that it is grounded in adult development. In other words, leader development occurs in the context of ongoing adult development, so understanding the former requires addressing the latter. That may sound like a reasonable proposition; however, it was only relatively recently (e.g., the last 30–40 years) that development was thought to continue during the adult years.

The classic Piagetian perspective is that most of the interior developmental changes in humans were complete by the early 20s. What emerged in more recent times were neo-Piagetian perspectives grounded in post-formal operations in adulthood. This is an academic explanation that researchers built on and extended the theory formulated by Jean Piaget (1929) who postulated that development ceased once the stage of formal operations was achieved in late adolescence or early adulthood. Since the late twentieth century, there have been advances on several theoretical fronts in understanding what continues to develop well into the adult years. One focus of these efforts has been on the concepts of mental complexity and meaning-making (or sensemaking).

The point was made that, if fortunate, we will spend most of our lives in the adult years (post 20 years of age). Given what is known both anecdotally and empirically about such things as wisdom and aging (Grossmann, 2017) it makes sense to consider how individuals continue to develop across the lifespan. Humans can change across the life course, so it is not just a long slow decline over time (thankfully). As the eminent lifespan psychologist Paul Baltes (1987) noted, development involves a dynamic process of managing both gains and losses. Healthy aging therefore involves minimizing losses while simultaneously maximizing gains throughout adulthood. Developing wisdom might be seen in similar ways as developing expertise: It occurs over a long period of time and happens despite the well-documented cognitive declines associated with aging.

The implications of these more distal outcomes grounded in adult development theory and research is that some things in leader development take a long time to develop—years and even decades. This is one reason why owning your own development (First Principle #1) is so important. Few organizations that I am aware of take such a long-term perspective when it comes to leader development. The exception (that proves the rule) is the military where senior leaders are not hired from the outside but developed over the course of an entire career. In non-military organizations there is a pressure to show a return on investment (ROI) for leader development in relatively short order—months at the most and usually sooner than that.

Long-term outcomes in leader development are associated with deep changes in the leader's operating system. It is not merely the case of applying some newly acquired skills but making sense of the world in more complex and sophisticated ways, which have implications for morality and ethical reasoning, complex problem-solving of ill-structured problems, and understanding and enacting leadership in various ways. These all relate to Moshman's (2003) three domains of adult development: (1) identity formation, (2) moral development, and (3) the development of epistemic cognition. As noted in this chapter, each of these domains has major implications for leader development.

This sounds all well and good, but what is the payoff? It may not be measurable in financial terms such as ROI but it is about making an increasingly complex world—and leadership amidst that complexity—more manageable. This is at the heart of what some researchers have proposed in terms of individual requisite complexity (Lord et al., 2011). Does the mental complexity and sensemaking frames of a leader match with the level of complexity inherent in their leadership role? There is evidence to suggest that this so-called complexity gap continues to widen (Kegan & Lahey, 2016; Thornton, 2023). As researchers, we want to be clear that what we are focusing on primarily are changes in the indicators of development, both proximal and distal. The second question is documenting whether such development changes are associated with enhanced leadership effectiveness. Each of these questions is sufficiently rich (and complex!) to keep interested researchers occupied for quite some time.

The distal indicators proposed for leader development are grounded in the aspects of adult development that were reviewed in this chapter (see Day & Dragoni, 2015). The indicators can take the form of deep-seated changes in a leader's operating system allowing them to make complex environments more manageable and therefore the responses to the complex adaptive challenges in such environments more effective (in theory). This is the core tenet of the requisite complexity perspective. Unfortunately, leader development research lags in this regard. There are available measures of these kinds of mental complexity constructs (Loevinger, 2014; O'Fallon et al., 2020), but they have tended to involve time-intensive human scoring procedures.

The advent of artificial intelligence and machine learning algorithms is starting to change this traditional obstacle to scalability, which should make assessments of changes in outcomes such as mental complexity easier to implement. Evidence exists supporting the psychometric properties of some state-of-the-science assessments for related adult development constructs (https://lecticalive.org/about/las-reliability-validity). What are needed are longitudinal studies of changes in these measures of mental complexity, especially those focused on the leadership domain. Such studies do not need to be over the entire lifespan. A helpful start would be a multiyear examination of adult changes using a personal trajectory approach to modeling individual change. But, again, tracking changes in the personal trajectories of these kinds of skills and other characteristics should be the primary focus. Showing how such changes are related to leadership effectiveness is an entirely different research program.

Lengthier time scales also pertain to the focus on leadership as a type of expertise or expert performance. We can quibble about whether it takes 10,000 hours or less (or more) to develop expertise in a skill domain, but the central point is that it takes considerable time and involves a specific type of (deliberate) practice that comes with its own set of guidelines. To become an expert leader requires a long-term investment in terms of time and practice, which is one reason why internalizing a leader identity self-view is needed. Doing so motivates the kinds of resource allocation to help achieve such long-term outcomes.

Thinking of someone as an expert leader is a holistic assessment of the whole individual leader. It might make more sense to break down the notion of being an expert leader into smaller skill domains. What those skill domains might be is open to debate; however, we know there are a few things that most leaders would benefit from developing. These are skills such as having a big picture or strategic perspective (Dragoni et al., 2014) influence and persuasion, feedback giving, reflection, and active listening, among others (Day et al., 2009). Thinking about these individual skills from the perspective of dynamic skill theory (Fischer, 1980; Fischer & Bidell, 2006) suggests that these various leadership skills could be considered as separate strands in a web of development that connect and intertwine as they each develop. At higher levels, these individual strands may combine in ways that come to define an expert leader.

## Chapter Summary

- Leader development occurs in the context of ongoing adult development.
- Developing throughout the lifespan involves a commitment to lifelong learning.
- Individuals have personal agency over their learning and development. They can choose to challenge themselves to continue learning and developing as a leader—or not.
- The scholarly field of expert performance can help understand the role of deliberate practice in the development of lifelong leadership skills.
- Developing the proximal indicators of leader development (i.e., self-views and leadership KSAs) will shape the development of distal indicators of leader development (i.e., sensemaking and dynamic

skills) through extensive practice and support or over a considerable amount of time (e.g., years and decades).

- Adult development is different from child and adolescent development and therefore rests on different criteria. Those criteria for adult development involve qualitative, progressive, and internally directed changes (Moshman, 2003). These criteria also are relevant for evaluating long-term leader development.
- Three domains in which adults can develop are identity formation, moral development, and the development of epistemic cognition. Each of these domains is relevant for understanding leader development across the lifespan.
- One of the foundational self-views for leader development is identity. Most of the research has investigated the role of leaders' identity strength as a time-varying covariate of skill development. Another component of leader identity that has received less research attention is that of leadership meanings (Hammond et al., 2017).
- Changes in leadership meaning from personal dominance to interpersonal influence to relational dialogue meet the criteria for adult development proposed by Moshman (2003).
- Moral development is critically important for leaders in terms of being able to identify, diagnose, and effectively respond to ethical dilemmas.
- The development of epistemic cognition is summarized by the Reflective Judgment Model (King & Kitchener, 1994). It is especially appropriate for understanding how individuals develop the capabilities to identify and respond to ill-structured problems where there is no agreed-upon solution. Most adaptive challenges requiring leadership are forms of ill-structured problems.
- Adult development theories in the form of constructive-developmental approaches and dynamic skill theory offer insights into the prospective processes involved in developing as an adult and as an adult leader through the adult years.

## References

Baltes, P. B. (1987). Theoretical propositions of life-span developmental psychology: On the dynamics between growth and decline. *Developmental Psychology, 23*(5), 611–626. https://doi.org/10.1037/0012-1649.23.5.611

Belsky, J., & Pluess, M. (2009). The nature (and nurture?) of plasticity in early human development. *Perspectives on Psychological Science, 4*(4), 345–351. https://doi.org/10.1111/j.1745-6924.2009.01136.x

Christensen, C. M. (2017). *How will you measure your life?* Harvard Business Review Press.

Cohen, T. R., & Morse, L. (2014). Moral character: What it is and what it does. *Research in Organizational Behavior, 34*, 43–61. https://doi.org/10.1016/j.riob.2014.08.003

Dalio, R. (2017). *Principles.* Simon & Schuster.

Day, D. V., & Dragoni, L. (2015). Leadership development: An outcome-oriented review based on time and levels of analyses. *Annual Review of Organizational Psychology and Organizational Behavior, 2*, 133–156. https://doi.org/10.1146/annurev-orgpsych-032414-111328

Day, D. V., & Harrison, M. M. (2007). A multilevel, identity-based approach to leadership development. *Human Resource Management Review, 17*(4), 360–373. https://doi.org/10.1016/j.hrmr.2007.08.007

Day, D. V., Harrison, M. M., & Halpin, S. M. (2009). *An integrative approach to leader development: Connecting adult development, identity, and expertise.* Psychology Press.

De Cremer, D., & Moore, C. (2020). Toward a better understanding of behavioral ethics in the workplace. *Annual Review of Organizational Psychology and Organizational Behavior, 7*(1), 369–393. https://doi.org/10.1146/annurev-orgpsych-012218-015151

Deming, W. E. (2018). *The new economics for industry, government, education.* MIT press.

Dragoni, L., Oh, I. S., Tesluk, P. E., Moore, O. A., VanKatwyk, P., & Hazucha, J. (2014). Developing leaders' strategic thinking through global work experience: The moderating role of cultural distance. *Journal of Applied Psychology, 99*(5), 867–882. https://doi.org/10.1037/a0036628

Drath, W. (2001). *The deep blue sea: Rethinking the source of leadership.* Jossey-Bass.

Drath, W. H., & Palus, C. J. (1994). *Making common sense: Leadership as meaning-making in a community of practice.* Center for Creative Leadership.

Ericsson, K. A. (2008). Deliberate practice and acquisition of expert performance: A general overview. *Academic Emergency Medicine, 15*(11), 988–994. https://doi.org/10.1111/j.1553-2712.2008.00227.x

Ericsson, K. A., Hoffman, R. R., & Kozbelt, A. (Eds.). (2018). *The Cambridge handbook of expertise and expert performance* (2nd ed.). Cambridge University Press.

Ericsson, K. A., Krampe, R. T., & Tesch-Römer, C. (1993). The role of deliberate practice in the acquisition of expert performance. *Psychological Bulletin, 100*(3), 363–406. https://doi.org/10.1037/0033-295X.100.3.363

Ericsson, K. A., & Pool, R. (2016). *Peak: Secrets from the new science of expertise*. Mariner Books.
Ericsson, K. A., Prietula, M. J., & Cokely, E. T. (2007). The making of an expert. *Harvard Business Review, 85*(7/8), 114.
Feldman, D. H. (1995). Learning and development in nonuniversal theory. *Human Development, 38*(6), 315–321. https://doi.org/10.1159/000278337
Fischer, K. W. (1980). A theory of cognitive development: The control and construction of hierarchies of skills. *Psychological Review, 87*(6), 477–531. https://doi.org/10.1037/0033-295x.87.6.477
Fischer, K. W. (2008). Dynamic cycles of cognitive and brain development: Measuring growth in mind, brain, and education. In A. M. Battro, K. W. Fischer, & P. Léna (Eds.), *The educated brain* (pp. 127–150). Cambridge University Press.
Fischer, K. W., & Bidell, T. R. (2006). Dynamic development of action, thought, and emotion. In W. Damon & R. M. Lerner (Eds.), *Theoretical models of human development: Handbook of child psychology* (6th ed., Vol. 1, pp. 313–399). Wiley.
Fischer, K. W., & Rose, L. T. (2001). Webs of skill: How students learn. *Educational Leadership, 59*(3), 6–12.
Fulmer, R. M. (1997). The evolving paradigm of leadership development. *Organizational Dynamics, 25*(4), 59–72. https://doi.org/10.1016/S0090-2616(97)90037-1
Gladwell, M. (2008). *Outliers: The story of success*. Little, Brown and Company.
Grant, A. (2023). *Hidden potential: The science of achieving greater things*. Viking.
Greene, J. A., Sandoval, W. A., & Bråten, I. (2016). An introduction to epistemic cognition. In J. A. Greene, W. A. Sandoval, & I. Bråten (Eds.), *Handbook of epistemic cognition* (pp. 1–16). Routledge.
Grossmann, I. (2017). Wisdom in context. *Perspectives on Psychological Science, 12*(2), 233–257. https://doi.org/10.1177/1745691616672066
Hammond, M. M., Clapp-Smith, R., & Palanski, M. (2017). Beyond (just) the workplace: A theory of leader development across multiple domains. *Academy of Management Review, 42*(3), 481–498. https://doi.org/10.5465/amr.2014.0431
Heifetz, R. (1994). *Leadership without easy answers*. Harvard University Press.
Hoyer, W. J., & Touron, D. R. (2002). Learning in adulthood. In J. Demick & C. Andreoletti (Eds.), *Handbook of adult development* (pp. 23–41). Springer. https://doi.org/10.1007/978-1-4615-0617-1_2
Hultsch, D. F., Hertzog, C., Small, B. J., & Dixon, R. A. (1999). Use it or lose it: Engaged lifestyle as a buffer of cognitive decline in aging? *Psychology and Aging, 14*(2), 245–263. https://doi.org/10.1037/0882-7974.14.2.245

Jones, E. E. (1979). The rocky road from acts to dispositions. *American Psychologist, 34*(2), 107–117. https://doi.org/10.1037/0003-066X.34.2.107

Kegan, R. (1980). Making meaning: The constructive-developmental approach to persons and practice. *The Personnel and Guidance Journal, 58*(5), 373–380. https://doi.org/10.1002/j.2164-4918.1980.tb00416.x

Kegan, R. (1982). *The evolving self: Problems and process in human development*. Harvard University Press.

Kegan, R. (1994). *In over our heads: The mental demands of modern life*. Harvard University Press.

Kegan, R., & Lahey, L. L. (2016). *An everyone culture: Becoming a deliberately developmental organization*. Harvard Business Review Press.

King, P. M., & Kitchener, K. S. (1994). *Developing reflective judgment: Understanding and promoting intellectual growth and critical thinking in adolescents and adults*. Jossye-Bass.

King, P. M., & Kitchener, K. S. (2002). The Reflective Judgment Model: Twenty years of research on epistemic cognition. In B. K. Hofer & P. R. Pintrich (Eds.), *Personal epistemology: The psychology of beliefs about knowledge and knowing* (pp. 37–61). Erlbaum. https://doi.org/10.4324/9780203424964-5

Kitchener, K. S., & King, P. M. (1981). Reflective judgment: Concepts of justification and their relationship to age and education. *Journal of Applied Developmental Psychology, 2*, 89–116.

Kohlberg, L. (1984). *The psychology of moral development: The nature and validity of moral stages*. Harper & Row.

Komives, S. R., Owen, J. E., Longerbeam, S. D., Mainella, F. C., & Osteen, L. (2005). Developing a leadership identity: A grounded theory. *Journal of College Student Development, 46*(6), 593–611. https://doi.org/10.1353/csd.2005.0061

Loevinger, J. (2014). *Measuring ego development*. Psychology Press.

Lord, R. G., & Hall, R. J. (2005). Identity, deep structure and the development of leadership skill. *The Leadership Quarterly, 16*(4), 591–615. https://doi.org/10.1016/j.leaqua.2005.06.003

Lord, R. G., Hannah, S. T., & Jennings, P. L. (2011). A framework for understanding leadership and individual requisite complexity. *Organizational Psychology Review, 1*(2), 104-127. https://doi.org/10.1177/2041386610384757

Macnamara, B. N., Moreau, D., & Hambrick, D. Z. (2016). The relationship between deliberate practice and performance in sports: A meta-analysis. *Perspectives on Psychological Science, 11*(3), 333–350. https://doi.org/10.1177/1745691616635591

Mann, A., & Harter, J. (2016). The worldwide employee engagement crisis. *Gallup Business Journal, 7*(1), 1–5.

McCauley, C. D., Drath, W. H., Palus, C. J., O'Connor, P. M. G., & Baker, B. A. (2006). The use of constructive-developmental theory to advance the understanding of leadership. *The Leadership Quarterly, 17*(6), 634–653. https://doi.org/10.1016/j.leaqua.2006.10.006

Moshman, D. (2003). Developmental change in adulthood. In J. Demick & C. Andreoletti (Eds.), *Handbook of adult development* (pp. 43–61). Springer. https://doi.org/10.1007/978-1-4615-0617-1_3

Newstead, T., Eva, N., & Day, D. V. (2024, in press). Where are you coming from? A place-based approach to developing leader self-awareness. *Academy of Management Learning & Education.*

O'Fallon, T., Polissar, N., Neradilek, M. B., & Murray, T. (2020). The validation of a new scoring method for assessing ego development based on three dimensions of language. *Heliyon, 6*(3). https://doi.org/10.1016/j.heliyon.2020.e03472

Parrish, S. (2023). *The ultimate deliberate practice guide: How to be the best.* https://fs.blog/deliberate-practice-guide/

Perry, W. G., Jr. (1970). *Forms of intellectual and ethical development in the college years: A scheme.* Holt, Rinehart, and Winston.

Piaget, J. (1929). *The child's conception of the world.* Routledge.

Popper, K. (2005). *The logic of scientific discovery.* Routledge.

Rooke, D., & Torbert, W. R. (2005). Seven transformations of leadership. *Harvard Business Review, 83*(4), 66–76.

Rose, L. T., Rouhani, P., & Fischer, K. W. (2013). The science of the individual. *Mind, Brain, and Education, 7*(3), 152–158. https://doi.org/10.1111/mbe.12021

Schaie, K. W. (1983). What can we learn from longitudinal studies of adult development? In K. W. Schaie (Ed.), *Longitudinal studies of adult psychological development* (pp. 1–19). The Guilford Press.

Thelen, E., & Smith, L. B. (1994). *A dynamic systems approach to the development of cognition and action.* MIT Press.

Thoreau, H. D. (1854/2006). *Walden.* Yale University Press.

Thornton, A. (2023). *Facing the complexity gap: Developing leaders' reasoning skills to meet the complex task demands of their roles* [Doctoral Dissertation, University of Western Australia Business School], Crawley, Western Australia.

Vonnegut, K., Jr. (1952). *Piano player.* Charles Scribner's Sons.

Wallace, D. F. (2009). *This is water.* Little, Brown and Company.

Ward, P., Schraagen, J. M., Gore, J., & Roth, E. M. (Eds.). (2019). *The Oxford handbook of expertise.* Oxford University Press.

Weick, K. E. (1995a). *Sensemaking in organizations.* SAGE.

Weick, K. E. (1995b). What theory Is *not*, theorizing *Is*. *Administrative Science Quarterly, 40*(3), 385–390. https://doi.org/10.2307/2393789

CHAPTER 6

# Developing a Collective Capacity for Leadership

## Leadership Development at the Collective Level

It was argued earlier in this volume that much of the leadership field has adopted a romanticized, heroic, and leader-centric perspective and assumptions regarding the nature of leadership. At the top of the list is the assumption that leadership flows from a leader to followers, which is why the field is characterized as leader-centric. One implication of this view—even if not stated explicitly—is that the best way to develop leadership is to develop leaders (Day, 2000). Developing individual capacity for leadership by focusing developmental efforts on individual leaders is not wrong or lacking value, but it is limited. Whatever is developed in individuals to enhance or otherwise expand their capacity for leadership must be used or applied for it to matter. The most highly developed leader cannot have any impact without an interpersonal context. Most of what passes for leadership development is in effect leader development, and much of leader development occurs with little consideration of context, interpersonal or otherwise.

Leadership development is different in one important regard: It assumes that leadership is created through the ongoing interactions of people engaged in shared work. For our purposes, shared work refers to tasks involving interdependencies among individuals. The greater the task interdependencies, the more that work is shared. Where leadership can be found in this approach is not within any leader but in the interactions and



D. V. Day, *Developing Leaders and Leadership*,
https://doi.org/10.1007/978-3-031-59068-9_6

relationships between individuals, some of whom might be designated as formal leaders and others not. This is central to a social network perspective on leadership to be discussed in detail in the next chapter. A social network perspective considers the informal relations among members of a team or larger collective to be where the power or capacity to produce leadership can be found. Related to that power is *leadership efficacy*, which is not the same as leadership self-efficacy (LSE) discussed at the individual level. LSE is the strength of belief that an individual has about the capability to engage in leadership activities.

In their review of leadership development using the frames of time of levels of analyses, Day and Dragoni (2015) offered their perspective on the proximal and distal indicators of leadership development. Figure 6.1 provides a representation of the processes that link proximal with distal indicators of collective leadership development. As indicated at the bottom left of the figure, individual capabilities developed through leader development processes are aggregated to form collective leadership capabilities. This reinforces an important point about development that individuals as well as collectives start at different places and change in different ways as they develop.

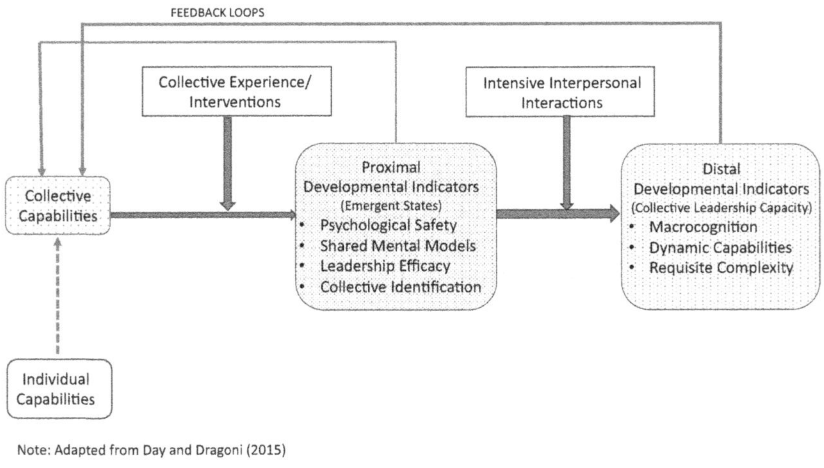


**Fig. 6.1** Collective leadership development with proximal and distal outcomes

### *Proximal Indicators: Collective Emergent States*

The level of analysis at the collective level translates into two or more individuals engaged in shared work over some unspecified length of time. What shapes leadership development at the first stage are collective experiences and interventions. These are shared experiences among the members of the collective. Shared experiences are what help shape the initial level of collective capabilities into a set of *emergent states* that are then transformed into distal indicators of leadership development through second-stage processes of intensive interpersonal interactions (see Fig. 6.1). It is also the case that emergent states can serve as inputs to a collective capacity for leadership that can help shape subsequent emergent states, as well as developmental processes and outcomes more distally.

Collective emergent states can be described as cognitive, affective, and motivational states of teams that are dynamic and vary as a function of context, inputs, processes, and outcomes (Marks et al., 2001). Emergent states differ from collective processes, the latter of which transform collective inputs into outcomes. Although it might be tempting to describe collective leadership development as a type of input-process-outcome model, be clear that proximal indicators of development are conceptualized as emergent states and not as collective processes.

The processes in this leadership development model are located as the first- and second-stage moderators based on shared experiences (stage 1) and shared interactions (stage 2). The feedback loops might also be considered as process mechanisms in a dynamic systems approach in which the respective emergent state operates as an input back to collective capabilities as well as indicating that more long-term or distal development is occurring at the collective level.

The origins of collective emergent states can be found in complexity science that has advanced the thinking about emergence as a construct (Goldstein, 1999). The fundamental characteristics of emergent states in groups are that they are: (1) global, (2) coherent, (3) ostensive, and (4) radically novel (Waller et al., 2016). As noted by Waller et al., these are not mutually exclusive categories but “are better conceptualized as filters through which we see different aspects of dynamisms come into relief” (p. 568). These characteristics have been used to understand complex adaptive systems, work teams, and group dynamics. The intent in this application is to adapt the filters of emergent states to help understand the development of leadership at a collective level of analysis.

Each of the defining characteristics of collective emergent states in leadership development is presented in Fig. 6.2. The most important issues to consider in assessing collective emergent states is that they are formed through dynamic interactions at a lower level (*global*), the emergent state persists over time but can also vary (*coherence*), the emergent state is experienced or felt by individuals in the collective (*ostensive*), and the emergent state does not exist in lower or underlying levels (*radically novel*). These characteristics are important considerations because they propose a set of criteria to evaluate whether something in the system can be considered an emergent state (Waller et al., 2016), thus setting some guidelines for establishing construct validity.

A review of the relevant literature identified the most often researched emergent states in the teams literature (Rapp et al., 2021). These findings are focused on teams of any kind, but mainly work teams; however, the focus is not on the development of leadership in these teams. Nonetheless, it may be of interest to note where most of the construct attention

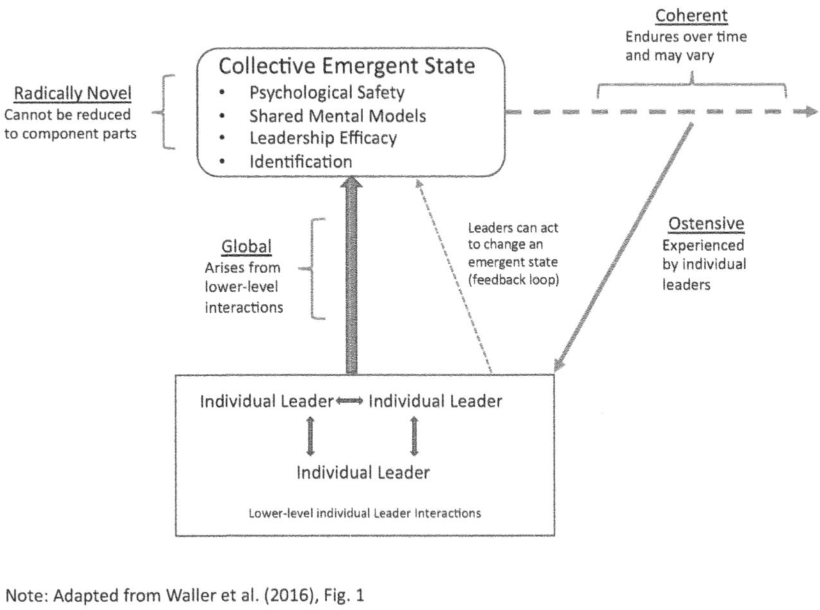


**Fig. 6.2** Characteristics of emergent states in leadership development

exists in the literature and serves as a novel application of the emergence constructs to collective leadership development.

Team emergent states can be categorized into cognitive, affective, motivation, and amalgam (combinations of two or more of the others) categories (Rapp et al., 2021). The most studied team emergent state constructs are: (1) team cognition, (2) team trust, (3) team climates, (4) team cohesion, (5) team psychological safety, (6) team confidence or efficacy, (7) team identification, and (8) team empowerment. These are not presented in any rank order suggesting respective popularity or frequency of study. Team cognition, trust, and climates all are forms of cognitive emergent states. Team cohesion and psychological safety are forms of affective emergent states. Team confidence/efficacy is a motivational emergent state and the team emergent states pertaining to team identification and empowerment are amalgam forms of cognitive/affective and cognitive/motivational categories, respectively.

In the present approach to conceptualizing collective leadership development, the proximal indicators of development are proposed in the form of four emergent states in the collective: (1) psychological safety (affective), (2) shared mental models (cognitive), (3) leadership efficacy (motivation), and (4) identification (cognitive/affective amalgam; Rapp et al., 2021). Each of these collective emergent states will be discussed in the next section. One point to consider is that these are not the only possible collective emergent states that could serve as proximal indicators of leadership development. Rather, these are the most likely emergent states based on current theory and research. Before turning to a more detailed discussion of these emergent states as proximal indicators, a brief overview of the more distal outcomes of collective leadership development is presented.

### *Distal Indicators: Collective Capacity for Leadership*

Distal indicators of leadership development can be characterized as long-term outcomes. These are not end states, per se, but indicators of the development of a collective capacity for leadership (Day et al., 2004) that is attained only after the collective emergent states have jelled and the collective has had ample opportunities for intensive interpersonal interaction. Any collective that interacts over time and endures as a collective has the potential to develop leadership capacity; however, just as with individual leaders this development of leadership potential is not inevitable. There must be an intention to develop the collective with the goal of enacting leadership in ways that are different from the typical leader-centric approach. How this can be done and what is involved in accomplishing this goal of developing a collective leadership capacity will be discussed a little later in this chapter in the section on long-term collective leadership development.

Much less is known about collective leadership development and the distal outcomes associated with those processes compared with leader development outcomes and processes. Three indicators of collective leadership capacity that will be discussed are macrocognition, dynamic capabilities, and collective requisite complexity. *Macrocognition* refers to a form of externalized cognition that emerges through intensive interpersonal interactions grounded in shared mental models (Fiore et al., 2010). *Dynamic capabilities* are similar to dynamic skills that were discussed at the individual level (Fischer & Bidell, 2006) except that they pertain to collective capabilities. There has been some discussion of how such dynamic capabilities are developed among a senior leadership team in corporate organizations (Day et al., 2024). The construct of requisite complexity was discussed at the individual level in terms of matching the level of mental complexity of the individual leader with the level of complexity in the leadership environment. Some attention has been given to how this construct is applicable at higher levels under the construct label of *collective requisite complexity* (Hannah et al., 2011). These process capabilities are fed back to influence the level of collective capabilities and the collective emergent states in the model, as proposed by open systems theory.

The remainder of this chapter will delve into greater detail on the proximal and distal indicators of collective leadership development. The processes parallel to some extent the individual leader development model in terms of incorporating a two-stage moderated mediational perspective. First-stage moderation occurs when shared experiences or more formal collective interventions help transform the initial level of collective capabilities into collective emergent states. Second-stage moderation proposes intensive interpersonal interactions over time as factors shaping these emergent states into long-term or distal indicators of leadership development.

Most of what is known about collective perspectives to various constructs, including leadership development, is based on the teams literature. What constitutes a team can range from a two-person dyad to a much larger collective. Although an organization is rarely conceptualized as a team, the approach described here could incorporate an entire organization as with those that have been designated as Deliberately Developmental Organizations in which the work of an organization is accomplished through supporting the individual and collective development of its members (Kegan & Lahey, 2016).

## Collective Emergent States in Leadership Development

When individuals join a collective such as a group, team, or organization, they bring certain individual capabilities with them. These are typically in the form of human capital such as knowledge, skills, and abilities and other intrapersonal capabilities. These contributions include individual leadership capabilities that may have been developed as part of a leader development system. Even if that is not the case, individuals do not join collectives as blank slates (*tabula rasa*) but bring leadership potential and capabilities that combine with others' leadership capabilities and potential in forming the initial collective capabilities. The trick is in turning these individual capabilities into something that is defined and operates synergistically at the collective level. This is the mandate of leadership development.

The first stage in this process of leadership development at the collective level is to have the designated group or team engage in shared experiences. These can either be designed as formal interventions guided by an external facilitator or more informal interactions that come about from engaging in shared work. Much as experience for development is thought to be an impactful way to develop individual leaders, providing or exposing a collective group to shared experiences offers first-stage opportunities to shape the collective capabilities into proximal indicators of leadership development. As introduced earlier in this chapter, these proximal indicators can be operationalized as collective emergent states. Each of these proposed emergent states are discussed next.

### *Psychological Safety*

What makes a collective group or team psychologically safe? What is the value of this emergent state to the collective? The construct of psychological safety has been around the literature on work organizations for decades but has experienced a recent resurgence of interest (Edmondson & Lei, 2014). Briefly stated, psychological safety is a shared belief (not an individual one) that interpersonal risk-taking with others in the collective will not result in harm (i.e., it is safe). Harm can be in the form of informal sanctions, ridicule, ostracizing behavior, or anything else that might jeopardize the psychological wellbeing or likelihood of speaking up (i.e., exercising voice) of one or more members of the collective. In short, psychological safety is a group norm that emerges in a collective (typically studied at the team level) in which members of the collective feel safe to expose personal vulnerabilities.

The individual best known for bringing psychological safety to the forefront in the scholarly literature is Dr. Amy Edmondson of the Harvard Business School. An empirical paper published in 1999 demonstrated that among 51 manufacturing work teams, psychological safety was positively associated with team learning (Edmondson, 1999). Furthermore, team learning mediated the relationship between psychological safety and team performance. The power of psychological safety has been demonstrated in all sorts of work teams, including surgical teams (Edmondson, 2003), healthcare and educational organizations (Edmondson et al., 2016), among others. An accessible summary of this research including cases and cogent discussions of important implications can be found in Edmondson's book titled "The Fearless Organization" (Edmondson, 2019).

The efficacy and impact of psychological safety on the learning and performance of work teams were evaluated by researchers at Google. Beginning around 2012, Google launched what they called Project Aristotle to determine the most important factors in building successful work teams (Duhigg, 2016). Of the hundreds of groups that they studied internally, researchers identified "group norms"—those informal rules about how the collective operates—as the single most important factor in influencing successful groups and teams. Of those group norms, of which there are hundreds of possibilities, it was those norms around interpersonal trust and mutual respect in which individuals could share their personal vulnerabilities and be themselves that were most important. In short, having psychological safety was determined to be the most important factor in creating successful Google work groups.

Meta-analytic review of over 130 independent samples and 22,000 individuals nested with approximately 5,000 groups/teams indicated that psychological safety was positively related to task performance and organizational citizenship behaviors over and beyond related concepts such as positive leader relations and work engagement (Frazier et al., 2017). It was also found that psychological safety is related to other desirable team features, including behavioral (e.g., learning, information sharing) and affective outcomes (e.g., engagement, satisfaction). As reminder, psychological safety is an affective collective emergent state (Rapp et al., 2021) indicating that it pertains to feelings, attitudes, and emotions of the collective as a whole.

But what about development? If psychological safety is important to leadership development as a proximal emergent state at the collective level as proposed, how does it help facilitate that development? Two underlying mechanisms are team learning and interpersonal trust. Development rarely if ever occurs when the members of a collective are holding back in terms of what they are thinking and feeling. Having the trust that others in the collective will not hurt someone for showing vulnerability is a prerequisite for sharing information, learning at the collective level, as well as developing a shared mental model about leadership. Shared mental models are the next collective emergent state to be discussed.

### *Shared Mental Models*

The notion of a so-called group mind has been in the scholarly literature for a long time, with questions raised as to whether it is a metaphor or a viable scientific construct (Klimoski & Mohammed, 1994). In more recent times, researchers have operationalized and measured team mental models in ways that have shown they are more than a metaphor, demonstrating empirically that mental model convergence predicts team effectiveness as mediated by team processes (Mathieu et al., 2000). In essence, developing a shared mental model enhances the adaptability of collectives in facing task and environmental challenges through better decision-making (Cannon-Bowers et al., 1993).

Shared mental models represent a cognitive form of collective emergent states (Rapp et al., 2021). Meta-analytic evidence accumulated across 231 correlations ($k = 65$ independent studies) of team cognition (another term for shared mental models) and its relationship to teamwork processes, motivational states, and performance outcomes suggests that team cognition predicts a variety of team outcomes and is related to effective teamwork (DeChurch & Mesmer-Magnus, 2010a). When it comes to leadership development, the shared mental model of interest is around leadership. To what extent does a collective share an understanding of how leadership is enacted when faced with complex adaptive challenges (i.e., those issues that require leadership as opposed to being solved by a technical solution)? Having a shared understanding of leadership, how it should be enacted collectively, and when leadership is needed is thought to enhance the adaptability of a collective and therefore enhancing its effectiveness.

Although performance and effectiveness are important outcomes associated with the application of leadership development across situations, they are not the same thing as development. In a similar way to what was discussed at the individual level, the evaluation of developmental outcomes should focus on a longitudinal study of changes in the specific target of developmental interest and not on performance outcomes, either at the individual or collective level. The thinking is that what is developed as a function of leadership development needs to be applied in appropriate leadership situations to enhance effectiveness and, ultimately, performance. But, again, leadership performance effectiveness and leadership development are two different questions and should be studied separately.

Shared mental models have been measured in different ways (Mohammed et al., 2000), but the good news is that they can be measured! Meta-analyses have indicated that there are differences in empirical relationships with performance outcomes depending on how shared mental models are measured, but regardless of the operationalization or measurement there are positive effects with different outcomes (DeChurch & Mesmer-Magnus, 2010b). Again, the focus here is on the development of leadership and not collective performance. Understanding how collective mental models of leadership are developed as emergent states is an important proximal indicator that more long-term collective development is occurring, especially in terms of macrocognition. As will be discussed later in this chapter, macrocognition is conceptualized as a distal indicator of leadership development.

### *Collective Leadership Efficacy*

Collective efficacy is defined as a shared belief in a collective's capabilities to organize and execute appropriate courses of action (Bandura, 1997). It is a form of collective confidence to successfully engage in a particular set of actions rather than confidence in general. That is why it is important to reference leadership as the target of this collective confidence (i.e., efficacy) and to ensure it refers to the collective and not individual unit of analysis.

Collective efficacy is a type of motivational collective emergent state (Rapp et al., 2021). Specifically, collective leadership efficacy motivates the enactment of leadership. Having a shared mental model is also important, but unless the collective feels some shared sense of being able to "execute appropriate courses of action" (Bandura, 1997, p. 477) when it comes to leadership, there is less likelihood of engaging in collective leadership.

When referring to leadership, collective efficacy pertains to a shared belief that the collective can successfully engage in leadership processes when facing a complex adaptive challenge. Although there are differences between team efficacy and collective efficacy (Gully et al., 2002), it is mainly a matter of levels of analysis. Team efficacy is focused on the shared beliefs of a team whereas according to Gully et al. collective efficacy can refer to departments, organizations, and even nations. Collective efficacy is the more inclusive construct and is used here, although the research evidence is mainly focused on team efficacy and the application to leadership development is mainly at the team level. A straightforward explanation of this approach, which is foundational to multilevel research, is provided by renowned scholars in the field of multilevel methods and analysis (Klein & Kozlowski, 2000, p. 216):

> Team or collective efficacy…is quite different than team members' average self-efficacy. Recall the example of the orchestra: Orchestra members may rate their individual musical self-efficacy high, but nevertheless rate their team efficacy—their confidence in the ability of the orchestra as a whole—quite low.

Measuring collective leadership efficacy is straightforward having only one recommended approach as compared with shared mental models that can be operationalized in several different ways. Collective efficacy is measured via self-reports; however, the referent is the collective and not the individual. In other words, the recommended approach does not ask members to rate their individual leadership self-efficacy and then averages those ratings. Instead, the referent for the rating is the collective. An important evaluation tool is the degree to which members agree on their ratings. There are statistical procedures to estimate the degree of within-group agreement or homogeneity. If the evidence suggests relatively modest or low agreement among member of the collective in their ratings of collective leadership efficacy (the rule of thumb is at least 80% agreement) then the evidence does not support the existence of the efficacy construct at the collective level. It would be individual-level perspectives on collective leadership efficacy that varies across members of the collective. There is no "sharedness" to the construct.

The lack of agreement in collective leadership efficacy ratings can be important diagnostic information at the practical level. It suggests that the collective could benefit from additional opportunities to engage in collective leadership activities to develop a stronger sense of a shared sense of leadership efficacy at the collective level. Having a strong sense of a collective leadership efficacy is important to develop as an emergent state as it is something that supports the development of dynamic capabilities as more distal indicators of leadership development.

### *Collective Leadership Identification*

The notion of collective identification is grounded in the social identity literature and refers to the degree that members identify with a collective (Carmeli & Shteigman, 2010). Researchers have proposed that the self consists of three fundamental self-representations: (1) *individual* self that is based on unique traits and values, (2) *relational* self that is based on different dyadic relationships, and (3) *collective* self that is based on group membership (Sedikides & Brewer, 2001). It has a different meaning when the referent is leadership and that is an important distinction when the focus is on leadership development.

The three levels of self were extended to the literature on leader development. Researchers have proposed that as leaders develop their identities expand in focus from individual to include relational and then collective levels (Day & Harrison, 2007; Lord & Hall, 2005). Thus, leader identity is thought to change in terms of its underlying level of inclusiveness, ranging from least inclusive (individual) to most inclusive (collective) as a function of the developmental process. The focus in leadership development is on collective identification and is one of the key emergent states serving as a proximal indicator of collective development. When the focus of identification is on collective leadership, it is an amalgam or hybrid of cognitive, affective, as well as motivational emergent states (Rapp et al., 2021).

One way to think about this change is that the referent in leadership shifts from "I" as individual leader, to "us" as in dyadic leadership such as leader-member exchange theory (Liden et al., 1997), to "we" in terms of collective identification as the source for leadership. To have a collective leadership identity, it recognizes that leadership is a product of systems structure and processes (Salancik et al., 1975). That is, leadership is a resource that is drawn from the collective and not solely something that an individual in a formal leadership position provides as input. This is not a conventional way of thinking about leadership. It requires developing shared mental models that support this novel and collective way of thinking about leadership as a systems resource. Chapter 7 addresses this issue and elaborates on how collective leadership identification can be operationalized and measured using social network analysis.

Collective leadership identification does not negate either an individual or relational leadership identity. Individuals have numerous identities at different levels, most of which are latent or dormant at any given time. An emergent state involving collective leadership would not prevent falling back to a relational or individual leader identity when appropriate. It is like other aspects of mental complexity and leadership. A more complex and inclusive way of thinking about leadership transcends but does not replace those lower level models.

One of the biggest obstacles to developing a collective emergent state that identifies leadership at a collective level are dominant stakeholders in the system (e.g., the CEO and other top-level leaders) who see leadership as their responsibility (Day et al., 2024). Leadership and power are intertwined practically and theoretically (Sturm et al., 2021). Some leaders view the development of more collective and inclusive leadership to be a threat to their position—and their egos! As noted by Day et al. (p. 306):

> By being overly directive, autocratic, and establishing the illusion of infallibility, a CEO can undermine any collective sense of leadership identity among the senior team. What is necessary is a CEO who sets the appropriate norms around transparency...and models behavior that reinforces those norms.

More insightful leaders recognize that no individual can have all the answers, especially in such dynamic and complex environments where most organizations operate. The alternative is to develop a collective capacity for leadership rather than relying on a few individuals to create the kind of leadership needed for successful adaptation to complex, ill-structured problems that do not have a single recognized correct solution, which are sometimes called wicked problems (Rittel & Webber, 1973).

As the focus of leadership development is a collective—usually an intact organizational team such as a senior leadership team—the developmental experiences needed to be shared by that collective. The emergent states proposed as integral to development in the form of psychological safety, shared mental models of leadership, collective leadership efficacy, and collective leadership identification are not mutually exclusive. Instead, these collective emergent states are mutually reinforcing in facilitating longer term development of a collective leadership capacity. Although it is possible to cultivate a smaller set of these emergent states, they will not be as potent in the long term as having all four emerge in the collective.

The next section addresses these distal indicators of collective leadership development. One important consideration is that these are not end states because there are no end states in development! These are indicators of a collective capacity for leadership that are returned as inputs into the developmental system through feedback loops.

## Long-term Collective Leadership Development

When considering or studying collective leadership development the focus is on the relationships or connections among members of the collective. That is why the second stage of the leadership development model proposes intensive interpersonal interactions as the process that shapes collective emergent states at the proximal level to more distal indicators of leadership development in the forms of macrocognition, dynamic capabilities, and requisite complexity that denote a collective capacity for leadership.

Proposing that leadership "exists" between members of some collective (e.g., team, work group) acknowledges that commitments, trust, and respect are forged through relationships and interactions among people engaged intensively in shared work. This is at the core of a social capital perspective on leadership development, which extends beyond dyadic relationships to consider the structural properties of the collective (Carter et al., 2024). Fortunately, there are statistical tools and techniques to facilitate the operationalization and understanding of the structured pattern of relationships among members of a collective. Social network analysis is a powerful way to understand social capital in a collective and how it can change (i.e., develop) over time.

Before turning attention to a network approach to leadership development in Chapter 7, this section will next review the individual components proposed as key indicators of more distal leadership development. A caveat to note is that these more long-term characteristics of leadership development have less supporting evidence as compared with the indicators of individual leader development. The work is mainly at the theoretical level for the time being.

### *Macrocognition*

Cognition is a stalwart of individual psychology and research going back decades. Much of the research on cognition has been conducted as experiments in laboratory settings where an overarching goal is to understand cognitive processes through reducing cognition to its smallest parts. Another term for this longstanding experimental approach might be *microcognition* given the emphasis on deconstructing things into its essential building blocks. Some researchers have argued that this traditional approach to studying cognition is useful as basic science, but it overlooks that "cognition in the wild" (Hutchins, 1995) is a very different matter. What happens in natural settings (i.e., in the wild) occurs under conditions that are different from the typical laboratory context.

One approach to studying what has been called *macrocognition* is through naturalistic decision-making processes. That is, through the study of cognition in naturalistic contexts, which often include complex decisions involving a great deal of information, made under time pressure with real-world implications, ambiguous goals, and many extraneous variables that cannot be controlled (Klein et al., 2003). Such conditions make naturalistic decision-making messy. Given that leadership development is targeted at developing collectives that will make decisions under these kinds of natural (i.e., messy) conditions it makes sense to focus on macrocognition and its underlying processes.

Another way to conceptualize macrocognition assumes that a cognitive system is not necessarily bounded in a single individual but can be distributed across multiple people and the environment (Clark, 2001; Fiore et al., 2010; Hutchins, 1995). In terms of problem-solving, a perspective based on this form of macrocognition assumes that problem solutions emerge through interaction among members of a collective.

Leadership can be considered as one form of complex problem-solving. Leadership development is therefore relevant for collective forms of conceptualizing and enacting leadership in complex environments dealing with ill-structured (i.e., wicked) problems. A key question thus becomes how can macrocognition be developed in teams and other collectives?

Understanding how macrocognition develops is on the cutting edge of team science. At present, there are more questions than answers; however, the field continues to develop theoretically and to a lesser extent empirically. One developmental practice that has been discussed in the macrocognition literature is that of scaffolding (Fiore & Wiltshire, 2016). There is a parallel in the individual development literature in which scaffolding refers to providing guidance and support to an individual that facilitates thinking or doing that is slightly beyond their current capability (Fischer, 1980; Vygotsky, 1978, 2012/1934). The form of scaffolding addressed in the macrocognition literature involves technological scaffolds that:

> help teams externalize and share knowledge by allowing for the representation and discussion of information and ideas, provide storage and access to team-level information allowing for more informed comparisons and evaluations, and act as a means for social-cognitive interaction that facilitates conversation, communication, and collaboration (Fiore & Wiltshire, p. 11).

Given the rapid advances in artificial intelligence—and no doubt with more breakthroughs to come—the notion of technological scaffolds in facilitating collective macrocognition as part of long-term leadership development is intriguing. But technology alone is insufficient to motivate collective leadership development because it still requires intensive interpersonal interactions among members of a collective. There is little if any research evidence on how technology can help scaffold and support collective development, but the macrocognition literature provides sound reasons why this potentially valuable prospect should be further developed theoretically and tested empirically.

### *Dynamic Capabilities and Collective Requisite Complexity*

The constructs of dynamic capabilities and collective requisite complexity will be discussed together as it is difficult to disentangle their interrelationships. The origins of dynamic capabilities can be found in the macro strategy literature focused on sources of competitive advantage for firms in times of accelerated technological change (Teece et al., 1997). Although the origins of the construct are macro, there are microfoundations of these firm-level advantages (Teece, 2007). One such advantage can be found in the dynamic capabilities developed in a senior leadership team (Day et al., 2024) or other strategic collectives. What are such dynamic capabilities at the team or collective level and how are they developed?

At the level of a leadership collective, dynamic capabilities are needed to help adapt to the complexity in which an organization operates. Relatedly, *requisite complexity* refers to the match between an individual, team, or organization's level of complexity and the associated level of complexity in the environment. Within organizational collectives, especially those with strategic decision-making responsibilities, greater complexity promotes a deeper understanding of environmental forces and is essential in devising novel responses to complex adaptive challenges (Hannah et al., 2011). Developing the senior leadership team or other strategic collective for dynamic capabilities is inherently about enhancing the collective requisite complexity of a collective in relation to its external operating environment.

Researchers working in this area have differentiated static versus dynamic forms of collective requisite complexity (Hannah et al., 2011). The static form is like an emergent state and can be considered as something of a "snapshot" of the level of requisite complexity in the collective. The dynamic form is more interesting because it is, well, dynamic! Dynamic is interesting because it implies change over time. Dynamic requisite complexity is a capability that creates the necessary amount of collective complexity needed in facing a particular complex adaptive challenge requiring leadership. The assumption is that every leadership challenge does not present the same level of complexity, so the collective must generate the appropriate requisite complexity to match with the specific adaptive challenge in the environment. This is a dynamic process that makes sense at a conceptual or theoretical level; however, there are few examples of this in action and no empirical study of it in the leadership or leadership development literatures. It is blue sky territory for future researchers.

An assumption on which collective requisite complexity rests is that the external leadership environment is, indeed, complex. If the environment is not sufficiently complex, then the capacity that is developed in the team is not of much use and might even be counterproductive. That said, it is difficult to imagine any competitive environment nowadays that is not complex. Given the trends toward deregulation, increasingly rapid technological advances, and intense global competition in many industries there is plenty of evidence to suggest that many leadership teams across most if not all industries are wrestling with rapidly increasing complexity. It is also a certainty that no single leader can figure it all out on their own. That is one big reason why there is such a need to think in terms of a collective capacity for leadership rather than only developing individual leaders.

There is no single developmental recipe and very few operating examples of where such dynamic capabilities and collective requisite complexity have been realized (although see Day et al., 2024, for a few case study examples). Part of the issue besides the general ambiguity of the construct of dynamic capabilities is that old devil time. It takes time for a collective to develop and that cannot happen solely in a classroom or artificial laboratory setting. The collective needs time working together (but how much?) in ways that require intense interpersonal interactions for these distal indicators of leadership development to gel.

An example of this can be found in a global cosmetics company in which the CEO made significant training investments in developing feedback skills among members of the senior leadership team and modeled shared leadership (see Day et al., 2024, pp. 301–302). One way this is done is by soliciting views from members of the senior team on topics outside of their functional expertise. This type of intensive interpersonal interaction broadens the perspectives of the team beyond their individual portfolios, which is supported by regular assignments outside the executives' respective areas of core expertise. The CEO also involves board members in developing knowledge and skills in various areas outside of an executive's core functional expertise. The key leverage point in this is the implementation of ongoing interpersonal interactions among the team members and the board to help further develop a shared mental model into things that could be considered dynamic capabilities and macrocognition.

Despite this case study example, what is being discussed is mostly aspirational rather than reality in organizations. Nonetheless, the world is not getting any less complex. Being able to work collaboratively as a leadership collective will require a lot of intensive work over a long period of time. The specifics around these parameters (i.e., intensity of interactions, time scales) need further theoretical scrutiny and much more empirical research.

## Implications of Developing Collective Capacity for Leadership

The definition of leader development proposed earlier in this volume and elsewhere (e.g., Day, 2000; Day & Dragoni, 2015) suggests that it is based on enhancing the capacity of an individual to be effective in leadership roles and processes. The case has also been made that leadership development is different because the focus is on developing a collective capacity for leadership that is greater than the sum of its parts. One implication of this assertion is that investing solely in individual development will take an organization only so far in the complex world of today and tomorrow in terms of its collective leadership potential.

To develop a collective capacity for leadership—regardless of the organizational level—the focus of development must be on the collective and not the individual leader. That does not mean that individual leader development can or should be ignored. Rather, collective leadership development requires highly developed individual leaders because it challenges individuals to think and act in ways that are different from the norm. To do so requires at least a modicum of attention on individual leader development in terms of enhancing leadership-related skills, competencies, and self-views. But different thinking also means thinking that is more advanced, more complex, with more potential for adapting to so-called wicked problems (Rittel & Webber, 1973) that require nontraditional methods and perhaps nonlinear collective thinking to address.

Rather than developing intrapersonal-based human capital, a leadership development focus is on the relationships or connections among members of the collective. In this manner, the value creation is grounded in social capital, or the potential for leadership that resides between people that is created through ongoing interpersonal interactions. Instead of adopting a strict individualistic, leader-centric premise regarding leadership and its development, a collective approach adopts a relational perspective grounded in commitment, mutual respect, and interpersonal trust (Day, 2000).

A relevant question to consider is how does leadership development differ from team development interventions? There is a robust evidence-based literature on team development (Lacerenza et al., 2018). Some of the focus associated with team development is related to leadership, but the evidence-based recommendations provided by Lacerenza and colleagues are directed at enhancing individual leader development and not collective leadership development. Team training and team development are also relevant to the discussion but the focus there is on directly enhancing team performance and not on developing a collective capacity for leadership. There is a difference. As reminder, the focus of this volume is on development and not performance. Development has potential value in improving performance, but these are different foci involving different research questions.

Much of traditional team building involves developing individual teamwork skills. These are important for effective team functioning and performance. But skills building stops short of developing a collective capacity for leadership because much of the recommended approach to team development flows from the literature on individual training, including leadership training (Lacerenza et al., 2017). Developing a collective capacity requires a focus on the collective to engage in shared ways of thinking and acting around leadership based on collective emergent states of psychological safety, shared mental models, collective leadership efficacy, and collective leadership identification. These are not the constructs that current evidence-based team interventions deploy, partly because these collective emergent states require both a focus on the collective as well as longer time scales to achieve compared to the typical training intervention (Day et al., 2021).

The value added by developing a collective capacity for leadership through leadership development initiatives is in enhancing the amount and type of leadership resources that are available. It has been noted that "the issues faced by organizations today are complex and dynamic, requiring responsive, quick, adaptive, and diverse groups of individuals" (Lacerenza et al., 2018, p. 528). It is also the case that assembling a group of highly skilled individual leaders does not ensure that effective collective leadership will result. That is where the value of leadership development adds value in terms of enhancing the leadership resources available to contemporary organizations.

The next chapter takes a deeper look at social network analysis—which is not the same as social networking!—as a lens through which to measure and understand how collectives might develop an overall capacity for leadership. Although the empirical research that has used social network analysis to study development of any kind is sparse, there is a viable proof of concept in the approach. As will be demonstrated, social network analysis and network theory more generally offer concrete recommendations on how to potentially proceed in making further theoretical and empirical advances in the nascent scientific field of leadership development.

## Chapter Summary

- Leadership development refers to developing the capacity of a collective to produce leadership.
- Collectives are usually work groups or teams, but can be larger entities such as departments, business units, or entire organizations.
- The collective comprises the aggregate of individual levels of leadership capacity to determine its initial collective capacity.
- The aggregate collective capacity is transformed to collective emergent states through shared collective experiences or interventions.
- Collective emergent states in the form of psychological safety, shared mental models, leadership efficacy, and collective identification represent the proximal indicators of leadership development.
- Collective emergent states can be transformed into distal indicators of collective leadership development through intensive interpersonal interactions over time.
- The most appropriate markers or indicators of a collective capacity for leadership—which is the long-term target of leadership development—are macrocognition, dynamic capabilities, and collective requisite complexity, especially the dynamic form of requisite complexity.
- Leadership development differs from team development in that the typical unit focus is on the collective rather than the individual and that longer time scales are involved.

- Developing a collective capacity for leadership adds valuable resources in the form of additional ways for collectives to meet the complex adaptive challenges across increasingly uncertain competitive environments.

## References

Bandura, A. (1997). *Self-efficacy: The exercise of control*. Freeman.

Cannon-Bowers, J. A., Salas, E., & Converse, S. (1993). Shared mental models in expert team decision making. In N. J. Castellan (Ed.), *Individual and group decision making: Current issues* (pp. 221–246). Lawrence Erlbaum Associates.

Carmeli, A., & Shteigman, A. (2010). Top management team behavioral integration in small-sized firms: A social identity perspective. *Group Dynamics: Theory, Research, and Practice, 14*(4), 318. https://doi.org/10.1037/a0018254

Carter, D. R., Cullen-Lester, K. L., Solanelles, P., Jones, J. M., & Wormington, S. V. (2024). Uncovering patterns of strategic leadership networks to support organizational agility. In S. Zaccaro, N. J. Hiller, & R. Klimoski (Eds.), *Senior leadership teams and the agile organization* (pp. 140–165). Routledge.

Clark, A. (2001). *Mindware*. Oxford University Press.

Day, D., Bastardoz, N., Bisbey, T., Reyes, D., & Salas, E. (2021). Unlocking human potential through leadership training and development initiatives. *Behavioral Science & Policy, 7*(1), 41–54. https://doi.org/10.1177/237946152100700105

Day, D. V. (2000). Leadership development: A review in context. *The Leadership Quarterly, 11*(4), 581–613. https://doi.org/10.1016/S1048-9843(00)00061-8

Day, D. V., Conger, J. A., & Dannhäuser, L. (2024). Developing the senior leader team for dynamic capabilities. In S. J. Zaccaro, N. J. Hiller, & R. Klimoski (Eds.), *Senior leadership teams and the agile organization* (pp. 291–316). Routledge. https://doi.org/10.4324/9780429353161-11

Day, D. V., & Dragoni, L. (2015). Leadership development: An outcome-oriented review based on time and levels of analyses. *Annual Review of Organizational Psychology and Organizational Behavior, 2*, 133–156. https://doi.org/10.1146/annurev-orgpsych-032414-111328

Day, D. V., Gronn, P., & Salas, E. (2004). Leadership capacity in teams. *The Leadership Quarterly, 15*(6), 857–880. https://doi.org/10.1016/j.leaqua.2004.09.001

Day, D. V., & Harrison, M. M. (2007). A multilevel, identity-based approach to leadership development. *Human Resource Management Review, 17*(4), 360–373. https://doi.org/10.1016/j.hrmr.2007.08.007

DeChurch, L. A., & Mesmer-Magnus, J. R. (2010a). The cognitive underpinnings of effective teamwork: A meta-analysis. *Journal of Applied Psychology, 95*(1), 32–53. https://doi.org/10.1037/a0017328

DeChurch, L. A., & Mesmer-Magnus, J. R. (2010b). Measuring shared team mental models: A meta-analysis. *Group Dynamics: Theory Research and Practice, 14*(1), 1–14. https://doi.org/10.1037/a0017455

Duhigg, C. (2016, 25 February). What Google learned from its quest to build the perfect team. *The New York Time Magazine*. https://www.nytimes.com/2016/02/28/magazine/what-google-learned-from-its-quest-to-build-the-perfect-team.html

Edmondson, A. (1999). Psychological safety and learning behavior in work teams. *Administrative Science Quarterly, 44*(2), 350–383. https://doi.org/10.2307/2666999

Edmondson, A. C. (2003). Speaking up in the operating room: How team leaders promote learning in interdisciplinary action teams. *Journal of Management Studies, 40*(6), 1419–1452.

Edmondson, A. C. (2019). *The fearless organization: Creating psychological safety in the workplace for learning, innovation, and growth*. Wiley.

Edmondson, A. C., Higgins, M., Singer, S., & Weiner, J. (2016). Understanding psychological safety in health care and education organizations: A comparative perspective. *Research in Human Development, 13*(1), 65–83. https://doi.org/10.1080/15427609.2016.1141280

Edmondson, A. C., & Lei, Z. (2014). Psychological safety: The history, renaissance, and future of an interpersonal construct. *Annual Review of Organizational Psychology and Organizational Behavior, 1*, 23–43. https://doi.org/10.1146/annurev-orgpsych-031413-091305

Fiore, S. M., Rosen, M. A., Smith-Jentsch, K. A., Salas, E., Letsky, M., & Warner, N. (2010). Toward an understanding of macrocognition in teams: Predicting processes in complex collaborative contexts. *Human Factors, 523*(2), 203–224. https://doi.org/10.1177/0018720810369807

Fiore, S. M., & Wiltshire, T. J. (2016). Technology as teammate: Examining the role of external cognition in support of team cognitive processes [Hypothesis and Theory]. *Frontiers in Psychology, 7*, 1531. https://doi.org/10.3389/fpsyg.2016.01531

Fischer, K. W. (1980). A theory of cognitive development: The control and construction of hierarchies of skills. *Psychological Review, 87*(6), 477–531. https://doi.org/10.1037/0033-295x.87.6.477

Fischer, K. W., & Bidell, T. R. (2006). Dynamic development of action, thought, and emotion. In W. Damon & R. M. Lerner (Eds.), *Theoretical models of*

*human development: Handbook of child psychology* (6th ed., Vol. 1, pp. 313–399). Wiley.
Frazier, M. L., Fainshmidt, S., Klinger, R. L., Pezeshkan, A., & Vracheva, V. (2017). Psychological safety: A meta-analytic review and extension. *Personnel Psychology, 70*(1), 113–165. https://doi.org/10.1111/peps.12183
Goldstein, J. (1999). Emergence as a construct: History and issues. *Emergence, 1*(1), 49–72. https://doi.org/10.1207/s15327000em0101_4
Gully, S. M., Incalcaterra, K. A., Joshi, A., & Beaubien, J. M. (2002). A meta-analysis of team-efficacy, potency, and performance: Interdependence and level of analysis as moderators of observed relationships. *Journal of Applied Psychology, 87*(5), 819. https://doi.org/10.1037/0021-9010.87.5.819
Hannah, S. T., Lord, R. G., & Pearce, C. L. (2011). Leadership and collective requisite complexity. *Organizational Psychology Review, 3*(3), 215–238. https://doi.org/10.1177/2041386611402116
Hutchins, E. (1995). *Cognition in the wild*. MIT Press.
Kegan, R., & Lahey, L. L. (2016). *An everyone culture: Becoming a deliberately developmental organization*. Harvard Business Review Press.
Klein, G., Ross, K. G., Moon, B. M., Klein, D. E., Hoffman, R. R., & Hollnagel, E. (2003). Macrocognition. *IEEE Intelligent Systems, 18*(3), 81–85. https://doi.org/10.1109/MIS.2003.1200735
Klein, K. J., & Kozlowski, S. W. J. (2000). From micro to meso: Critical steps in conceptualizing and conducting multilevel research. *Organizational Research Methods, 3*(3), 211–236. https://doi.org/10.1177/109442810033001
Klimoski, R., & Mohammed, S. (1994). Team mental model: Construct or metaphor? *Journal of Management, 20*(2), 403–437. https://doi.org/10.1016/0149-2063(94)90021-3
Lacerenza, C. N., Marlow, S. L., Tannenbaum, S. I., & Salas, E. (2018). Team development interventions: Evidence-based approaches for improving teamwork. *American Psychologist, 73*(4), 517. https://doi.org/10.1037/amp0000295
Lacerenza, C. N., Reyes, D. L., Marlow, S. L., Joseph, D. L., & Salas, E. (2017). Leadership training design, delivery, and implementation: A meta-analysis. *Journal of Applied Psychology, 102*(12), 1686–1718. https://doi.org/10.1037/apl0000241.supp
Liden, R. C., Sparrowe, R. T., & Wayne, S. J. (1997). Leader-member exchange theory: The past and potential for the future. *Research in Personnel and Human Resource Management, 15*(1), 47–119.
Lord, R. G., & Hall, R. J. (2005). Identity, deep structure and the development of leadership skill. *The Leadership Quarterly, 16*(4), 591–615. https://doi.org/10.1016/j.leaqua.2005.06.003

Marks, M. A., Mathieu, J. E., & Zaccaro, S. J. (2001). A temporally based framework and taxonomy of team processes. *Academy of Management Review, 26*(3), 356–376. https://doi.org/10.5465/amr.2001.4845785

Mathieu, J. E., Heffner, T. S., Goodwin, G. F., Salas, E., & Cannon-Bowers, J. A. (2000). The influence of shared mental models on team process and performance. *Journal of Applied Psychology, 85*(2), 273. https://doi.org/10.1037/0021-9010.85.2.273

Mohammed, S., Klimoski, R., & Rentsch, J. R. (2000). The measurement of team mental models: We have no shared schema. *Organizational Research Methods, 3*(2), 123–165. https://doi.org/10.1177/109442810032001

Rapp, T., Maynard, T., Domingo, M., & Klock, E. (2021). Team emergent states: What has emerged in the literature over 20 years. *Small Group Research, 52*(1), 68–102. https://doi.org/10.1177/1046496420956715

Rittel, H. W. J., & Webber, M. M. (1973). Dilemmas in a general theory of planning. *Policy Sciences, 4*(2), 155–169. https://doi.org/10.1007/BF01405730

Salancik, G. R., Calder, B. J., Rowland, K. M., Leblebici, H., & Conway, M. (1975). Leadership as an outcome of social structure and process. In J. G. Hunt & L. L. Larson (Eds.), *Leadership frontiers* (pp. 81–101). Kent State University.

Sedikides, C., & Brewer, M. B. (Eds.). (2001). *Individual self, relational self, collective self*. Psychology Press.

Sturm, R. E., Herz, H., & Antonakis, J. (2021). The science of leader power. *The Leadership Quarterly, 32*(4), 101550. https://doi.org/10.1016/j.leaqua.2021.101550

Teece, D. J. (2007). Explicating dynamic capabilities: The nature and microfoundations of (sustainable) enterprise performance. *Strategic Management Journal, 21*(13), 1319–1350. https://doi.org/10.1002/smj.640

Teece, D. J., Pisano, G. P., & Shuen, A. (1997). Dynamic capabilities and strategic management. *Strategic Management Journal, 18*(7), 509–533. https://doi.org/10.1002/(SICI)1097-0266(199708)18:7%3C509::AID-SMJ882%3E3.0.CO;2-Z

Vygotsky, L. (1978). *Mind in society: The development of higher psychological processes*. Harvard University Press.

Vygotsky, L. (2012/1934). *Thought and language* (A. Kozulin, Trans.; revised and expanded ed.). MIT Press.

Waller, M. J., Okhuysen, G. A., & Saghafian, M. (2016). Conceptualizing emergent states: A strategy to advance the study of group dynamics. *Academy of Management Annals, 10*(1), 561–598. https://doi.org/10.1080/19416520.2016.1120958

CHAPTER 7

# Networks and Leadership Development

## Overview of Social Network Analysis (SNA)

The first thing to consider is that social networks are not the same as social networking. The latter is reserved for events where people make professional connections with others, or different websites and apps that track how many connections someone has in the form of friends, professional acquaintances, or some other type of relationship. Social network analysis (SNA) is the more serious science of how individuals are connected to each other and in what ways they are connected in a bounded space. There is even a scholarly, interdisciplinary journal titled *Social Networks* that publishes works on all things related to social networks. Social networking is fun on a personal level (e.g., Facebook) and possibly helpful professionally (e.g., LinkedIn). SNA is a serious science. But make no mistake: These networking organizations use SNA to track you and your relationships. How else would they know what to sell you?

Here is a brief example of how these two different kinds of network perspectives intersect. In 2022, researchers at LinkedIn and a few premier academic institutions such as Harvard, Stanford, and MIT published an article in *Science*, which is one of the best journals in all of, well, science (Rajkumar et al., 2022). The results were based on data collected across multiple large-scale randomized experiments with LinkedIn users over a five-year period involving the professional networks of over 20 million people. Big data meets network science.



D. V. Day, *Developing Leaders and Leadership*,
https://doi.org/10.1007/978-3-031-59068-9_7

Of scientific interest was testing a well-known theory involving the so-called strength of weak ties (Granovetter, 1973), which predicts that who you are connected to indirectly through others (i.e., weak ties) is more likely to provide you with successful job leads compared to those who you are connected to directly (i.e., strong ties). The theory behind this thinking is that weak ties provide novel or fresh information whereas direct ties involve individuals motivated to help with someone known directly.

Researchers randomly manipulated the LinkedIn algorithm called "People You May Know" that recommends new connections to users. The bottom line is that the results supported the strength of weak ties theory and because it was a randomized experiment that varied the prevalence of weak ties in a user's network, it allowed for strong causal inferences to be drawn. This was a longitudinal study in which two billion new ties and 600,00 new jobs were created. How do we know? Well, that is what LinkedIn does! It allows users to post job and career mobility. Although LinkedIn is a professional networking site, researchers were able to conduct a rigorous field experiment using SNA to test a highly regarded network theory. And all this was done without the users having a clue their network recommendations were being manipulated. We will cover research ethics a little later in the chapter. Just kidding.

The notion of ties or links is a core SNA concept. This is familiar to Facebook and LinkedIn users because the number of "friends" (whether they are really friends doesn't seem to matter) and professional contacts is known to users. This is an overall count of the number of ties (called degree in SNA terminology) in an egocentric network. What can also be estimated quantitatively and displayed visually in a sociogram is the pattern or structure of those links across the entire network. This is one of the biggest contributions of SNA to understanding human cognition and behavior, and potentially leadership development. What kinds of value are created by different patterns of SNA links or connections? This is the essence of social capital (Adler & Kwon, 2002; Kwon & Adler, 2014), which will be discussed in more detail a little later in the chapter.

Before going into further detail, it might be helpful to provide a primer of sorts on SNA. There are a lot of different terms, which is not jargon as much as it is specific scientific and statistical terminology. A key point to remember is that SNA is a potentially important methodology and analytic approach to understanding collective leadership development, how it is created, and how it changes over time. These important issues have an underlying connection to network science and SNA, which is why a clear and concise overview of the core concepts and metrics of SNA is needed.

### *SNA Primer*

At the risk of coming across as a nitpicker, primer when used in the way it is intended here (i.e., a small introductory piece of writing) is pronounced as "primmer" and not "pry-mer." The latter is a material used to prepare a surface for painting or finishing with a different material. I apologize for the pedanticism, but I am a product of an elementary school teacher who always corrected me when mispronouncing this word. Lesson over!

There are some excellent resources to learn more about SNA in the social sciences, including books (Borgatti et al., 2024; Kilduff & Tsai, 2003; Wasserman & Faust, 1994), book chapters (Brass, 2012), and journal articles (Borgatti et al., 2009; Kilduff & Brass, 2010; Kilduff & Lee, 2020). To be as clear as possible, ***social*** refers to interpersonal relationships, ***network*** refers to an underlying pattern or structure, and ***analysis*** refers to the various ways to systematically understand a social network. For our purposes of understanding leadership development systematically, a social network consists of individuals (such as friends, acquaintances, and coworkers) connected by interpersonal relationships.

There are inherent levels of analysis in SNA such that individuals (also called actors or nodes in the network) can occupy more favorable or less favorable positions in the network. At a higher level, the entire network can be analyzed as a collective, with metrics and analytical techniques available to understand social networks at both levels. SNA originated in the sociology literature with a primary concern focused on understanding the structure of social relationships in some bounded space (i.e., a network). That helps explain why the fields of psychology and organizational behavior were slow to pick up on the approach and use it in research. This has changed thanks to researchers who have shown that individual differences in psychological constructs such as cognition and personality are important predictors of an individual's network position (Kilduff & Krackhardt, 1994; Kilduff & Lee, 2020). A social network does not just happen; individuals make choices about who they affiliate with, and those choices are often shaped by what they are like.

*Network Types*

Social networks reflect the informal organization that operates behind the scenes as compared with the formal organization represented in an organizational chart. But just as informal power and informal leadership are often potent forces in how things get done—or not—in organizations, the underlying social networks have a lot of explanatory potential. Note that networks as used here are plural and not singular because there are any number of possible networks of interest in any space. This reflects that there are numerous informal organizations that undergird the formal structure. The type of informal network is based on the type of resources that are flowing or being exchanged in the system.

When trying to understand any social network one of the first questions to ask is what kind of network is this? What is the referent? Some of the more common social networks that have been studied are those related to friendship (who is a friend?), advice (who do you go to for advice?), and communication (who do you communicate or share information with?). There may be some overlap in these different networks, but they refer to different types of resources and SNA is all about understanding how resources flow informally across and among individuals.

A question to consider is whether it makes sense to conceptualize and measure an informal leadership network. There has been some attention to SNA and leadership networks (Balkundi & Kilduff, 2006; Carter et al., 2015; Hoppe & Reinelt, 2010) but it is not a mainstream approach and even less attention given to leadership development (although see Cullen-Lester et al., 2017). What is proposed here is a bit different. The network resource is leadership in the form of informal, emergent leadership (Badura et al., 2022) in terms of leadership perceptions granting leadership status to another informally (DeRue & Ashford, 2010). Rather than attempting to understand who is considered a friend (informal social support resources) or an advisor (informal expertise), the notion of who is considered a leader goes directly to the development of a collective capacity for leadership. That is the intended outcome of leadership development initiatives. Thus, it is not only important to be able to measure collective leadership in a network, but also being able to understand and study how it changes over time. This does not negate the potential importance of other types of networks that are related to leadership emergence, such as influence networks or communication networks.

*SNA Concepts and Measures*

There is a great deal of SNA terminology, which can be daunting. It is especially challenging when dealing with the many different SNA measurement concepts, most of which have a mathematical or statistical foundation. The purpose here is to not try and cover all those possibilities but to focus on the core concepts and principles to provide a general understanding of network theory and SNA. The first thing to remember is that networks are inherently multilevel, and the associated measures can be at the level of the individual actor or the whole network. The five most important concepts at each level are reviewed next. A more complete treatment of individual and whole network measures can be found in Brass (2012).

*Individual Level Concepts and Measures*

A summary of the five most relevant SNA concepts and measures at the individual level is provided in Table 7.1. An *actor* is an individual in a network that is also called a *node* in a network diagram or *sociogram*. Nodes are connected by *links* or *ties*, which are connections between nodes that indicate some sort of relationship (e.g., friendship, advice, communication). These ties can be nondirectional indicating there is some connection but not specifying the direction of the flow of resources. Ties can be directional indicating a one-way flow of resources and usually depicted as a one-way arrow in a sociogram. Ties can also be reciprocal or bidirectional indicating a two-way flow of resources.

The overall pattern of nodes and ties is what is displayed in a sociogram, which can be modeled statistically using techniques such as Exponential Random Graph Modeling (Harris, 2014). The technique was developed to handle the non-independence of network data that also allows for testing predictive hypotheses in a form like logistic regression. The details of the procedure are beyond what is needed to know at a general level about SNA. I mention it to reinforce the point that there is a scientific, mathematical, and statistical basis to social networks and related hypothesis testing procedures.

One of the simplest ways to quantify anything is to count. A concept of interest in SNA pertains to the number and type of links. The number of direct links from an actor to all others in a network is called *degree*. More specifically, *in-degree* refers to the number of incoming links to an actor or node and *out-degree* refers to the number of direct outgoing links to other actors/nodes. In terms of friendships, how many others (*alters*)

**Table 7.1** Five SNA Measures at the Individual Level

| *Measure* | *Description* |
|---|---|
| 1. **Degree**: | Number of direct links with others in the network |
| a. **In-degree**: | Number of direct links to the actor from others (incoming links) |
| b. **Out-degree**: | Number of direct links from the actor to others (outgoing links) |
| 2. **Closeness:** | How easily an individual actor can reach all others in the network |
| 3. **Betweenness**: | Extent to which an individual actor falls between any other two actors on the shortest path between those individual actors |
| 4. **Centrality**: | Extent that an individual actor is central to the network |
| 5. **Structural hole**: | Extent that an individual actor is connected to others (i.e., alters) who are not otherwise connected |

*Note* Adapted from Brass (2012), Table 21.1

identify you as a friend is in-degree whereas how many alters you identify as friends is out-degree. *Closeness* refers to how easily others are reached in a network and is typically measured by averaging the direct and indirect links to all others. The most weight is given to direct links (i.e., strong ties) and indirect links (i.e., weak ties) are assigned weights depending on the number of intervening ties needed to reach an actor more distally in a network. Betweenness gages the extent that an actor mediates the flow of resources between any other two actors. *Centrality* is measured by how central each actor is in the network. Finally, a ***structural hole*** is a gap in the network in which an actor connects otherwise unconnected others (i.e., alters).

There is a very rich literature on structural holes as related to individual and collective competition (Burt, 1992). An actor who occupies a structural hole might hold a competitive advantage in a network because it allows for a tighter control over the flow of resources. But what might be good for an individual actor might not be good for the overall health or competitiveness of the network. An actor who occupies a structural hole is also called a broker or a bridge in the network. A general network sociogram illustrating the concepts of actors, ties, and a structural hole is presented in Fig. 7.1.

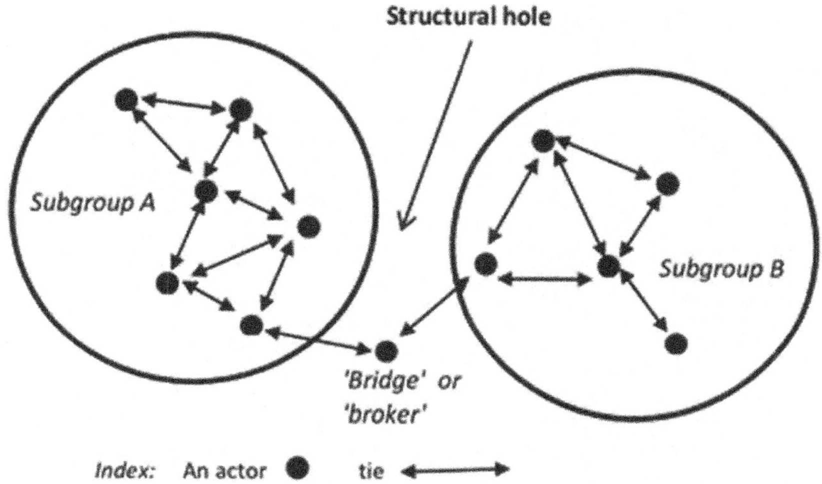


**Fig. 7.1** Sociogram illustrating actors, ties, and a structural hole

*Network Level (Collective) Concepts and Measures*
A summary of the five most relevant SNA concepts and measures at the network or collective level is provided in Table 7.2. These and other SNA measures used to describe entire networks are especially relevant to the discussion on leadership development where the focus is on the collective development of the capacity to produce effective leadership. The *size* of a network is a straightforward count of the number of actors. This implies that there is a boundary around network membership, which can be an arbitrary decision or, more typically, is based on some recognized group membership. *Inclusiveness* is a count of the total number of actors in a network minus the number who have no connections. Another term for these actors with no connections (either in-degree or out-degree) is *social isolate*. Sounds bad and probably is because these actors are considered network members but are unconnected to any other network member directly or indirectly. The ratio of the number of actual ties in a network to the number of possible ties is called *density*. In a leadership network, it is probably desirable to have high inclusiveness and high density in complex envrionments. Both indicators suggest that leadership is distributed in the network. But as will be discussed, sometimes distributed leadership

**Table 7.2** Five SNA measures at the network level

| *Measure* | *Description* |
|---|---|
| 1. **Size**: | Number of nodes or actors in the network |
| 2. **Inclusiveness**: | Size of network minus the number of isolated actors who are not connected to any others |
| 3. **Density**: | Ratio of the number of actual links to the number of possible network links |
| 4. **Centralization**: | Extent to which the network is centered around a few versus many actors |
| 5. **Transitivity**: | Extent that any three actors are connected compared to the possible number of transitive triples |

*Note* Adapted from Brass (2012), Table 21.2

is unnecessary as when the nature of the adaptive challenge is simple and straightforward.

A more direct indicator of distributed leadership is *centralization*. There is a ratio score computed based on the centrality scores of the most central actor relative to others in the network. Ideally, this score is low for a distributed leadership network indicating that leadership is relatively widely shared. The final concept discussed here is *transitivity*, which pertains to the structural balance in the network. It is beyond the scope of this treatment to try and explain the mathematical foundations of this network concept. If interested, more information on network transitivity can be found elsewhere (see Wasserman & Faust, 1994, Chapter 6, on structural balance and transitivity). Briefly, this concept is grounded in Heider's (1958) balance theory that describes a balanced state as one in which the ties between any given triad of actors are positive (or negative) in all aspects. More simply, a balanced triad exists when a friend of a friend also is a friend. An unbalanced tried is when two actors are friends, but the third actor (or alter) is friends with only one of the two others.

The purpose of this section was to provide a brief introduction to SNA and network theory by reviewing a few key concepts. One takeaway is that social networks are inherently multilevel. Measures are available to describe an individual actor's place in the network and there are measures available to describe the network in holistic terms (i.e., whole network). A second takeaway is that at the individual level, network position of an actor is key. It is not so much the raw number of "friends" or "likes" (i.e., ties) that matter as much as the structural position of the actor relative to alters (i.e., other actors) in that network. At the level of the network, the key concern is how that network can be described in terms of density, inclusiveness, and centralization. A composite of these factors at the network level can be used to describe its *social capital*, which is where attention is focused next.

### *Social Capital*

The origins of the social capital construct can be found in the sociology literature. The field of sociology is focused on the scientific study of society; thus, sociological theory and research generally are focused on macro kinds of issues. Sociology is less focused on the scientific study of the individual. That would be psychology. Nonetheless, sociology is interested in ways that macro structural factors can influence individuals, mainly in terms of their economic wellbeing. Even though SNA addresses levels from the individual all the way up to and including world systems (Kilduff & Lee, 2020), the notion of social capital as incorporated into leadership development is focused mainly on the macro network level encompassing a collection of individual actors. Social capital is mainly about the leadership resources embedded in a collective.

The earliest contemporary exploration of social capital was produced by the renowned sociologist Pierre Bourdieu, who defined the concept as "the aggregate of the actual or potential resources which are linked to possession of a durable network of more or less institutionalized relationships of mutual acquaintance or recognition" (Bourdieu, 1985, p. 248). Indeed, that is a very academic definition. A more straightforward description if not a definition of social capital is a set of resources that is inherent in the structure of relations between individual actors (Oh et al., 2004).

Although there is an historical connection between social capital and economic capital (Portes, 1998), that is not the focus here. The resources that are thought to result from collective leadership development are leadership resources. These leadership resources might be predictive downstream of economic advantage through collective adaptability, creative responses, and other factors; however, the key concern is enhancing the collective's capacity to produce effective leadership (Day, 2000).

Not to confuse things, but there are multilevel effects to consider. Network membership confers resources and other benefits on individual actors (Portes, 1998). Researchers have proposed a multilevel and multidimensional theoretical perspective on group or collective social capital (Oh et al., 2006). Research on this concept of collective social capital has demonstrated that the effectiveness of a collective is maximized under certain structural considerations that optimize the flow of social capital, including intragroup closure and bridging relationships that span intergroup boundaries (Oh et al., 2004). Sociological researchers have also claimed that social capital creates human capital through network resources gained by individual members (Coleman, 1988). But it is also the case that "human capital can create social capital, and social capital can create even more social capital" (Brass, 2012, p. 680).

How can this occur in leadership development? A primary way is through feedback loops. Social capital that is created in the development of leadership is fed back to the initial state that is an aggregate of individual leadership capabilities of the members. But it is also the case that the human capital of individual members in the form of leadership capabilities dictate the initial level of collective capabilities. Through developmental processes and feedback loops at the collective level, social capital can create even more social capital related to leadership.

### *Network Change or "Churn"*

Early in this volume there was a discussion of longitudinal research methods. It was argued that development is inherently about change, whether it is at the individual or some broader collective level. Studying change requires appropriate methodological and analytical tools grounded in longitudinal research. This applies to the study of network change as well. Studying leadership development from the perspective of social networks requires a focus on the current network structure as well as how that structure changes because of experience and other more structured interventions. The study of network change is also termed "churn" in the SNA literature. As recommended by top researchers in the field, "We need new theory to capture the benefits and drawbacks of network change in organizations" (Kilduff & Lee, 2020, p. 170). The nascent field of network dynamics is on the cutting edge of SNA theory and research.

There are not many, but there are a few empirical examples of network churn research. One of the earliest published pieces in the management and organizations literature on network churn investigated the role of individual self-monitoring personality in occupying brokerage or bridging positions in a network of employees at a Dutch radiology department (Sasovova et al., 2010). The research results suggest that certain personality types (i.e., high self-monitors or those who are attuned to interpersonal cues from others) were more likely to create and then bridge structural holes in work-related friendship networks. A drawback of this study is that it was not truly longitudinal because it only included two waves of data. As a reminder, longitudinal research requires a minimum of three waves of data. A true longitudinal network study examined the coevolution of network position and individual attitudes across three separate waves of data (Tröster et al., 2019). Both empirical studies were focused mainly on the individual (i.e., actor or node) level of analysis.

A whole network study was conducted to understand leadership churn (i.e., turnover among organizational leaders) and organizational learning in a school district (Caduff et al., 2023). The approach involved a longitudinal exploratory mixed-methods case study that included social network analysis. The purpose was to examine the association between a district restructuring and changes in social structure and organizational learning. The study collected two waves of data across three years and reported (among other things) whole network statistics in years 1 and 3 in the form of number of nodes, and number of ties, network density, average degree, centralization, as well as other SNA statistics. In general, the results suggested that the organizational learning culture within district school sites decreased across time based on leaders' reports, and that leader churn was associated with reduced trust within schools in the district.

This mixed-method (qualitative and quantitative) study incorporating SNA methods and measures might be a relevant model for future researchers to emulate in the study of collective leadership development, especially as early contributions. As noted, SNA approaches to leadership development are nonexistent at least at the empirical level. Starting with a mixed-methods approach to understand leadership development inductively could be very useful in advancing the field.

A final example concerns what the researchers called *network oscillation* (Burt & Merluzzi, 2016). The concept is grounded in the assumption that networks change and evolve with or without formal interventions. Networks are not static entities and that has implications for organizations and its members. Network oscillation refers to a period of deep engagement (i.e., dense connections) in a collective in what can be called a closed network, followed by a period of connecting more selectively (i.e., sparse connections) in an open network in which there are one or more structural holes. This is followed by another period of deep engagement followed by more selective brokering, and so on in repeated cycles of creating a closed and then an open network.

The research reported by Burt and Merluzzi (2016) demonstrated that those actors who created patterns of network oscillation were more successful than those who only engaged in brokering (i.e., occupying a structural hole). At the group or more collective level, others have argued (Oh et al., 2006) and demonstrated empirically (Oh et al., 2004) that there are more and less optimal network configurations in creating resources that define social capital.

A version of these kinds of network oscillation changes has implications for leadership development. Previously, the distal outcome of dynamic capabilities was presented as a collective outcome of leadership development. One type of dynamic capability might be the capability of the network to reconfigure into either a closed or more open configuration depending on the type and complexity of the leadership challenge. Sometimes leadership does not need to be produced by the entire network, such as in cases of strong expertise being held by a particular member in the collective (i.e., network actor). In such instances, the network can reconfigure in a more centralized or open form. But when the adaptive challenge is such that there is no single expert with a solution or viable way forward, the network reconfigures into a more distributed or closed form.

The next section addresses this issue of different network forms and their relevance for leadership and leadership development. Further elaboration on the relationships between distal outcomes of leadership development (macrocognition, dynamic capabilities, and collective requisite complexity) and network configurations will be a specific focus.

## Social Networks and Leadership Development

There has been little attention given to a networks-based perspective of leadership development (although see Cullen-Lester et al., 2017). One potential explanation for this paucity of scholarship is that the field is still focused heavily on leader-centric approaches to development. As noted previously in this volume, that is not wrong, but it is limited and limiting. It might be tempting to have the pendulum of theory and research swing more fully in the opposite direction by focusing only on collective development. This would have its own limitations, mainly that we know comparatively little about collective leadership development.

It is not an either-or proposition but an and-both one when it comes to developing leaders and leadership. The most highly developed leadership system will include leaders who are advanced in terms of their respective leadership self-views and knowledge, skills, and abilities (KSAs). A highly developed leadership system will also have the capability to configure into collective forms of leadership capacity in which leadership is an outcome of system structure and processes when needed. Knowing when different structural forms of leadership are appropriate to the adaptive challenge at hand is another system capability grounded in shared mindsets and macrocognition. Having extensive capabilities requires investments in both individual leader and collective leadership development. How these different structural configurations might happen in creating leadership is a function of what was described in the previous section as network oscillation.

To help facilitate an understanding of how network oscillation might work in the context of leadership, and to help see the connection to development, a brief overview of basic network structures is presented. The three general network structures or network forms that will be discussed are centralized, decentralized, and distributed networks.

### *Three Types of Network Structures*

Sociograms depicting three basic types of social networks are presented in Fig. 7.2. As reminder, the small circles represent nodes or actors in the network and the lines are nondirectional ties between nodes. Although the different networks depicted in the figures have somewhat different sizes (i.e., number of nodes), it is possible to think of these as different structural configurations of the same respective network size. The important point is to consider the different network structures in terms of leadership and what the benefits that each leadership type confers individually and collectively.

The first question to consider in examining Fig. 7.2 is to identify the leader. Most would say that the leader is easy to spot in the centralized and decentralized networks because the leader surely occupies the most central position (i.e., high actor centrality). In the centralized network everything in terms of resources either flows into or from that central

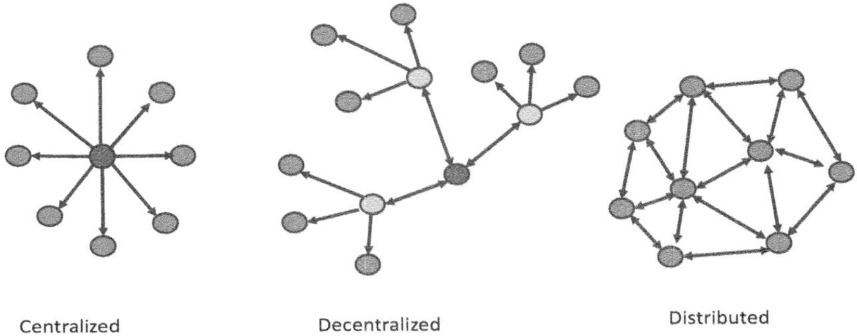


**Fig. 7.2** Three types of network structures

node. In the decentralized network the central actor (our leader) occupies a structural hole and is serving as a broker or bridge to four subgroups in the network. The central actor controls the flow of resources across the subgroups.

But what about the distributed network? There might be educated guesses about which of the nodes is "the" leader because some nodes are more central in the network and others more on the periphery of the network. Most would not consider an actor on the network margins to be a leader because most implicit leadership theories that people hold consider the leader to be one if not the most influential and powerful actors in any network. More than either the centralized or decentralized networks—both of which are open networks—the origin of leadership in the distributed network is less obvious. Indeed, it could be that the leadership is not located in any of the individual nodes but is distributed as an overall capacity across the network. That is a nontraditional way of conceptualizing leadership, but it offers another way of engaging in leadership that is best suited for certain situations (i.e., highly complex adaptive challenges).

In considering potential network efficacy—defined as how well the network uses its resources—it makes little sense to try an identify the more effective structure in addressing the entirety of possible leadership challenges. Leadership challenges define the situation, and it has been noted historically that the situation is an important consideration in effective leadership (Green et al., 2023). The three network structures depicted in Fig. 7.2 can be effective, but in different leadership situations. A goal of leadership development is to develop the capacity to align the leadership network structure with the situation in which it is most likely to contribute to adaptability and effectiveness. The capability of a collective to accomplish these network reconfigurations is an important source of dynamic capabilities at the collective level. Thus, it is an important consideration in leadership development.

### *Network Structure as Dynamic Capability*

In Chapter 5 of this volume addressing adult development influences and individual leader development, three different leadership principles or ways in which leadership can be enacted were reviewed. The simplest form is personal dominance, next more complex is interpersonal influence, and the most complex—and rarest of all in enacting leadership—is relational dialogue. Based on developmental theory it was argued that if the most complex form of leadership could be conceptualized and enacted then it was highly likely that the less complex or simpler forms could also be enacted when needed, but there is intransitivity in this relationship. Being only able to do leadership at the simplest level of personal dominance makes the probability of engaging in influence or dialogue when needed unlikely. The reason is that there needs to be development in place to think and act as a leader in more complex ways. The same holds at the collective level.

The centralized network structure depicted in Fig. 7.2 is like a personal dominance approach. Everything flows to and from a centralized leader. This type of structure can be effective if the leader has experienced the type of situation before and knows how it should be handled. In such situations, research has shown that this type of network structure is associated with the fastest problem-solving (Borgatti et al., 2009). A classic example of this is a crisis type of situation in which the leader holds an effective solution and there is no need for interdependencies among the followers. It is pretty much taking orders and responding as a follower. This could be the typical command-and-control type of leadership. This type of network structure can be effective, but only in a limited number of situations. As the situation becomes more ambiguous and complex where the leader reaches the limits of individual expertise, this type of structure will start to unravel in accomplishing an effective response. It might still be quick in offering problem solutions, but those solutions might not be accurate or effective. A more complex way of structuring for leadership may be needed.

A decentralized network in Fig. 7.2. is where the leader occupies a structural hole and brokers the necessary resources to various subgroups (e.g., departments, units, project teams). There is still a high degree of leader control in this type of network structure, but there are interdependencies and resource flows among the subgroup members. The leader has direct contact with each of four "lieutenants" who each occupy a structural hole in their respective subunits. Again, this network form assumes that the leaders (plural in this case) have the necessary expertise to respond adaptively to the leadership challenge.

This type of structure might be the most effective one in cases in which each subunit has a different piece of the leadership challenge to address, the different subunits do not need to interact differently with each other as the leader serves as the hub to coordinate responses across the subunits. The limits of this type of decentralized network structure are reached when there are interdependencies across the subunits in terms of resource flows. In this case the leader is more of a bottleneck than an efficient conduit of network efficacy by slowing down and controlling the resource flows, especially in terms of information and expertise.

A fully distributed network is one that is best suited for a completely novel adaptive challenge in the form of what Karl Weick (1993) called *vu jadé* experiences where the group has no idea what is happening, has never experienced this type of event before, and has no idea how to adapt to the challenge. This type of leadership network is slower and more cumbersome in diagnosing situations and making decisions but is well-suited for the kinds of novel VUCA events (volatile, uncertain, complex, ambiguous; Bennett & Lemoine, 2014) that are becoming more commonplace. It is also an adaptive form of leadership when there are significant interdependencies among network actors or subgroups and the challenge is novel and complex. It is also the case that these kinds of challenges might be best addressed through relational dialogue. But as noted, dialogue takes time and cannot be enacted without first having that capacity developed among network members. It does not automatically happen without intense developmental preparation.

In terms of dynamic complexity and collective requisite complexity, which are two of the distal outcomes of leadership development proposed in this volume, the more developed leadership collective would be able to structure itself in all three forms as the situation requires. Burt and Merluzzi (2016) have noted that networks are inherently dynamic, although the way in which networks are studied does not reflect this dynamism. Most research treats the focal network as static. In future leadership development research, examining network change or churn is an imperative. It is also of interest to understand how such network structures can be sufficiently flexible to adapt to changing complexities regarding the challenges faced by collectives.

Before discussing the implications of SNA to the development of collective leadership capacity in leadership development, a brief mention of network methods, measures, and analyses is in order. It is beyond the scope of this section to provide an intensive review of how to use network analysis in research primarily because it can take so many different forms. SNA can be used at every level of analysis from individual to the broadest collectives that can be imagined. Data can be collected directly from participants in the form of nominations or ratings or indirectly through data archives such as email transactions or online platforms such as Twitter (now X). Analyses can be conducted using open access techniques such as R or more specialized software such as UCINET (Borgatti et al., 1999).

A recommended reading that summarizes much of the information about social network data, including data collection strategies and applications can be found in Chapter 2 of Wasserman and Faust (1994). There is a lots of flexibility in how SNA can be applied to all sorts of organizational issues, including leadership development. Readers are encouraged to explore those many and varied possibilities in their research.

## Implications of a Social Network Approach to Developing a Collective Capacity for Leadership

This chapter has taken a social network analysis (SNA) approach to understanding leadership development. SNA is a powerful set of tools and techniques that can be applied in charting and understanding how collectives develop and create greater leadership capacity, which is the foundational marker of leadership development. The notion of a collective or even an entire organization operating as a network of leaders is not new. Marvin Bower, who was CEO of McKinsey & Company consultancy for many years and widely credited (or blamed) for the rise of global management consulting, wrote about just that idea some time ago

(Bower, 1997). What is relatively novel is that idea of a collective capacity for leadership that does not reside in any single leader or multiple individual leaders and that SNA can be used to study this capacity and its development. From SNA and social capital perspectives leadership exists as a resource embedded in the relationships among actors in a bounded network.

With novel ideas there is a lag in terms of research evidence. There have been theoretical contributions to advancing an understanding of leadership capacity in teams (e.g., Day et al., 2004) but there is scant available empirical evidence on collective leadership development. Perhaps the closest to the kind of direct evidence on this topic is from the team development literature (Lacerenza et al., 2018). But even in that literature there is little that is directly targeted at interventions designed to enhance a collective capacity for leadership.

Despite the nascent state of the collective leadership development field, there are bright spots offering related types of evidence to build upon. The proximal indictors of leadership development proposed in this volume are based on collective emergent states of psychological safety, shared mental models, collective leadership efficacy, and collective identification. There is a good amount of theory and evidence for each of these proposed proximal leadership development outcomes. It is also the case that these four emergent states do not represent the entirety of possible emergent states to consider in leadership development. Additional theorizing and theoretical development are needed along with research evidence focused on the core topic of developing a collective capacity for leadership, which is the Holy Grail of leadership development. There is a lot yet to learn about these important aspects of developing a collective to engage in creating the kinds of leadership that enhances adaptability to complex novel challenges.

Where things are especially weak in terms of evidence-based understanding is with the long-term indicators of leadership development that are proposed to support a collective leadership capacity. But it is the case that research evidence on all sorts of long-term developmental outcomes is sparse, even at the individual level. That means what is proposed here as the distal indicators of leadership development could be tentative and speculative propositions. That means they might change over time or include other outcomes that have yet to be studied. So goes science, which is a self-correcting system. What is proposed in this volume around leadership development is what makes sense based on what is known presently about leadership development and related factors.

Something that is more certain is the potential to use SNA tools (data, methods, analyses) to help advance the field. Network science is developing at a rapid pace, and we are learning about leadership in networks, leadership as networks, and leadership in and as networks (Carter et al., 2015). How such perspectives apply to leadership development is lagging even more, but there is interest and preliminary contributions (Cullen-Lester et al., 2017). Although the foundation for further advancing a science of leadership development is far from complete, there are a few pieces in place on which to build. This is exciting!

The study of development inheres the study of change. This applies to the study of collective leadership development as well as individual leader development. To date, by far the most work on social networks has adopted a static, single-shot perspective on a given network. Networks are dynamic whether it is in the form of ongoing oscillations (Burt & Merluzzi, 2016) or because of more structured developmental interventions. More needs to be known about how to effectively model dynamic networks, which is a critical piece needed to integrate SNA more fully with the study of leadership development.

The good news is that there are ongoing advances in the theory and analysis of network dynamics. Researchers have proposed stochastic actor-based models that can incorporate a wide variety of influences on network change, estimate parameters expressing such influences, and test corresponding hypotheses (Snijders et al., 2010). There is at least one recognized set of analytic techniques for these stochastic actor-based models of network dynamics that is found in the Simulation Investigation for Empirical Network Analysis (SIENA) statistical program. SIENA consists of a set of methods that can be implemented in a computer program such as R that carries out the statistical estimation of models for repeated measures of social networks (Ripley et al., 2023). An example of its use in a published article is available, demonstrating how the stochastic actor-based model of network change can be implemented using SIENA (Tröster et al., 2019). A nice feature of this empirical study is that it incorporated three waves a data, thus making it a true longitudinal study.

Looking ahead to the final chapter in this volume, the focus will be on advancing the science of developing leaders and leadership. It will take a holistic perspective on the underlying conceptual framework specifying how leaders and leadership develop and their interrelationships.

Given that researchers interested in these topics is intended as a primary audience for this volume, there will be a focus on remaining research questions. The intent is to help provide a map of sorts of where the scientific contributions are most needed in advancing our science. It is not intended as an exhaustive list.

## Chapter Summary

- Social network analysis (SNA) is not the same as social networking. SNA is a scientific approach to understanding the pattern and structure of relations in some bounded space.
- SNA offers a powerful set of tools for mapping and analyzing networks across different levels of analysis from individual to broad collectives.
- Social networks track the flow of resources across individuals engaged in shared work and maps the informal organization.
- Social networks vary by the type of relationships under study. The most studied social networks are based on friendship, advice, and communication.
- A social network can also inform researchers about the leadership capacity of a collective.
- A sociogram depicts the pattern and structure of relationships in a network.
- At the individual level of analysis, relevant terms include a node or actor (individual), ties or links (connections or relationships), as well as statistical summaries of the pattern of nodes and ties.
- A structural hole exists when an actor connects two or more unconnected alters (other actors) in a network, which can be a source of individual competitive advantage because the actor controls the flow of resources.
- At the whole network level, important considerations include the network size, its inclusiveness, the density of relationships, how centralized it is, and the extent of transitivity among connections.
- Social capital refers to the advantage provided by a particular network structure. In terms of leadership, it refers to the leadership-related resources that reside between actors.

- At the cutting edge of SNA is the notion of network change or churn. Because leadership development is inherently about change, SNA needs to adopt a dynamic perspective on how the collective develops and changes in terms of network metrics over time.
- Three basic types of network structures are centralized, decentralized, and distributed. Each of these network types can be effective, but only in certain situations related to different levels of the complexity of the underlying adaptive challenge.
- A dynamic capability related to network change is the collective's capability to reconfigure relationships to match the leadership challenge.
- There are various ways to collect network data and to conduct relevant analyses. The application of SNA techniques to the field of leadership development is in its infancy, which means there are myriad opportunities to help advance the field empirically and theoretically.

## References


Adler, P. S., & Kwon, S.-W. (2002). Social capital: Prospects for a new concept. *Academy of Management Review, 27*(1), 17–40. https://doi.org/10.5465/amr.2002.5922314

Badura, K. L., Galvin, B. M., & Lee, M. Y. (2022). Leadership emergence: An integrative review. *Journal of Applied Psychology, 107*(11), 2069–2100. https://doi.org/10.1037/apl0000997

Balkundi, P., & Kilduff, M. (2006). The ties that lead: A social network approach to leadership. *The Leadership Quarterly, 16*, 941–961. https://doi.org/10.1016/j.leaqua.2006.01.001

Bennett, N., & Lemoine, G. J. (2014, Jan/Feb). What VUCA really means for you. *Harvard Business Review, 92*, 27.

Borgatti, S. P., Everett, M. G., & Freeman, L. C. (1999). *UCINET 5 for Windows: Software for social network analysis*. Analytic Technologies.

Borgatti, S. P., Mehra, A., Brass, D. J., & Labianca, G. (2009). Network analysis in the social sciences. *Science, 323*, 892–895. https://doi.org/10.1126/science.1165821

Borgatti, S. P., Everett, M. G., & Johnson, J. C. (2024). *Analyzing social networks (*3rd ed.*)*. SAGE Publications.

Bourdieu, P. (1985). The forms of capital. In J. G. Richardson (Ed.), *Handbook of theory and research for the sociology of education* (pp. 241–258). Greenwood.

Bower, M. (1997). *The will to lead: Running a business with a network of leaders*. Harvard Business School Press.
Brass, D. J. (2012). A social network perspective on organizational psychology. In S. W. J. Kozlowski (Ed.), *The Oxford handbook of organizational psychology* (Vol. 1, pp. 667–698). Oxford University Press. https://doi.org/10.1093/oxfordhb/9780199928309.013.0021
Burt, R. S. (1992). *Structural holes: The social structure of competition*. Harvard University Press.
Burt, R. S., & Merluzzi, J. (2016). Network oscillation. *Academy of Management Discoveries, 2*(4), 368–391. https://doi.org/10.5465/amd.2015.0108
Caduff, A., Daly, A. J., Finnigan, K. S., & Leal, C. C. (2023). The churning of organizational learning: A case study of district and school leaders using social network analysis. *Journal of School Leadership, 33*(4), 355–381. https://doi.org/10.1177/10526846221134006
Carter, D. R., DeChurch, L. A., Braun, M. T., & Contractor, N. S. (2015). Social network approaches to leadership: An integrative conceptual review. *Journal of Applied Psychology, 100*(3), 597–622. https://doi.org/10.1037/a0038922
Coleman, J. S. (1988). Social capital in the creation of human capital. *American Journal of Sociology, 94*(Supplement: Organizations and Institutions: Sociological and Economic Approaches to the Analysis of Social Structure), S95–S120. https://doi.org/10.1086/228943
Cullen-Lester, K. L., Maupin, C. K., & Carter, D. R. (2017). Incorporating social networks into leadership development: A conceptual model and evaluation of research and practice. *The Leadership Quarterly, 28*(1), 130–152. https://doi.org/10.1016/j.leaqua.2016.10.005
Day, D. V. (2000). Leadership development: A review in context. *The Leadership Quarterly, 11*(4), 581–613. https://doi.org/10.1016/S1048-9843(00)00061-8
Day, D. V., Gronn, P., & Salas, E. (2004). Leadership capacity in teams. *The Leadership Quarterly, 15*(6), 857–880. https://doi.org/10.1016/j.leaqua.2004.09.001
DeRue, D. S., & Ashford, S. J. (2010). Who will lead and who will follow? A social process of leadership identity construction in organizations. *Academy of Management Review, 35*(4), 627–647. https://doi.org/10.5465/amr.35.4.zok627
Granovetter, M. S. (1973). The strength of weak ties. *American Journal of Sociology, 78*(6), 1360–1380. https://doi.org/10.1086/225469
Green, J. P., Dalal, R. S., Fyffe, S., Zaccaro, S. J., Putka, D. J., & Wallace, D. M. (2023). An empirical taxonomy of leadership situations: Development, validation, and implications for the science and practice of leadership. *Journal*

*of Applied Psychology, 108*(9), 1515–1539. https://doi.org/10.1037/apl0001083

Harris, J. K. (2014). *An introduction to exponential random graph modeling*. SAGE Publications.

Heider, F. (1958). *The psychology of interpersonal relations*. Wiley.

Hoppe, B., & Reinelt, C. (2010). Social network analysis and the evaluation of leadership networks. *The Leadership Quarterly, 21*(4), 600–619. https://doi.org/10.1016/j.leaqua.2010.06.004

Kilduff, M., & Brass, D. J. (2010). Organizational social network research: Core ideas and key debates. *Academy of Management Annals, 4*(1), 317–357. https://doi.org/10.5465/19416520.2010.494827

Kilduff, M., & Krackhardt, D. (1994). Bringing the individual back in: A structural analysis of the internal market for reputation in organizations. *Academy of Management Journal, 37*(1), 87–108. https://doi.org/10.5465/256771

Kilduff, M., & Lee, J. W. (2020). The integration of people and networks. *Annual Review of Organizational Psychology and Organizational Behavior, 7*, 155–179. https://doi.org/10.1146/annurev-orgpsych-012119-045357

Kilduff, M., & Tsai, W. (2003). *Social networks and organizations*. SAGE Publications.

Kwon, S.-W., & Adler, P. S. (2014). Social capital: Maturation of a field of research. *Academy of Management Review, 39*(4), 412–422. https://doi.org/10.5465/amr.2014.0210

Lacerenza, C. N., Marlow, S. L., Tannenbaum, S. I., & Salas, E. (2018). Team development interventions: Evidence-based approaches for improving teamwork. *American Psychologist, 73*(4), 517. https://doi.org/10.1037/amp0000295

Oh, H., Chung, M.-H., & Labianca, G. (2004). Group social capital and group effectiveness: The role of informal socializing ties. *Academy of Management Journal, 47*(6), 860–875. https://doi.org/10.5465/20159627

Oh, H., Labianca, G., & Chung, M.-H. (2006). A multilevel model of group social capital. *Academy of Management Review, 31*(3), 569–582. https://doi.org/10.5465/amr.2006.21318918

Portes, A. (1998). Social capital: Its origins and applications in modern sociology. *Annual Review of Sociology, 24*(1), 1–24. https://doi.org/10.1146/annurev.soc.24.1.1

Rajkumar, K., Saint-Jacques, G., Bojinov, I., Brynjolfsson, E., & Aral, S. (2022). A causal test of the strength of weak ties. *Science, 377*(6612), 1304–1310. https://doi.org/10.1126/science.abl4476

Ripley, R. M., Snijders, T. A. B., Boda, Z., Vörös, A., & Preciado, P. (2023). *Manual for RSiena (version September 29, 2023)*. University of Oxford, Department of Statistics, Nuffield College. http://www.stats.ox.ac.uk/~snijders/siena/RSiena_manual.pdf

Sasovova, Z., Mehra, A., Borgatti, S. P., & Schippers, M. C. (2010). Network churn: The effects of self-monitoring personality on brokerage dynamics. *Administrative Science Quarterly, 55*(4), 639–668. https://doi.org/10.2189/asqu.2010.55.4.639

Snijders, T. A. B., Van de Bunt, G. G., & Steglich, C. E. G. (2010). Introduction to stochastic actor-based models for network dynamics. *Social Networks, 32*(1), 44–60. https://doi.org/10.1016/j.socnet.2009.02.004

Tröster, C., Parker, A., Van Knippenberg, D., & Sahlmüller, B. (2019). The coevolution of social networks and thoughts of quitting. *Academy of Management Journal, 62*(1), 22–43. https://doi.org/10.5465/amj.2016.0914

Wasserman, S., & Faust, K. (1994). *Social network analysis: Methods and applications*. Cambridge University Press.

Weick, K. E. (1993). The collapse of sensemaking in organizations: The Mann Gulch disaster. *Administrative Science Quarterly, 38*(4), 628–652. https://doi.org/10.2307/2393339

CHAPTER 8

# Advancing the Science of Developing Leaders and Leadership

## Theorizing About the Science of Developing Leaders and Leadership

This volume reflects a unique perspective on developing leaders and leadership. It is unique in terms of differentiating leader development from leadership development and offering frameworks that specify the developmental pathways for each of these levels. The proposed pathways also incorporate unique indicators at different time scales, roughly categorized as proximal (or leading) and distal (or lagging) indicators of development. The unique perspective also takes a more inclusive, evidence-based approach to ongoing development. It is not about programs; rather, it is about cultivating systems that support the development of leaders and leadership.

The proposed approach presented in this volume is not intended for Human Resource (HR) or talent development specialists; rather, at a practical level it is mainly intended for those individuals who want to become (better) leaders and are willing to make the commitment in terms of the time and effort to invest in that journey. If those in professional practice find value in the approach, that is all the better. That said, the main focus of this volume is on advancing the science associated with developing leaders and leadership.

Although the previous 20 years have seen an incredible surge of interest in studying leader and leadership development scientifically, the fields



D. V. Day, *Developing Leaders and Leadership*,
https://doi.org/10.1007/978-3-031-59068-9_8

remain theoretically and empirically underdeveloped compared with the general leadership field. It is hoped that in furthering the development of the field of leadership development, which includes leader development in this discussion, that the same mistakes are not made.

Much scholarly energy was invested in discovering and promoting ***the*** leadership theory. This mistake led to an all-or-nothing type of turf battle among the proponents of different leadership theories. None of these theories are completely right and none completely wrong (ok there might be a few of the latter). Put differently, there is probably some truth in most of the leadership theories proposed and tested in the scholarly literature. Let's not make the same mistake going forward in advancing the science of developing leaders and leadership. Leader and leadership development are inherently eclectic, which is why no one theory will suffice.

An earlier volume that I co-authored proposed an integrative approach to leader development (Day et al., 2009). What was integrative about the approach was that it attempted to connect the scholarly disciplines of identity, expert performance, and adult development in the study of leader development. We did not propose this approach as a theory, per se, but as theorizing (Weick, 1995) in an eclectic fashion about the core topic. In that 2009 volume, the approach (not theory!) was positioned as a multilevel framework in which identity was at the most visible or accessible level, expert performance as a leader at an intermediate level, and relevant aspects of adult development at the deepest and least visible level. This theorizing was the forerunner of the proximal and distal indicators of leader development presented in this volume and elsewhere (Day & Dragoni, 2015). There are two related points: (1) theorizing is ongoing and the thinking about developing leaders and leadership is evolving, and (2) the nature of the problem is eclectic in that helpful ways of addressing the challenges of leader and leadership development will not be based in any one academic discipline.

Eclecticism is inherent to both leadership and development. Combining those terms into leadership development could be construed as a topic that is doubly eclectic. That might be a bit much, but it recognizes that leadership development combines two terms with different underlying scientific traditions that will require diverse modes of theorizing to be useful in improving their study and practice. A common assumption—although perhaps implicit—is that if we could only determine the correct leadership theory then what is needed is to train individuals on that theory and the problem of leadership development would be solved. That is both naïve and overly simplistic.

We need a separate field of leader and leadership development apart from the voluminous leadership literature because of the development component. The point was made earlier in this volume that providing leadership training "solutions" [sic] will take us only so far. A hallmark of science is that it is based on disciplined, systematic reasoning that can be deductive, inductive , or even abductive. Here is another type of eclecticism. Because the field is in its infancy, all forms of rigorous scientific reasoning can be helpful. There are hypotheses tested deductively using the hypothetico-deductive model, which is the traditional scientific approach. Observations in nature can lead to insightful research questions inductively through processes such as grounded theory (Glaser & Strauss, 2017). There are also ways of reasoning from a set of facts to a theoretical explanation(s) using abduction (Haig, 2018). Deduction, induction, and abduction—there are entire methodological toolkits to be applied using any of these scientific methods.

My scholarly background and training are mostly aligned with the traditional hypothetico-deductive approach to science in which experience with the world leads to temporary explanations (i.e., hypotheses) from which predictions are deduced and then tested through experimentation or other scientific methodologies. Rather than providing a litany of hypotheses to test, perhaps a better place to start is in articulating a smaller set of ontological assumptions reflecting the nature of leader and leadership development adopted in this volume. What can we say with some degree of certainty is true about leader and leadership development? A core set of these assumptions can be discerned from the First Principles presented in Chapter 1. Those First Principles are more like practical reflections of the underlying theoretical assumptions to be discussed a little later in this chapter. The purpose is not to (necessarily) convince you that they are the most correct assumptions; rather, it reflects the thinking that any system should rest on a set of explicit ontological and epistemological assumptions if it is to be considered scientific.

Building on these assumptions, the remainder of the chapter attempts a version of abductive reasoning in the form of educated guesses or logical inferences that seek the simplest and most likely conclusions based on the available data (Bamberger, 2019). Unlike deductive reasoning, abductive reasoning yields a plausible conclusion but does not verify it. Abductive conclusions do not eliminate uncertainty or doubt but provide inferences representing the best available explanation to a given phenomenon. The emphasis is on plausible and tentative inferences in the spirit of ongoing theorizing. These are best guesses in the most scientific ways that can be presented given the embryonic state of the field. Before articulating these theoretical assumptions through abductive reasoning, the next section briefly summarizes a few so-called truths about developing leaders and leadership.

## What is "True" About Leader and Leadership Development?

The summary presented here is just a partial list of truths when it comes to the broad field of leadership development. True is in quotation marks in the section header to reflect that what is true is not an absolute but something that holds a reasonable degree of certainty. There are likely to be others that can be nominated, and it is certainly the case that we continue to establish more truths through scientific means. Consider this list to be a snapshot of where we are in the first quarter of the twenty-first century and a guide to further elaboration on the theoretical assumptions that undergird these truths. Some of these truths may seem obvious no brainers, but they need stating as assumptions about the ontology of leader and leadership development reflected in this volume. Assumptions should always be understood and tested whenever possible.

### *Individuals Can Develop as Leaders and Collectives Can Develop Leadership*

An asterisk should go on this truth because we have more evidence that leaders can develop than collectives can develop leadership. Why would it be surprising to discover that individuals can develop as leaders? It goes to the longstanding debate about nature or nurture, born or made when it comes to leaders. There is still the belief among many—ironically, usually highly successful leaders—that you either have it, or you don't when it comes to leadership. There is no doubt that genetics play some role in leadership (De Neve et al., 2013), but it does not explain everything about what it takes to be a leader.

Just as any other set of skills, research results are clear that individuals can develop leadership skills and related self-views. These may not make any individual a world-class leader of an organization, movement, society, or other large-scale entity; however, with sufficient effort and support, those leadership skills and self-views can change in positive ways. The truth that collectives can develop leadership rests mainly on what is known from the science of team development (Lacerenza et al., 2018) that has shown various interventions to help develop more effective teamwork. It is true that teamwork is not the same as leadership, but it may be a precursor to collective leadership capacity.

Although it is asserted that individuals and collectives can develop leadership capacity, it does not necessarily mean that it develops as proposed in this volume. There may be different and possibly better developmental pathways (practices and processes) that have yet to be proposed and tested. This is how science works as an incremental and self-correcting system. The point made here is that we have a high level of certainty that leaders and leadership can develop and are not inherently bestowed, at least not completely.

### *Leader Development and Leadership Development Involve Different Levels of Analysis*

The truth behind this claim is that developing leaders does not inherently mean that better leadership will result. That is the typical expectation, however, and a primary reason behind why so much is invested in what is typically billed as leadership development. Where the leadership takes place is in the application of the developmental outcomes. It is a two-stage process in which development of leadership-related qualities occurs first with the second stage involving the appropriate application of these attributes and characteristics. That is why the study of leader development needs to focus on both the proximal and distal outcomes. Leadership effectiveness is one form of job/role performance and involves the appropriate application of what has been developed.

The traditional assumption is that leadership is the result of the actions of an individual leader. It is a leader-centric line of thinking in which it is assumed that leadership resides with or in the individual leader. If the focus is intended to be on leadership development, then the appropriate level of analysis is the collective (e.g., dyad, group, team, unit, department, organization). The origin of leadership is in the connections or relationships between individuals. That is why it is apt to conceptualize leadership as being drawn from the collective rather than originating from a singular leader. Nonetheless, there is an application piece with leadership development as well. Determining when leadership is drawn forth and that the form of leadership matches with the complexity of the adaptive challenge are important considerations in predicting leadership effectiveness at the collective level.

### *Some Individuals and Collectives Need to Work Harder to Achieve the Same Developmental Outcomes that Others Attain More Readily*

This truth is grounded in the principle of individual differences, roughly defined as enduring psychological characteristics that distinguish one individual from another. Although there may be some universals in development that are driven by biological maturation in childhood (Piaget, 1929), there is a great amount of variability in most other types of attributes and processes. In terms of development, some individuals and collectives are fortunate to have certain advantages. At the individual level, those who are extraverted have an easier time being seen by others, or emerging, as leaders because of their preference for speaking up in social situations (also known as the babble effect). Introverted individuals can still develop and be seen as leaders, but those individuals need to overcome their dispositional discomfort associated with putting themselves and their ideas forward in a group.

At the collective level, there are differences in the overall initial leadership capabilities across collectives based on experience, collective personality, and other factors. Due to these and other reasons, one collective might need to work harder together than another to create the kinds of collective emergent states that have been proposed in this volume as the proximal indicators of leadership development. This truth also rests on the fact that individuals and collectives start at different places and change in different ways on their respective developmental journeys. This is part of the developmental imperative that differentiates it from most training scenarios in which changes are thought to occur in a more regimented manner.

### *Leader Development and Leadership Development Occur in Context*

Leadership does not occur in a vacuum, nor does development. Again, this sets it apart from most (but admittedly not all) training approaches that adopt a more generic or acontextual approach. Leader development occurs in the context of ongoing adult development (Day et al., 2009) as well as the context provided by ongoing experience (i.e., the life gym). Of course, experiences take place in classrooms and other more formal instructional spaces; however, to the extent that leadership is learned it tends to be learned through ongoing everyday experience (McCall, 2010).

Different contexts provide different learning opportunities, which means that it facilitates the development of different things. Something similar applies to leadership development at the collective level. Groups of individuals are embedded in different organizational contexts that can be conceptualized and operationalized using the frameworks of social network analysis (Cullen-Lester et al., 2017). To better study and understand the development of leaders and leadership, there is the need to understand the contexts in which they occur (Johns, 2006) and this is especially relevant to the leadership field in general (Johns, 2023).

### *Development Has No Endpoint*

Leader development has been framed as an ongoing, lifelong endeavor, although it might be better to consider it as an investment. There is no point at which one can say that development is finished, it is complete, I am done. That would be like saying there is nothing more to learn. This applies as much to collectives as it does to individual leaders. Collectives and individuals can fall prey to hubris, which is excessive confidence to the point of arrogance. Based on Greek mythology, hubris essentially boils down to a false belief that there is nothing to be learned from others or the environment. It is a leading cause of leader derailment (Van Velsor & Leslie, 1995) as well as organizational failure (Picone et al., 2014).

A major reason why development is never finished is because the type and complexity of challenges faced by individual leaders and leadership collectives is always changing. In the previous discussion of requisite complexity, the objective was to at least match individual or collective complexity with the level of environmental complexity. If the adaptive challenge in the environment was more complex than what a responding entity can handle cognitively or otherwise, then failure is the likely result. The antidote to hubris is continuous learning and continuous learning is the foundation of continuous development. The philosophical roots to this way of thinking might be best found in the principles of *wabi sabi* that state: Nothing lasts, nothing is finished, nothing is perfect (Takahashi, 2020). The current state of development does not last if one is

**Table 8.1** Five truths* about leader and leadership development

| |
|---|
| 1. Individuals can develop as leaders and collectives can develop leadership |
| 2. Leader development and leadership development involve different levels of analysis |
| 3. Some individuals and collectives need to work harder to achieve the same developmental outcomes that others attain more readily |
| 4. Leader development and leadership development occur in context |
| 5. Development has no endpoint |

* As known at the time of this writing

learning. Development is never finished if one is learning. Nothing is perfect because all knowledge is subject to revision.

This simple philosophy applies to the development of individuals and collectives. In Japanese Zen culture this is called *Kaizen* or the art of continuous growth and improvement. Some readers may have come across this term as it has been applied in manufacturing contexts in Japan and other places. But it is a broader term that includes the philosophy of using small steps to make big changes, which is something discussed in this volume as a way of tackling the challenges of motivating ongoing development.

In the spirit of *wabi sabi*, it is admittedly the case that what is represented above as developmental truths are far from perfect or complete. As the field continues to develop and the science behind leader and leadership development advances these truths will likely be challenged, amended, revised, or extended to include others. That is how science works. Even gravity, which is typically heralded as a basic scientific truth, is nothing more than a hypothesis that can be refuted by contravening data. Science marches on! (see Table 8.1 for a summary list of these five truths).

The next section explores theoretical assumptions that stem from what is considered to be true in leader and leadership development currently. It is necessary and important to state these assumptions explicitly because they support recommendations about further advancing the science of developing leaders and leadership.

## Theoretical Assumptions Guiding the Study of Leader and Leadership Development

Underlying theoretical assumptions are often implicit. They are what we take for granted as being true. These theoretical assumptions reflect what is valued and guide the practices of what we do in terms of developing leaders and leadership (in the present case). This section articulates a few of those theoretical assumptions for leader development and leadership development, respectively. These assumptions serve as the foundation for the novel perspectives reflected in this volume on the topics of leader and leadership development. Making these assumptions explicit offers the possibility of exploring their veracity scientifically. Each of the research questions could spawn testable hypotheses to help advance the science behind leader and leadership development. The assumptions presented here are not necessary **THE TRUTH** (yes, in all caps!) but are taken as such. But as with any scientific endeavor, a healthy dose of scientific skepticism is advised.

### *Leader Development*

1. ***Everyone has leadership potential***. Leadership is not a rare gift that is exclusively distributed in the human population. Everyone has leadership potential. In a recent book, Adam Grant addresses the notion of hidden potential (Grant, 2023). There is hidden potential in us all, including leadership potential. The American statesman John Gardner expressed a similar sentiment (Gardner, 1990) that was quoted in Chapter 3 of this volume. Gardner opined that most people go through their lives using only a fraction of their potential and pointed out that there is a lot of untapped potential when it comes to "leadership gifts" (p. xix). The context in which he was quoted in Chapter 3 was in response to the common practice of having so-called high potential leadership programs in organizations. Given that typically fewer than five percent of the employees in an organization are considered high potential, the implicit assumption is that leadership is a rare and exclusive gift. How much potential is wasted in assuming this? Would any organization find it acceptable to potentially waste 95% of the potential in any other asset? A final point about this assumption is that we cannot continue

at a societal level to waste so much leadership talent given the challenges we face now and in the future. A common saying among Finnish educators is "We can't afford to waste a brain" (Grant, p. 158). We should adopt a similar ethos in that we cannot afford to waste leadership potential. This volume offers some specific recommendations on how to develop that untapped leadership potential, which is related to the next assumption.

**Research Questions:**

- What is the relative level of leadership potential among emerging (i.e., new) leaders? How does this potential compare to that of more experienced leaders?
- What are various ways of measuring leadership potential and how well do these measures perform in terms of psychometric properties and in predicting relevant outcomes?
- What is the relationship between leadership potential and a capacity for leadership? Recall that the definition of leader development posed earlier in this volume is that it is about enhancing the capacity of individuals to be effective in leadership roles and processes. Are these essentially identical constructs or if they are different, then how are they different?

2. ***Everyone is the author of their own development as a leader***. This underlying assumption is like the First Principle #1 in Chapter 1, which states that you cannot make anyone develop as a leader. By being an author of one's development, the underlying assumption is that of personal agency. Development is an active process and not a passive one. By assuming agency—whether it's called ownership or self-authorship or something else—the onus for motivating development as a leader over a long period of time is on the individual. That is one reason why internalizing a strong leader identity is important: We devote resources to those things we value and what we value is part of our overall identity.

    There are two general observations related to this assumption. The first observation is that often individuals wait too long before commencing on their developmental journeys as leaders. There is a lot of focus on gaining technical specialty skills—and this is especially the case in higher education—that are thought to be the basis of career success. What typically happens is that after a few years a good technical specialist is promoted to supervise or lead a group of other technical specialists. Some wags have noted that this is a double loss: The organization loses a high-performing technical specialist and gains an unprepared leader. The time to start preparing for leadership is in the present and not once someone has gained a formal leadership position. By then it is too late because development takes time.

The second observation is that too often we wait for others to develop us—whether it is a teacher or professor, or more commonly, HR or talent management professionals. Dr. Martin Luther King commented on this notion of "hold on, just wait" when it came to Civil Rights. Paraphrasing from his *Letter from Birmingham Jail* (King, 1963), Dr. King noted that "wait" almost always meant "never" and that justice too long delayed is justice denied. Please note that I am not equating leader development with the historic struggle for Civil Rights; rather, there is a parallel phenomenon associated with telling someone to wait on their leader development. This voice telling someone to wait could even be their own voice.

Everyone owns their development and should start as soon as possible in preparing (i.e., developing) themselves for leadership, even if they do not have a formal leadership position. This is a fundamental assumption that those who own their development as leaders are predicted to perform more effectively as leaders than those who do not own their development. One obstacle to this self-authorship recommendation when it comes to leader development is that individuals do not know where to start or how to develop themselves. This volume has attempted to provide sound evidence-based recommendations on how that can be done, especially around designing experiences that include the important aspects of assessment, challenge, and support.

**Research Questions:**

- How early should individuals start developing leadership capacity? Is there a point where too early might be a detriment over the longer term?

- Does owning one's development help accelerate leader development beyond what is accomplished in traditional programs and practices?
- What are examples of systems designed by individuals to facilitate their leader development? Which types of system designs are most helpful in terms of longer term motivation as well as development of holistic leadership capacity?

3. ***Everyone has a unique personal trajectory of development***. A promising methodology for studying leader development is through charting and understanding personal trajectories of development. From some of the personal trajectory studies that have been conducted on leader development (e.g., Day & Sin, 2011; Kragt & Day, 2020), it is evident that individuals start at different places and change in different ways as they develop. From these findings it can be assumed that every individual has a potentially unique developmental trajectory.

   When it comes to estimating these personal trajectories, there are usually some aggregations made to understand the overall or average trends. Research has found subcategories of different types or classes of trajectories. In one of the earliest personal trajectory studies of leader development, we found that the majority trend was curvilinear in a J-shaped manner for bother leader identity and ratings of leader effectiveness in small teams (Day & Sin, 2011). But there was a smaller class of trajectories representing about 10 percent of the sample that were positive and linear. This second trajectory class was found using a set of estimation techniques called growth mixture modeling estimating empirically whether there was a mix of different types of trajectories represented in the sample. To further individualize the analysis, the intercept and slope parameter estimates for each participant could be considered as either independent or dependent variables in subsequent analyses. What kinds of attributes predict intercept and slope values? What do the intercept and slope values predict that might be related to more long-term development? These kinds of questions have yet to be examined empirically in the leader development literature.

**Research Questions:**

- Are there individual attributes that predict slope and intercept parameter estimates in the study of personal trajectories of developing leaders?
- Do trajectory parameter estimates (i.e., slopes and intercepts) predict more distal indicators of leader development?
- What can be learned from the trajectories of effectively developing leaders that can be used to intervene on the trajectories of less effectively developing individuals?

4. ***Some leadership-related attributes change quickly, others change more slowly***. Because individuals start at different places and change in different ways as they develop as leaders, it is assumed that the various attributes that compose leadership capacity do the same. There are certain attributes that have shorter and steeper trajectories and those that have longer and less steep trajectories. There are even those kinds of attributes that have curvilinear trajectories, such as leader identity (see Day & Sin, 2011). It has been proposed here and in other work (e.g., Day & Dragoni, 2015) that leadership self-views and KSAs develop relatively quickly as compared with other attributes associated with adult development such as mental complexity and dynamic capabilities. There is surely much more that goes into the development of an effective leader, and to paraphrase John Gardner (1990), we have only scratched the surface in terms of what we know about leader development that is evidence-based. Going forward, we need to give much more careful attention to the role of time.

**Research Questions:**

- What is the more specific timeline for the development of various leadership-related attributes?
- Besides self-views and KSAs, what other kinds of "low hanging" attributes can be addressed. By low hanging I mean other attributes that are important to leader development and can change in relatively quick order that have yet to be studied.

- Are there practices, processes, or technologies that accelerate developmental timelines? If so, what are they?

5. ***Leadership potential is transformed into various indicators of development through experience.*** It was noted in Chapter 3 that developmental programs and other interventions do not directly cause the developmental of anything. Instead, developmental experiences in the so-called life gym provide the underlying processes that shape individual capabilities into the proximal indicators of development in the form of leadership self-views and KSAs/competencies. The proximal indicators suggest whether longer term development might occur provided there is deliberate practice over an extended amount of time.

   In this form, deliberate practice is a specific type of experience that is guided by the developing leader. In more formal terms, the experience and practice serve as first- and second-stage moderators in leader development. This raises an important scientific point about causality. Establishing cause-and-effect relationships is a hallmark of the scientific method and it is achieved primarily through applying experimental methods. Of those methods, random assignment of participants to experimental and control conditions is the main way of demonstrating that something like a leader development intervention causes changes in relevant outcomes. Having this kind of experimental control is very difficult in non-laboratory settings in which most leader development research occurs. Although difficult, it is not impossible to conduct true field experiments as a few studies focusing on charismatic (Antonakis et al., 2011) and transformational leadership training interventions (Barling et al., 1996; Dvir et al., 2002; Jacobsen et al., 2022) have shown.

   By far most research studies on leader development are correlational in nature meaning that strong causal inferences cannot be made. This would especially be the case in using ongoing experiences for leader development. There is no way to randomly assign participants to life experiences, especially when the participants have agency in designing their development. Positioning experience and practice (which is a type of experience) as moderators in the developmental process also better reflects the open systems nature of development discussed in Chapter 2.

**Research Questions:**

- Is there a priority or preferred ratio of the components of assessment, challenge, and support in making experience more developmental?
- What other experiential features enhance developmental punch or potency in leader development?
- How can causality be established in using ongoing experience for development?

6. ***Leader development changes do not directly translate into performance improvements or greater effectiveness as a leader***. It is tempting to use job performance as the outcome of interest when studying leader development, but that would not be appropriate. Doing so would embrace an erroneous assumption that any developmental gains will translate directly and immediately into better performance. Approaches to estimating the potential return on investment (ROI) of developmental interventions have adopted some version of job performance as the outcome of interest (Avolio et al., 2010; Phillips et al., 2015).

   There are two different questions underlying this scenario. Studying developmental change should focus on what is expected to change because of a developmental intervention. In leader development, these are most likely proximal outcomes associated with self-views and leadership KSAs. Performance as a leader or in one's job more generally may improve, but only to the extent that these developmental gains are applied appropriately back in the leadership environment. The first phase is demonstrating empirically that what was expected to change has indeed changed in the expected manner. The second phase involves testing hypotheses about leadership performance improvements that are due to developmental gains in the relevant indicators (either proximal or distal). For these reasons, performance is not the appropriate outcome in studies of leader development. Leader development does not inherently develop more effective leadership. Then what is the potential return on investment (ROI)? That remains an ongoing research question.

**Research Questions:**

- How do developmental outcomes in leader development translate into more effective leadership? What is involved in that transfer from development to performance and what are the various time scales involved?
- How can ROI be estimated if the outcome of interest is development and not performance?
- What does ROI mean and how can it be estimated in non-business contexts?

A final point is not about the ontology of leader development, but the methods used to study it. Put simply, the scientific study of leader development requires a longitudinal focus. Development implies change. It does not seem possible to study change through static snapshots of leadership phenomena. What is needed is a longitudinal focus and that involves more than just two measurement waves or points of data collection. The reason is that the only possible change trajectory with two data points is linear. We are learning through the application of personal trajectories methods and analyses that some changes in leader development are curvilinear. Leader identity is a specific example (Day & Sin, 2011; Miscenko et al., 2017). Identity strength as a leader has been shown to decline or weaken before it begins to strengthen and take on a positive slope (i.e., following a J-shaped trajectory). This trend would not have been detected if the corresponding research design was a two-wave, pre-post approach. The research questions associated with this underlying assumption build on the previous assumption about the timing of developmental effects (see Table 8.2 for a summary).

### *Leadership Development*

This section addresses the underlying (implicit) assumptions associated with collective leadership development. As noted above and previously, leader development and leadership development operate at different levels of analysis. It is also the case that more evidence has been collected about leader development; thus, the assumptions presented here should

**Table 8.2** Recommended theoretical assumptions for leader development research

| |
|---|
| 1. Everyone has leadership potential |
| 2. Everyone is the author of their own development as a leader |
| 3. Everyone has a unique personal trajectory of development |
| 4. Some leadership-related attributes change quickly, others change more slowly |
| 5. Leadership potential is transformed into various indicators of development through experience |
| 6. Leader development changes do not directly translate into performance improvements or greater effectiveness as a leader |

be considered even more tentative than those for leader development and there are fewer of them. Nonetheless, the goal is to summarize where the leadership development field is now and to offer suggestions about theoretical assumptions. As with the section on leader development, a few pressing research questions (not hypotheses!) are provided for each assumption.

1. ***The collective is greater than its individual parts, eventually***. A key difference between leader development, which is at the individual level of analysis, and leadership development, which is at the collective level, is the latter involves more than one individual. Because individuals compose the collective this is essentially a multilevel issue. Researchers have proposed different types of collective unit properties: (1) global, (2) shared, and (3) configural (Kozlowski & Klein, 2000). Global collectives have properties that originate at the collective unit level. These properties do not have a basis in individual phenomena such as perceptions, personality, or experience but are a property of the collective as a whole and work in a top-down manner. This type of collective property is not relevant for the present discussion of leadership development because we are interested in how individuals come to form a collective and how that collective develops a sense of sharedness. The question therefore is whether the individual attributes and characteristics brought into the collective that form the initial level of leadership capability can be transformed into shared unit properties. Rather than some pattern of individual contributions that reflects a configural representation of the individuals in a collective,

> [s]hared until properties are based on *composition* models of emergence, in which the central assumption is one of isomorphism of constructs at different levels; the constructs share the same content, meaning, and construct validity across levels. (Kozlowski & Klein, p. 30, italics in original)

As example, the content, meaning, and construct validity of individual leadership self-efficacy is the same at the collective level except that the referent is the collective rather than the individual regarding the level of confidence to engage in leadership tasks and processes. But this form of sharedness only emerges through collective engagement in leadership over time. How much time? The best guess—and currently it is only a guess—is that these collective emergent properties come about only after weeks or months at the earliest. That is why it is imperative that members of the collective stay together over time. In terms of research, the kinds of "bottom-up emergent effects necessitate long-term longitudinal or time-series designs" (Kozlowski & Klein, 2000, p. 47). Time is not on our side if short-term changes are expected in collectives from a configural states to a shared unit property.

**Research Questions:**

- How does an initial collection of individual leadership capabilities transform into shared unit properties that are manifested in collective emergent states?
- What time-scale differences are involved in creating different shared unit properties and collective emergent states?
- Does leadership development occur if there are no shared properties among the collective? What does that leadership look like?

2. ***Distributed leadership provides greater collective leadership capacity than centralized leadership.*** The way in which collective leadership capacity has been conceptualized in this volume is based on the flexibility to enact leadership at various complexity levels. A highly centralized leadership network is one in which there is a central leader who controls the flow of resources (e.g., information, strategic material, leadership). Essentially, everything is controlled by a single leader. This form of leadership may be effective in specific

situations where that leader knows how to best respond to an adaptive challenge; however, leadership in this form will start to reach its limits as the nature of the challenge increases in complexity beyond the capabilities of that leader. A more decentralized network involves multiple leaders whereas a distributed leadership network operates in a way in which every individual is engaged in leadership (see Fig. 7.2). An issue with distributed leadership networks is that they are not very efficient, but they are potentially the most effective form in facing complex adaptive challenges that exceed the capabilities of any single leader.

An assumption made about these different leadership networks is that if a collective can conceptualize and enact leadership in a more complex distributed way then that collective can do leadership in a simpler more centralized way when needed. But the converse is not true. If the collective only knows top-down, centralized leadership, that collective cannot restructure itself in a distributed manner when needed. There is a lack of transitivity due to the greater complexity associated with leadership in less traditional forms. It is also why investments in leadership development are needed to create the type of dynamic capability in which a collective can restructure its informal network to best meet the complexity of the presenting challenge.

**Research Questions:**

- How does the leadership network develop in a collective? What are the prerequisites for more distributed leadership development?
- At what level of complexity does a challenge benefit from distributed leadership as compared with centralized or decentralized leadership?
- How can leadership capacity be measured using social network analysis metrics? How does capacity change or churn?

3. ***Collective leadership capacity is based on human capital and social capital***. The primary difference between human and social capital is that the former is an intrapersonal (within-person) resource, and the latter is an interpersonal (between-person) resource. Although leadership development in the collective form focuses on the creation of social capital (Day, 2000) in which leadership is based on the

relationships among members of a collective, it does not mean that human capital is irrelevant. At the initial state, collective leadership capabilities are a compilation of individual human capital contributions. In other words, the investments made in individual leader development are leveraged by a collective in forming its initial leadership capacity. But that initial capacity is mostly an aggregation of each leader's intrapersonal capabilities. Over time, through shared experiences and intensive interactions that initial capacity is transformed into leadership resources that reside between individuals (i.e., social capital). This aggregation of human capital therefore is integral in developing the social capital of a collective; it is also the case that the emergent social capital can further develop human capital through feedback mechanisms in the developmental system (Coleman, 1988). In this manner the overall leadership capacity is a function of both individual human capital and collective social capital.

**Research Questions:**

- How do human capital and social capital interact in creating collective leadership capacity?
- What is the optimal human capital mix in leadership development for creating leadership resources?
- How does the social capital embedded in collective leadership capacity create human capital? Put differently, how can leadership development enhance leader development?

4. ***Collective emergent states mediate the relationships between initial leadership capabilities and the development of distal collective leadership capacity***. The systems model of leadership development proposes that initial leadership capabilities in a collective are transformed into key emergent states enroute to developing a collective capacity for leadership. Another way of stating this is that the collective emergent states mediate that set of relationships. The proposed emergent states discussed in Chapter 6 are psychological safety, shared mental models of leadership, collective leadership efficacy, and collective identification. The specific emergent states are less important than the proposed mediating effects. That is because what

is learned through future research might amend or expand the list of emergent states that are deemed most critical in collective leadership development.

The full leadership development model can be described as a two-stage moderated mediational model. The first-stage moderator is a history of shared or collective experience that shapes the transformation of initial leadership capabilities into the collective emergent states. The second-stage moderator are intensive interpersonal experiences that shape the collective emergent states into the proposed distal indicators of collective leadership capacity (i.e., macrocognition, dynamic capabilities, and requisite complexity). Because the model is proposed formally in terms of moderated mediation it means that it could be directly tested empirically. For now, that is a remote possibility given the lengthy time scales involved. For that reason, is it better to think of this model in more theoretical terms including the underlying theoretical assumptions.

**Research Questions:**

- Mediation implies causality. How can causal claims be established in leadership development?
- What are other relevant collective emergent states that can serve as proximal indicators of leadership development?
- Are there alternative ways to conceptualize leadership development that might be simpler or more accurate?

These four theoretical assumptions represent the implications stemming from the truths about leadership development as they are known now. There are some assumptions that spill over from individual leader development such as development does not translate directly or immediately into better performance of enhanced leadership effectiveness. As with individual leader development, performance is not the appropriate outcome in studies of leadership development. The scientific study of leadership development should focus on what changes occur in the proposed developmental outcomes represented by proximal and distal indicators.

Enhanced effectiveness is, of course, important but there are many reasons for leadership effectiveness, and only some might be attributable to what is proposed developmentally. The environment and the broader

**Table 8.3** Recommended theoretical assumptions for leadership development research

| |
|---|
| 1. The collective is greater than its individual parts, eventually |
| 2. Distributed leadership provides greater collective leadership capacity than centralized leadership |
| 3. Collective leadership capacity is based on human capital and social capital |
| 4. Collective emergent states mediate the relationships between initial leadership capabilities and the development of distal collective leadership capacity |

context in which leadership is enacted are also important considerations. This is a challenging scientific endeavor going forward because it involves sorting out causal relations. The kind of experimental control, especially random assignment into different treatment groups, is difficult for studying something like leadership development that transpires outside of the laboratory. Nonetheless, there may be available research designs such as interrupted time-series approaches that can help establish some level of causal claims in research on leadership development (see Table 8.3 for a summary of leadership development theoretical assumptions).

## Summary Perspectives on Developmental Systems Design and Conclusions

Attempting to propose a full-fledged theory of leadership development (inclusive of leader development) is unwise for now. The field is still in a very early state, so it would be premature to propose some sort of Grand Unified Theory. It is also the case that "few things that are full-fledged theories" (Weick, 1995, p. 389) and what might be most needed according to Weick are attempts at theorizing a given phenomenon. Think about it as an interim rather than end state. Here is a related perspective:

> Theory belongs to the family of words that includes guess, speculation, supposition, conjecture, proposition, hypothesis, conception, explanation, model. The dictionaries permit us to use theory for anything from "guess" to "a system of assumptions, accepted principles, and rules of procedure devised to analyze, predict, or otherwise explain the nature or behavior of a specified set of phenomena" (Runkel & Runkel, 1984, as cited in Weick, p. 386).

The notion of theory being guess, supposition, conjecture and so forth is especially apt. Science is an evolving and self-correcting system. Some things included in theory—perhaps even major assumptions and suppositions—turn out to be wrong. We want theories and hypotheses to be falsifiable (Popper, 2005), otherwise they are not good science.

In invoking abductive reasoning in this section, it recognizes that theorizing at this juncture holds more risk than something set forth as a formal theory with a great deal of empirical evidence behind it. Please be clear that there is empirical evidence on developing leaders and leadership, but perhaps not as much as what would be needed to engage in more formal theoretical development. It is also the case that the available empirical evidence is not always directly testing a theory, but different components of what is conceptualized as a broader—and do I dare say eclectic—process involving human development. Perhaps a preferable way of thinking about what is needed going forward is to take smaller bites of the leadership development apple. Find relevant pieces to gather evidence and test relationships with various development outcomes. That is how the science of leadership development will advance.

## *Conclusions*

In bringing this chapter and the entire volume to a close, it is a good place to remind readers of the importance of the focal topics. From my experience, organizations care little about the "right" theory of leadership. That can be left to the academics to debate (and my, have they done that!), but there seems little likelihood that there will ever be the one overarching theory of leadership upon which all agree. Leadership ontology continues to evolve as the nature of the challenges that leaders face continue to change. What many if not most organizations care deeply about is how to better develop their leaders and enhance an overall capacity for leadership to face ever-increasing complex adaptive challenges.

The approach adopted in this volume embraces the scientist-practitioner ethos that defines certain fields such as organizational psychology. That said, my approach is more aligned with a capital "S" science and a lower-case "p" for practice. There are many books and other products that emphasize the practice and minimize the science, or completely ignore it. Practice should be guided by and grounded in science, which stipulates that science should proceed evidence-based practice. Unfortunately, should does not always mean that it does because of competing values between those in science and those in practice.

The tasks of developing leaders and leadership are important practically, and the arguments set forward in this volume propose that these are important scientific concerns as well. Historically, too much ownership and control has been ceded to those holding values that are not necessarily aligned with science. When this happens—as is the case with the leadership development field—it opens the gates for those who want to provide services (i.e., make a buck or two) that may not be evidence-based. Despite my tendency to engage in polemic diatribes about some of the products and services provided in the name of leadership development, it is not the case that every consultant or consultancy offers rubbish. Many do, a few don't. But it is the case that the primary values associated with consulting are financial rather than scientific. This volume has been an earnest call to bring science more fully into leader and leadership development.

Science is about finding truth, especially about the causes of various phenomenon. When we talk about something being evidence-based (or not), it refers to science. Is there empirical data and results to back up claims that something like a leader development intervention works? Science is based on a set of agreed-upon methods. These can be based on hypothesis testing using the hypothetico-deductive model described earlier in this chapter. Evidence can also be gathered using inductive qualitative methods. I will go out on a philosophical limb by stating that science does not prefer how or where the data originates—although individual scientists tend to have strong opinions about that—if its consumers are aware of the limitations inherent in that data especially concerning causal claims. Although better evidence is usually reported in reputable scientific outlets because the data and results have gone through extensive peer review, there are differences in the scientific merit of what journals publish. A quick—albeit imperfect—metric of quality can be found in a journal's impact factor. It essentially reports how many scientific citations are made to works published in that journal controlling for the total number of papers published in a specific year. Assessing the impact of a scholarly work is done mainly by seeing how many others have referred to a published scholarly work, which is summarized in citation counts.

A problem with peer review and citation counts (well, one of many) is that both the review and publication process and subsequent citations to a work takes time. Often it is a lot of time, like in years. This is frustrating to many in practice who want immediate state-of-the-science solutions to their leadership challenges. Science and business work in very different ways and with completely different time scales. There are some attempts to improve the scientific publishing process such as advocating for open science that involves greater transparency that might also accelerate the dissemination of scientific evidence (i.e., knowledge).

Despite all the issues associated with the marketplace of leadership development and the goals of some to prioritize the monetization of products and services in its name, I remain optimistic about the future of the leadership development field. I wholeheartedly agree with the sentiment expressed by John Gardner (1990, p. xix): "We can do better. Much, much better."

It is hoped that this volume has provided insights into how we can do much better by focusing on advancing a science of leader and leadership development.

## Chapter Summary

- Advancing the science requires a summary of a few things we know to be "true" about developing leaders and leadership.
- These truths (or what we believe to be true right now) lead to a set of theoretical assumptions about leader and leadership development, respectively.
- The scientific process behind this approach is based on abductive reasoning in the form of educated guesses (or logical inferences) that seek the simplest and most likely conclusions based on the available data.
- The approach can be described as theorizing rather than formal theoretical development.
- Going forward, scientific values rather than marketplace dominance should guide the development of the field.
- We can and should do much better when it comes to developing leaders and leadership, and in advancing a science that grounds practice.

## References

Antonakis, J., Fenley, M., & Liechti, S. (2011). Can charisma be taught? Tests of two interventions. *Academy of Management Learning & Education, 10*(3), 374–396. https://doi.org/10.5465/amle.2010.0012

Avolio, B. J., Avey, J. B., & Quisenberry, D. (2010). Estimating return on leadership development investment. *The Leadership Quarterly, 21*(4), 633–644. https://doi.org/10.1016/j.leaqua.2010.06.006

Bamberger, P. A. (2019). On the replicability of abductive research in management and organizations: Internal replication and its alternatives. *Academy of Management Discoveries, 5*(2), 103–108. https://doi.org/10.5465/amd.2019.0121

Barling, J., Weber, T., & Kelloway, E. K. (1996). Effects of transformational leadership training on attitudinal and financial outcomes: A field experiment. *Journal of Applied Psychology, 81*(6), 827–832. https://doi.org/10.1037//0021-9010.81.6.827

Coleman, J. S. (1988). Social capital in the creation of human capital. *American Journal of Sociology, 94*(Supplement: Organizations and Institutions: Sociological and Economic Approaches to the Analysis of Social Structure), S95–S120. https://doi.org/10.1086/228943

Cullen-Lester, K. L., Maupin, C. K., & Carter, D. R. (2017). Incorporating social networks into leadership development: A conceptual model and evaluation of research and practice. *The Leadership Quarterly, 28*(1), 130–152. https://doi.org/10.1016/j.leaqua.2016.10.005

Day, D. V. (2000). Leadership development: A review in context. *The Leadership Quarterly, 11*(4), 581–613. https://doi.org/10.1016/S1048-9843(00)00061-8

Day, D. V., & Dragoni, L. (2015). Leadership development: An outcome-oriented review based on time and levels of analyses. *Annual Review of Organizational Psychology and Organizational Behavior, 2*, 133–156. https://doi.org/10.1146/annurev-orgpsych-032414-111328

Day, D. V., Harrison, M. M., & Halpin, S. M. (2009). *An integrative approach to leader development: Connecting adult development, identity, and expertise*. Psychology Press.

Day, D. V., & Sin, H. P. (2011). Longitudinal tests of an integrative model of leader development: Charting and understanding developmental trajectories. *The Leadership Quarterly, 22*(3), 545–560. https://doi.org/10.1016/j.leaqua.2011.04.011

De Neve, J.-E., Mikhaylov, S., Dawes, C. T., Christakis, N. A., & Fowler, J. H. (2013). Born to lead? A twin design and genetic association study of leadership role occupancy. *The Leadership Quarterly, 24*(1), 45–60. https://doi.org/10.1016/j.leaqua.2012.08.001

Dvir, T., Eden, D., Avolio, B. J., & Shamir, B. (2002). Impact of transformational leadership on follower development and performance: A field experiment. *Academy of Management Journal, 45*(4), 735–744. https://doi.org/10.2307/3069307

Gardner, J. W. (1990). *On leadership.* The Free Press.

Glaser, B., & Strauss, A. (2017). Discovery of grounded theory: Strategies for qualitative research. *Routledge.* https://doi.org/10.4324/9780203793206

Grant, A. (2023). *Hidden potential: The science of achieving greater things.* Viking.

Haig, B. D. (2018). An abductive theory of scientific method. In B. D. Haig (Ed.), *Method matters in psychology: Essays in applied philosophy of science* (pp. 35–64). Springer International Publishing. https://doi.org/10.1007/978-3-030-01051-5_3

Jacobsen, C. B., Andersen, L. B., Bøllingtoft, A., & Eriksen, T. L. M. (2022). Can leadership training improve organizational effectiveness? Evidence from a randomized field experiment on transformational and transactional leadership. *Public Administration Review, 82*(1), 117–131. https://doi.org/10.1111/puar.13356

Johns, G. (2006). The essential impact of context on organizational behavior. *Academy of Management Review, 31*(2), 386–408. https://doi.org/10.5465/amr.2006.20208687

Johns, G. (2023). The context deficit in leadership research. *The Leadership Quarterly, 101755*, https://doi.org/10.1016/j.leaqua.2023.101755

King, M. L., Jr. (1963). Letter from Birmingham jail. Retrieved 18 November 2023, from https://minio.la.utexas.edu/webeditor-files/coretexts/pdf/1963_mlk_letter.pdf

Kozlowski, S. W. J., & Klein, K. J. (2000). A multilevel approach to theory and research in organizations: Contextual, temporal, and emerging processes. In K. J. Klein & S. W. J. Kozlowski (Eds.), *Multilevel theory, research, and methods in organizations: Foundations, extensions, and new directions* (pp. 3–90). Jossey-Bass.

Kragt, D., & Day, D. V. (2020). Predicting leadership competency development and promotion among high-potential executives: The role of leader identity. *Frontiers in Psychology, 11*, 1816. https://doi.org/10.3389/fpsyg.2020.01816

Lacerenza, C. N., Marlow, S. L., Tannenbaum, S. I., & Salas, E. (2018). Team development interventions: Evidence-based approaches for improving teamwork. *American Psychologist, 73*(4), 517. https://doi.org/10.1037/amp0000295

McCall, M. W. (2010). Recasting leadership development. *Industrial and Organizational Psychology-Perspectives on Science and Practice, 3*, 3–19. https://doi.org/10.1111/j.1754-9434.2009.01189.x

Miscenko, D., Guenter, H., & Day, D. V. (2017). Am I a leader? Examining leader identity development over time. *The Leadership Quarterly, 28*, 605–620. https://doi.org/10.1016/j.leaqua.2017.01.004

Phillips, P. P., Phillips, J. J., & Ray, R. (2015). *Measuring the success of leadership development: A step-by-step guide for measuring impact and calculating ROI*. ATD Press.

Piaget, J. (1929). *The child's conception of the world*. Routledge.

Picone, P. M., Dagnino, G. B., & Minà, A. (2014). The origin of failure: A multidisciplinary appraisal of the hubris hypothesis and proposed research agenda. *Academy of Management Perspectives, 28*(4), 447–468. https://doi.org/10.5465/amp.2012.0177

Popper, K. (2005). *The logic of scientific discovery*. Routledge.

Takahashi, S. (2020). *Wabi sabi: The Japanese art of impermanence*. Author.

Van Velsor, E., & Leslie, J. B. (1995). Why executives derail: Perspectives across time and cultures. *Academy of Management Perspectives, 9*(4), 62–72. https://doi.org/10.5465/ame.1995.9512032194

Weick, K. E. (1995). What theory is *not*, theorizing *Is*. *Administrative Science Quarterly, 40*(3), 385–390. https://doi.org/10.2307/2393789

# Index




D. V. Day, *Developing Leaders and Leadership*,
https://doi.org/10.1007/978-3-031-59068-9

The manufacturer's authorised representative in the EU is Springer
Nature Customer Service Centre GmbH, Europaplatz 3, 69115 Heidelberg,
Germany. If you have any concerns regarding our products, please
contact ProductSafety@springernature.com

Printed and bound by CPI Group (UK) Ltd, Croydon, CR0 4YY
28/09/2026
02224072-0007